The Harcourt Brace Sourcebook
for Teachers of Writing

Patricia Roberts
University of Missouri

HARCOURT
BRACE

HARCOURT BRACE COLLEGE PUBLISHERS

Fort Worth   Philadelphia   San Diego   New York   Orlando   Austin   San Antonio
Toronto   Montreal   London   Sydney   Tokyo

ISBN: 0-15-508158-6

Address for orders:
Harcourt Brace College Publishers
6277 Sea Harbor Drive
Orlando, Florida 32887-6777
1-800-782-4479

Address for editorial correspondence:
Harcourt Brace College Publishers
301 Commerce Street, Suite 3700
Fort Worth, Texas 76102

Web site address:
http://www.harbrace.com/english

Printed in the United States of America
890123456 023 987654321

Contents

Chapter 1
General Introduction

Perhaps the greatest change in the teaching of composition in this century is that composition pedagogy has become increasingly rhetorical. That is, it has tended to move from a concern with certain rules to a sense that good writing is the result of *kairos*. As James Kinneavy argues, *kairos*, a central concept in classical rhetoric, is the notion of appropriateness to situation. Kinneavy argues that what makes a particular piece of discourse effective is not that it has a specific form, which will always be effective, but that effective discourse strategies are appropriate to audience, author's intention, and rhetorical situation.

This same notion is extremely helpful in teaching because numerous teaching strategies have worked beautifully in some situations and have fallen short in others—the success or failure of these strategies depending largely upon *kairos*. In other words, the effectiveness of any given pedagogical practice is strongly influenced by the personality and general approach of the teacher, the needs of the program, the specific needs and experience of the students, and even such elements as the classroom or time of the semester.

For instance, instructors of first-year composition are often required to teach research; however, to plan that aspect of the course, an instructor must first consider various questions about the situation: What are the students supposed to learn by doing research? Should research instruction provide basic instruction in library skills, or are students expected to get that elsewhere? How much emphasis should the instructor place on evaluating the credibility of sources, or critical reading of studies, in relation to the basic instruction or material regarding form and citation method? Is "research" synonymous with "library research," or might students do primary research (such as conducting their own surveys)? Is the instructor expected to provide advice which will apply in all other disciplines (such as teaching alternate methods of citation, or how to evaluate the reliability of the study)? Is there a particular research strategy which the instructor must require (such as using three-by-five cards)? Is the instructor required or encouraged to have only one paper, which requires library research, or is library research supposed to be part of the writing process of every paper? Is "the research paper" being taught as a special genre of paper, or is research being taught as a part of every writing process?

The answers to these questions depend upon the instructor, rhetorical situation, and present and future experiences of the students. For instance, students who will be going on to writing intensive courses that will assume, but not provide, library skills will need skills instruction in their first-year courses. If, however, the students are in a program in which that instruction is provided in a required bibliographic methods course (or university life course), then instructors might choose to forgo such instruction in composition courses.

As the aforementioned example illustrates, considering the rhetorical situation of writing instruction is crucial. It is also important to note that no single teacher can do everything and that no single strategy will work for all teachers and all students. Instructors who rely simply on the successes described in various books, journal articles, and conference papers may end up with an odd sense of inadequacy. They may come to think that a good teacher is someone who succeeds at all the things that every article describes and that instructors who have time only to do a few of these things are guilty of terribly flawed teaching. Or, such instructors might feel that there is something terribly wrong with their approach because the strategy so glowingly described in the literature has not worked terribly well in their classes.

The teachers I have most admired do not seem to share any one approach, but they do have a similar attitude: Like a good rhetorician, they tend to think carefully and recursively about their teaching, setting well-articulated goals and strategies—however different from each other—that are appropriate to those goals. Their strategies, by their own description, change over time and from one course to another. They rely on *kairos*.

In the following article, "Three Views of English 101," Erika Lindemann explores the three different perspectives of the first-year composition course, based on the views of writing "as a product, a process, or a system of social actions". Lindemann's article provides an introduction to the many pedagogical concerns surrounding the teaching of first-year composition and, thus, assists in creating the context for the thirteen articles that appear in the remaining nine chapters of this guide. Chapters two and three, which make up Part I—"Writing Processes and Audience Awareness"—of *The Harcourt Brace Sourcebook for Teachers of Writing,* present current research concerning the teaching of writing processes and audience through cornerstone articles by Linda Flower and John R. Hayes, Mike Rose, Peter Elbow, and Lisa Ede and Andrea Lunsford. Part II, "Pedagogical Issues and Trends," offers current perspectives on a variety of pedagogical issues and trends—group work (chapter 4), writing in communities (chapter 5), grammar and usage (chapter 6), and grading and responding (chapter 7)—and features articles by Peter Smagorinsky and Pamela K. Fly, Marilyn M. Cooper, Patrick Hartwell, and Elaine O. Lees. Part III, "Writing Genres and Assignments," presents a mixture of cornerstone and contemporary research concerning the teaching of personal essays and exploratory writing (chapter 8), argument (chapter 9), and research (chapter 10) from composition researchers including Susan Swartzlander, Diana Pace, and Virginia Lee Stamler; William Zeiger; Jeanne Fahnestock and Marie Secor; Catherine E. Lamb; Richard L. Larson; and Matthew Wilson.

Three Views of English 101
Erika Lindemann

This essay resumes a discussion that began in 1992, when Gary Tate and I debated the place of literature in Freshman English during the annual meeting of the Conference on College Composition and Communication. Those presentations, revised for *College English,* appeared in the March 1993 issue and generated several responses, four of which were published in the October 1993 issue. At that time, neither Tate nor I wished to respond to the responses, for our purpose had been to engage teachers in an important discussion about the nature and purpose of the first-year course. Having taken our turn in the conversation, we wanted others to have their say.

What they said was revealing. Most of the responses in *College English* take exception, not to Tate's position (that literature belongs in Freshman English), but to mine (that it does not). Though you will want to read the four responses as they originally appeared, let me abstract their principal claims here:

- If literature does not belong in the first-year writing course, then the first-year writing course does not belong in the English department.
- Reading books has become the occasion for [students'] own questions about human growth and change.
- Thus, combining composition and literature in required freshman English classes makes sense not only because it introduces first-year students to the type of writing necessary to succeed in college but also because, if it is done right, it is practical, enjoyable, an efficient way to develop critical thinking, and the easiest way to introduce large numbers of students to cultural diversity.
- We should not allow the misuse of literature to discourage us from "right use."

Both Tate and I find these and other responses to our debate engaging but also puzzling. Colleagues invite us to lecture on their campuses or to appear together at conferences; they include the *College English* essays in their course paks for graduate classes; they urge us to make up our differences, unaware that we have been friends for many years and have co-edited a book. What began (I thought) as a discussion about the nature and purpose of the first-year course appears now to be part of a much different conversation. In this essay, I propose to examine the "event" begun by the Tate-Lindemann debate. Though it signals an important opportunity to explore what English 101 is, or could become, it also illustrates significant differences in the assumptions teachers make about the course. Unless we take into account these differences in perspective, we will be unable to establish sufficient common ground for moving the discussion forward.

To continue the conversation requires me to write more than a response. It requires new arguments, based perhaps but not necessarily on those already advanced. I now realize that many readers regarded the Tate-Lindemann debate as a political argument. In advocating that poetry, fiction, and drama be excluded from English 101, I created the perception that I was anti-literature, had sided with the compositionists in the so-called lit/comp split, advocated removing the course from English departments, and found misguided those students and teachers who love books. Writers are responsible, of course, for the impressions they create, but readers too construct texts, and their ways of reading my original essay have reminded me again how truly beleaguered writing and literature teachers sometimes feel in each other's company. Nevertheless, reducing my essay to a political claim disparaging the use of literature in a writing course allows readers to co-opt the larger pedagogical argument I was making. Regarding me as one of "them," a politically suspect, anti-literature compositionist, makes my argument easier to dismiss, especially by those who love literature and regularly teach it in English 101. Reading the essay politically shifts the ground just enough so that we do not have to deal with the "prior question" I posed at the beginning of my original essay: "We cannot usefully discuss the role of imaginative literature (however defined) in freshman English without first asking what the purpose of a writing course is."

To my mind, we still have not addressed the prior question. In the rest of this essay, I wish to return to it. I propose to advance three ways of seeing English 101. I am interested primarily in exploring why we hold such different opinions about the course, but I also believe that whether or not we include literature in English 101 depends on how we see it. Though it is difficult to sort pedagogical arguments from political, historical, and theoretical ones, I intend to focus primarily on *instruction,* not institutional relationships, departmental politics, or rhetorical theories. What we do in the classroom, it seems to me, reveals most clearly our different ways of seeing English 101, and these pedagogical differences remain the greatest obstacle to defining a common ground that helps us explain the course to one another, to our students, and to people within and outside the academy. Until we can find some common ground in instructional practices (or articulate our differences when we cannot), other discussions seem irrelevantly secondary. Until we can say why teachers and students meet together to read and write in a place called college, we cannot address other practices —placement tests, teacher training, program administration, hiring, and so on— meant to advance this work.

Each view of English 101 outlined here proceeds from a definition of *writing*—what it is and how we teach it—that varies among teachers. I want to examine the term *writing* and the consequent perspectives that shape our notions about English 101 by borrowing a method of inquiry described in Richard E. Young, Alton L. Becker, and Kenneth L. Pike's *Rhetoric: Discovery and Change:*

> We have found three perspectives particularly useful in exploring a unit of experience. These three perspectives are identified in Maxim 4: *A unit of experience can be viewed as a particle, or as a wave, or as a field.* That is, the writer can choose to view any element of his experience *as if it were*

static, or as if it were dynamic, or as if it were a network of relationships or a part of a larger network. Note carefully that a unit is not *either* a particle *or* a wave *or* a field, but can rather be viewed as all three.

In fairness to Young, Becker, and Pike, the heuristic procedure they describe makes it theoretically possible to generate nine, not just three, views of *writing.* To select only three, as I do here, oversimplifies the ways in which they overlap. For my purposes, however, three approaches illustrate that, despite our different ways of seeing English 101, we can still engage in a constructive conversation about the nature and purpose of the course.

Regarding writing as a particle, wave, and field generates three views of English 101, each perspective depending on whether we see writing *primarily* as a product, a process, or a system of social actions. Each view is "right" for the person who holds it, but each view also is partial and calls up quite different assumptions about the course and our reasons for teaching it as well. Each view has its own historical antecedents, its own theory of language, its own notions about how students learn, and its own political implications. Each view also assigns different values to literature, reading, and the role of texts. Individual teachers do not need to know *consciously* what these antecedents, theories, implications, notions, and values are, but each of us customarily assumes that others share our perspective—until some difference of opinion reminds us that other views are possible. A teacher who regards writing primarily as a product is likely to encounter problems talking to a teacher who sees writing as a system of social actions. Neither teacher may be conscious of the difference in perspective, but unless they both can create an appreciable space for some shared assumptions about the term *writing,* their conversation about English 101 is likely to be unproductive.

In what follows, I want to explain these three views in greater detail and, for each one, examine the following four questions: Given this view, what is the principal focus of English 101? What roles does each perspective assign teachers and students? What function does reading have in the course? Why do students write and by what standards do we judge their work?

Writing as Product

The view that writing is a product is the oldest and most prevalent. Though its antecedents appear in classical rhetoric, its contemporary incarnation is not altogether classical because it slights invention and treats audience, language, and style differently. Even so, this view predominates among parents, students, many teachers, and most college administrators. Many product-centered teachers do not read *College English;* they may be unfamiliar with professional developments that have changed English 101 since they themselves took the course. Though teachers who regard writing as a product probably received no formal training in teaching either literature or composition, their coursework prepared them to be intelligent readers. They teach English 101 by remembering the writing courses they took (or what they heard about them) but do not rely on memory alone. Their instructional practices have changed in their encounters with students, in responding to their students' and their own successes and failures.

Seeing writing as a product appeals to these teachers because they already are oriented toward texts. They tend to be biographical or philosophical critics, who regard writing as a moral or aesthetic act. They believe that poetry, fiction, and drama convey important messages to readers about how to live well: "Reading books has become the occasion for [students'] own questions about human growth and change."

Product-centered or so-called traditional pedagogy regards English 101 as a content course centered in texts. If students read enough, they will encounter sufficient ideas to write about and eventually will write better. Given this view, reading texts, especially important works of belletristic literature, is essential to teaching writing well because literature offers ideas for students to write about and stylistic models to emulate. Students read these works, discuss them with the teacher and their classmates, and then address comparable subjects in their own essays.

Thinking is the most important form of invention in product-centered courses. Though what is meant by *thinking* is not always clear, many traditional teachers attempt to teach this skill by discussing logical fallacies and syllogistic reasoning or by designing exercises in "critical thinking." Other invention strategies receive scant attention perhaps for historical reasons, Renaissance rhetoricians having divorced invention from rhetoric to realign it with logic. Be that as it may, students in a product-centered English 101 course typically plan their responses to an assignment by reading a text and then thinking about it. Their reading and thinking may culminate in writing an outline, a "product" with its own formal requirements that nevertheless is intended to help writers arrange their material in some "logical" order.

When students write in a product-centered course, they usually write essays. The essay is the "product" traditional English teachers know best because it is a conventional form for interpreting poetry, fiction, and drama. However, other products are alive and well in traditional English 101 courses: outlines, five-paragraph themes, practice paragraphs, sentence diagrams, and workbook exercises. Because product-centered courses assign primacy to texts, teachers pay considerable attention to form. They assume that proficiency in constructing essays depends on developing confidence about "lesser forms." First, students may examine small units of language—parts of speech, for example—then practice writing sentences and paragraphs before composing whole essays. This sequence of instruction proceeds from studying the smallest units of language to constructing increasingly larger ones. It assumes that students must command the parts of a text—words, sentences, and paragraphs—before constructing the whole, before doing "real" writing. This piecemeal approach is especially common in community colleges where an entire course may focus exclusively on parts of speech as on writing paragraphs. In product-centered courses, literary texts support invention, but the building blocks of language provide the "content" for discussing arrangement and style.

Product-centered courses advance a notion of style defined rather narrowly to include principles governing sentence structure, word choice, mechanics, and usage. The stylistic principles students learn may derive from the study of literature, grammar, or a handbook. The teacher discusses these principles in class and encourages their imitation through exercises and eventually essay writing. Presumably, by imitating these principles, students will learn to apply them to forms of writing required in other college courses and beyond. Imitation is the watchword. Most traditional teachers accept without question the value of imitation in a pedagogical principle. Pedagogies based on imitation have never been subject to the scrutiny or controversy that attend newer teaching methods such as group work.

The teacher in this course assumes the role of an expert, a literary critic imparting knowledge about texts, ways of reading them, and principles governing their form and style. She uses primarily lecture and discussion to convey these subjects. She may give tests and pop quizzes (other products) to insure that students have learned the material. Her writing assignments carefully spell out formal and stylistic requirements expected in students' final drafts. Because the topics of these assignments tend to derive from readings, invention or planning receives less attention than revision, an activity that enables students to correct their drafts and bring them closer stylistically to the models under study. Avoiding plagiarism is a concern because the teacher rarely sees early drafts; the focus is on the students' final product.

Because students write primarily for the teacher-as-critic, the teacher's standards for "good writing" apply. Teachers, in turn, often express frustration that their students' writing rarely exhibits the formal or stylistic competence of the models explicated so patiently in class. Given the evidence of students' writing, many product-centered teachers conclude that students do not command the knowledge of subject matter, form, and style to succeed, that they seem unable to learn by imitation, or that they are deficient in the expertise the teacher brings to class—a command of literature, or of grammar, or of the essay form. A few teachers may question altogether the legitimacy of the course. Though they believe in the timelessness of good writing, they rarely see it in students' papers and may persuade themselves that their expertise has fallen on deaf ears.

Because students are regarded as novices, deficient experts, or worse, unruly and incorrigible people, many traditional teachers mark students' papers as copy-editors would, rarely commenting on content but copiously "correcting" the text, generally at the level of the word or sentence. They attempt to note all errors, in part to justify the grade but also perhaps to signal to students (by referring them to the handbook) that they still have much to learn about style, usage, and mechanics. The teacher-as-critic works from a tradition of rules about form and style, matching students' texts against exemplary models characterizing this tradition. Annoyed by students who still haven't learned these principles after twelve years of schooling, the traditional teacher may express students' grades in tense mathematical formulas: three misspelled words or one comma splice earns an F. Though no points get added back for making sense or saying something meaningful, split grades sometimes reward content, even though mechanics are flawed.

Teachers who regard writing as a product make English 101 a product-centered course. Though such a course may draw its content from essay anthologies, newspapers, or television and movies, the majority of product-centered courses require students to read and write about literature. Literature provides ideas for students to contemplate, enables the teacher to assume the role of expert, and determines which stylistic principles are worth emulating. The curriculum moves students through discussions of principles, terminology, and subject matters that represent things to *know,* not what writers *do.* The exercises and assignments progress from the smallest to increasingly larger units of discourse, from the study of grammar to sentences to paragraphs to essays. Through practice based largely on imitation, students eventually should understand the etiquette of these forms and duplicate them. Though traditional teachers hope to make students sensitive to the possibilities of language, they generally focus on forms, formulas, terminology, and rules.

Writing as Process

The view that writing is a process has antecedents in classical rhetoric too, but in American education its intellectual parents are Ralph Waldo Emerson, Henry David Thoreau, and American Romantic writers. It enjoyed a resurgence during the late 1960s and influenced writing courses primarily through the work of Janet Emig, Ken Macrorie, Peter Elbow, and Donald M. Murray. To see writing as a process is to be concerned not so much with what writers *know* but with what they *do.* This view assumes that all writers negotiate similar processes in planning, drafting, and revising their work, yet every writer also approaches composing with unique cognitive abilities and strategies for solving the problem a writing task presents. Teachers who regard writing as a process may have training in literature or in composition, but what attracts them to the approach is that it focuses primarily on students.

Process-centered or so-called expressivist teaching assumes that, if students write often, on subjects of interest to them, they will discover who they are as writers and will gain confidence in making their ideas and feelings known. The student writer is the expert, commanding subjects and strategies for composing that the teacher has no access to because they are born of the writer's experience. The student has a self to discover, some truth to express, a unique language and voice. The assignments in process-centered courses encourage self-expression and the discovery of self. Though students write essays, they also may write letters, dialogues, journal entries, autobiographical material, personal reactions to reading assignments, or exploratory pieces that examine career goals, life goals, and interpersonal relationships.

The teacher in a process-centered course does not see himself as an expert in literature, style, or some other "content." Instead, he considers himself a more experienced, confident writer, giving students permission to reflect self-consciously on their composing and providing opportunities for students to explore the self and the world. He tries to give writers confidence by encouraging honesty and by respecting what students have to say. He also writes with his students from time to time, sharing with them his own wars with words.

Process-centered courses pay considerable attention to invention. Journals, freewriting, heuristics, analogies, and other ungraded prewriting activities enable students to discover what they want to say. Unlike traditional courses that begin with the study of a genre or a unit of language, the parts leading to the whole, process-centered courses begin with a student-self who must discover her message. Planning permits her to find her purpose, audience, and voice. Each assignment offers her an opportunity to plan, draft, and revise. Students repeatedly practice solving problems in writing, making decisions, and experimenting with linguistic and rhetorical options. Practice, not imitation, is the watchword. Because process-centered courses also are student-centered, they encourage students to discuss with one another their plans for tackling assignments or successive drafts. These workshops not only help students talk out their ideas and find an authentic voice, but also make public the criteria for good writing, students helping other students attain them.

The most important text in such a course is student writing. Though reading is important, belletristic literature is not. Primarily, students read one another's work, their own creative acts, not works appearing in anthologies of essays or collections of poetry, fiction, and drama. Occasionally, published works may serve as examples of forms students are practicing (journal entries, dialogues, or autobiography) or of subjects they are exploring (growing up, learning about the self and others). Nevertheless, process-centered courses avoid large doses of literature for two reasons: it displaces the focus on student writing, and imitation, so central to traditional courses, has negative connotations.

Imitation is suspect because it can lead to dishonest uses of language and substitutes another's style for the writer's own fresh, original voice. Expressivist pedagogy supports a broad definition of style, defined as all of those choices writers make to create an honest voice expressing a message to an interested reader. Though writers must conform their messages to reasonable conventions of spelling, mechanics, and usage, these same rules and principles may prove confining. So, students in process-centered courses have permission to play with language, especially metaphor and analogy, figures that help readers understand the writer's personal world. An individual style that avoids clichés, jargon, and stereotypes is preferable to pretentious or derivative language (Macrorie calls it "Engfish"). Only by regarding language as suspect and sometimes stifling can students pierce Emerson's "rotten diction" and learn to develop their own voices.

Because process-centered courses assume that students have important messages to share, students write for one another as well as for the teacher. The criteria for good writing do not always derive from literary standards applied to finished drafts. Process is more important than product, so teachers may review (but do not grade) the scratchwork and multiple drafts for evidence of thoughtful planning and revision. Students see a great deal of writing as they discuss their work-in-progress and comment on classmates' drafts. The teacher guides these discussions by means of sample student drafts, training the class to appreciate a writer's strengths and to offer constructive responses to guide revision. When it comes to evaluating the final draft, sometimes simply "publishing" the piece is sufficient. Students may read their work to one another or send it to an appropriate audience. They may contribute their best writings to a class-produced anthology distributed at the end of the term.

When the teacher evaluates students' work, he may write comments only on a draft, not the final version. This feedback establishes a dialogue, the voice of the experienced teacher-writer engaging the student's voice and suggesting changes to consider for the final version. Or the student and teacher may discuss the draft in conference. In either event, the teacher will note strengths as well as weaknesses, will react to the message as a sympathetic reader, and will offer guidance about particular strategies and processes to try in the next draft. He responds to students' writing, not with mathematical formulas or corrections, but with questions, suggestions for further writing, and encouragement. Though students may write and rewrite their work throughout the term, only some of it receives a grade; much of it remains ungraded. Eventually, students may add their finished pieces to a portfolio, which will receive a single grade at the end of the term. If the teacher grades individual assignments, he is likely to reward the honest voice, the truthful insight, and language that takes risks.

One important goal of a process-centered English 101 course is self-discovery, encouraging students to compose a self in language. Some teachers, however, find it difficult to balance the freedom and discipline necessary to cultivating truth-telling authentic voices. Some students quickly learn what sorts of selves the teacher would like to see in their writing. They invent a *dis*honest persona who will carry them to an A. Other students, those who remain truthful, may disturb the teacher even more. Their voices betray bigoted selves or selves so abused as children or so confused by experience that their writing embarrasses classmates and leaves the teacher wondering how to respond. Though English 101 is not the place for saving or improving souls, process-centered courses have contributed much to the teaching of writing. They have renewed our appreciation for invention and given us respect for the messages of our students.

Writing as System

The view that writing is a system emerged in the mid-1980s. Though it is as old as Aristotle's *Rhetoric,* its recent reappearance seems to be, in part, a reaction to the process-centered approach. It also reflects efforts to consolidate our understanding of how people write in contexts outside English 101. By studying writers in various professions as well as students writing for college courses, some teachers concluded that the process approach had oversimplified matters. In portraying writers as isolated individuals, it had divorced them from the social contexts in which language always operates. By restricting audience primarily to the self, expressivist pedagogy had stripped rhetoric of its important cultural, often political, force. Writers, these teachers claimed, live in a culture shaped by language, and language is always a form of social interaction. Writing, then, is a way of living in social groups, of interacting with others and having them interact with us. Though we write to make meaning and discover the self, we also write to make a difference in the world.

In an important essay first published in 1986, Marilyn Cooper responds to the process-centered view, with its images of the solitary author, by proposing instead an ecological model for writing. Just as natural environments comprise dynamic interlocking systems, in which organisms both respond to and alter their surroundings, writers are "continually engaged with a variety of socially constituted systems". The ecological model usefully complicates the learning and teaching of writing because it reminds us of the social context in which all writers work. Cooper identifies at least five systems that every writer is necessarily involved in:

> The system of ideas is the means by which writers comprehend their world, to turn individual experiences and observations into knowledge. . . .
>
> The system of purposes is the means by which writers coordinate their actions. . . .
>
> The system of interpersonal interactions is the means by which writers regulate their access to one another. . . .
>
> The system of cultural norms is the means by which writers structure the larger groups of which they are members. . . .
>
> The system of textual forms is, obviously, the means by which writers communicate.

Teachers who find the ecological model appealing are still defining its pedagogical implications. Their primary goal is to empower writers to membership in various discourse communities. Their classrooms are not always in a building on campus. They may teach writing in a community literacy project, a shelter for battered women, or a prison, where definitions of *community* and *empowerment* are complicated by social alienation and economic disenfranchisement. On campus, they may realize their goal best in cross-curricular courses that help students negotiate the demands of writing in varied disciplines. For these teachers, writing-across-the-curriculum is not a course in reading and then writing essays about issues such as global warming; such courses can be just as product-centered as traditional writing-about-literature courses are. Instead, these teachers encourage students to understand the systems that comprise the diverse discourse communities in which students find themselves. The ecological model suggests that, if students learn the systems and conventions characterizing particular discourse communities, they can successfully participate in and eventually even alter these communities.

To understand the discourses of the academy and gain confidence in approximating them, students must learn new ways of reading and writing. David Bartholomae's "Inventing the University" and Bartholomae and Anthony Petrosky's *Facts, Artifacts, and Counterfacts* help teachers understand how students encounter the academy and begin to find their place in it. No one seriously proposes that English 101 can prepare a first-year student to read and write the discourse of physics with the fluency of an experienced physicist. But English 101 can introduce students to some disciplinary assumptions about using language to make knowledge.

Seeing writing as a system contextualizes these disciplinary perspectives and raises questions student writers inevitably must answer for every course they take: What is a legitimate subject to write about in this discipline? What assertions and proofs are appropriate? What options do I have for defining my point of view and organizing my material? What should my writing look like, what conventions of form and style apply? Through careful reading and the analysis of a variety of texts, students examine how writers in the sciences, social sciences, and humanities handle these matters. Then they practice creating similar texts: journalistic essays, interpretations of music or art, case studies, analyses of data, and investigations of problems a discipline seeks to address. Assignments in this kind of English 101 course rarely call for self-expressive writing; instead, tasks resemble those that students encounter in the academy. They usually call for referential and persuasive writing because informing and persuading members of academic discourse communities (including professors) are significant functions of academic literacy.

Teachers adopting the ecological model attempt to forge their English 101 classes into a community of writers. They act as facilitators. Though students may begin the course having been schooled in the strategies of individual competition, the teacher deliberately fosters collaboration so that students must now learn from one another. In this model, students are always members of a stable writing group, working together for the entire term so that they develop trust in one another, accept responsibility for the group's successes and failures, and appreciate one another's diverse abilities and interests. Every class meeting involves group activities: developing schedules for a project and assigning research tasks, sharing information gained from independent reading and research, talking out plans for a draft, responding to and revising drafts, sometimes writing collaboratively. Discussions of readings also may begin in groups, each group talking about and writing out what it wishes to say about a text, then reporting its findings to the rest of the class. The teacher assumes responsibility for setting tasks that require learning by consensus, for monitoring students' work (intervening only to clarify tasks or help groups work efficiently), for synthesizing discussion, and for reporting on the quality of the work the groups have done. Community, collaboration, and responsibility are the watchwords.

System-centered courses treat invention, arrangement, and style as conventional, as practices admitting considerable variability. Each discourse community advances its own principles of good writing, which initiates must infer by reading and analyzing models intelligently and then imitating them. Because the opportunities for misreading are plentiful—as any student struggling to make sense of a difficult course knows—focusing exclusively on texts is not enough. Textual forms, as Cooper notes, are only one of several systems characterizing any discourse community. Students also must understand the community's culture, what subjects it finds worth writing about how readers and writers relate to one another, what value people place on experience, observation, interpretation, speculation, objectivity, and so on. In the process, students learn how flexible such concepts as audience, purpose, and style are. Students come to understand that "good writing" requires making effective choices in juggling the demands of a task, a language, a rhetoric, and an audience.

Because most writing teachers feel at home in the humanities, they can "know" firsthand only some of the conventions governing academic discourse communities. They may find it next to impossible to judge what a biologist might call "good writing." While this obstacle a together prevents some teachers from adopting the approach, other teachers have developed ways to learn more about the ecology of the academy. They learn much from talking with their students. They discuss writing with colleagues in other disciplines, requesting samples of their students' work and using their training in how to read texts to deduce rhetorical and linguistic principles that need attention in English 101. They invite faculty members to class to explain their expectations for effective student prose. Sometimes they team-teach writing courses linked to courses in other disciplines.

Adhering to the model can be difficult when it comes to evaluating students' writing. Ideally, the ecological model suggests that those most familiar with the system should judge the student's work, just as our own writing gets judged by those audiences for whom we intend it. By this logic, if an English 101 assignment asks students to approximate the discourses of the social sciences, social science faculty members should assess the responses. In some team-taught or linked courses they do, but for other types of system-centered English 101 classes, this arrangement is impractical. As a result, most teachers adopt an unhappy compromise. They maintain a faith that their students *eventually* will succeed in writing for other faculty members, but they adopt traditional methods of grading students' papers or borrow strategies that have worked well for process-centered teachers—a portfolio system, for example.

Dissatisfied with the compromise, a few teachers have explored an alternative emphasizing communal standards for good writing, standards developed in the context of the English 101 class itself. These teachers, trained in methods of holistic assessment, teach their students how to evaluate one another's work holistically. Guided by the requirements of a fully contextualized assignment, the class develops a scoring guide or a rubric. Because this rubric makes clear and public the criteria that will be used to assess students' responses, it also helps students plan, draft, and revise their work. After the teacher has collected the final drafts, students practice scoring actual responses (identified only by a "student number" such as the last four digits of a social security number) until they become calibrated to the rubric. Then they read and score their unidentified classmates' work. Anyone familiar with the literature on assessment understands the inherent dangers in such a system of evaluation. Nevertheless, with proper training, students can be as capable and conscientious as teachers in evaluating student writing responsibly. The method helps students internalize and apply criteria for effective writing much more quickly than teacher-controlled assessments do, and it reinforces the principle that students really are writing for one another, for the class-as-discourse-community, which will eventually judge their work.

Collaborative writing, group work, even students' evaluating one another's writing are not new. Nineteenth-century college students engaged in such practices in their debating societies, communities they formed to prepare themselves for the pulpit, the bar, and the lectern in ways that they believed their courses could not. While they are methods new to English 101 and likely to concern product- or process-centered teachers, pedagogies that foster active, communal learning nevertheless also enjoy the sanction of tradition. Moreover, the ecological model finds growing support among those faculty members and administrators outside English departments who believe that English 101 ought to prepare students for the writing they must do to succeed in the academy. In "Writing and Knowing: Toward Redefining the Writing Process," James A. Reither concludes that "writing and what writers do during writing cannot be artificially separated from the social-rhetorical situations in which writing gets done, from the conditions that enable writers to do what they do, and from the motives writers have for doing what they do". Teachers adopting the ecological perspective have helped us direct writing back into the world, reminding us of the social context of all rhetorical activity.

A Common Ground?

All three views of *writing* exist simultaneously in our profession. Yet each perspective promotes an English 101 course that differs from the others with respect to its principal focus, the roles it assigns teachers and students, the function reading has in the course, the reasons why students write, and the standards by which we judge their work. Reading, for example, is important in all three models, but reading literature may not be. To see writing as product is to assert the primacy of texts; consequently, reading and discussing belletristic literature may occupy considerable prominence in a traditional English 101 class. To see writing as process is to advocate the importance of what people do *as* they read and write; so *how* students read may matter more than *what* they read in a process-centered English 101. Expressivist pedagogy supports a definition of *literature* enlarged to include genres other than poetry, fiction, and drama and at the same time also narrowed to focus on texts that have a self-expressive aim. To see writing as a system is to value the complicated contexts in which writers and readers use language to interact with one another; reading, like writing, offers a way into the conversation. A literary text, however, may not be a form by which writers and readers communicate in a particular discourse community, or it may be only one of many forms. So an English 101 course that examines the function of reading in the academy (or in a community outside it) may omit belletristic literature, primarily because reading and writing about literature are activities peculiar to only one discourse community students encounter. To omit literature, however, is not to ignore reading or the multitude of interpretive practices disciplines use to make knowledge. Because all disciplines comprise dynamic interlocking systems, we cannot assume that the ways of reading practiced in one discipline necessarily apply to any other.

What then is our common ground? I would argue that it is teaching. Regardless of which perspective shapes our peculiar brand of English 101, *we all seek to give students practice with reading and writing.* We hope to guide this practice in constructive ways, designing assignments and class activities that encourage students to see the power and possibility of language. We hold students responsible, not only to themselves, but also to an audience, a larger society of readers. As surrogates for this audience, we offer feedback on the reading and writing students do, not only to help them improve their performance but also to make familiar and useful the standards by which they may judge their own work. *We do all this in the belief that what we teach is worth knowing and that our students are worth our respectful attention.*

At the same time, if these statements characterize our common ground, they are too general to govern consistent instructional practices. For example, while we might agree on the value of "designing assignments and class activities that encourage students to see the power and possibility of language," we disagree about how best to implement this goal. As we have seen, the assignments and class activities in product-, process-, and system-centered courses all look quite different. Similarly, every sentence in the preceding paragraph admits diverse possibilities for giving students practice with reading and writing, holding students responsible to themselves and an audience, offering feedback on the reading and writing students do, and so on. Though teaching may not be shabby common ground on which to stand, our divergent views of English 101 may promote greater disagreement than consensus about pedagogical issues. Even so, I do not believe that English 101 teachers hold such disparate views of the course that they cannot talk with one another, a conversation it seems to me increasingly urgent for us all to participate in.

I am not suggesting that all English 101 courses must look alike or that all teachers must hold the same view of writing, teaching, or learning. But we also cannot justify our work as a profession by giving every English 101 teacher license to do as he or she pleases. Some of the instructional practices I have described make sense, and others are ineffective. How do we best evaluate them?

It is clear to me that private criteria will not help us identify teaching strategies that merit either applause or condemnation. We now have access to considerable research and scholarship that deserves further discussion—in our journals, our conferences, and our classrooms. The pedagogical implications of this work need our collective, not merely our individual, attention. We need to adopt some of the strategies beginning teachers use to discuss with one another what they read and how it affects their teaching. In deciding what kind of teacher they wish to become, in developing a rhetoric of teaching, they not only ask questions about themselves, their students, and the purpose of English 101, but also keep testing their assumptions against the collective wisdom of a local as well as a national professional community.

Experienced teachers, however, too often suppose that the provisional answers they settled for after a year or so in the classroom will serve a lifetime. Because every writing teacher approaches his or her initiation into the profession individually, uniquely, each eventually comes to believe that "whatever works for me and my students is best." But such self-expressive assertions ignore the larger institutional and professional culture that in fact also has shaped our understanding of what it means to teach English 101 well. Private definitions of good teaching, persistent inconsistencies between what we say and what we do, and resistance to approaches that seem alien to us prevent the sort of communal thinking necessary to identifying our common ground and explaining our work to others, especially students, parents, and colleagues outside and within the profession.

In outlining here three views of English 101, I have tried to avoid arguing that one is "right." Making such a claim would amount to substituting my preference for judgments I believe we should make collectively. It would serve to close a conversation rather than continue it. My purpose instead has been to define in the differences I have described some important tensions to resolve. We ought not regard these differences as either a matter "simply" of personal taste or as implied criticisms of how some teachers conduct their classes. Paradoxically, pedagogical differences may represent opportunities to discover shared assumptions. Our differences may help us redefine those instructional practices that we, as a community of English 101 teachers, find essential to our work.

Works Cited

Bartholomae, David. "Inventing the University." *When a Writer Can't Write: Studies in Writer's Block and Other Composing Process Problems.* Ed. Mike Rose. New York: Guilford P, 1985. 134–65.

Bartholomae, David, and Anthony Petrosky, eds. *Facts, Artifacts and Counterfacts: Theory and Method for a Reading and Writing Course.* Portsmouth: Boynton/Cook, 1986.

Cooper, Marilyn M. "The Ecology of Writing." *College English* 48 (April 1986): 364–75. Rpt. in Marilyn M. Cooper and Michael Holzman. *Writing as Social Action.* Portsmouth: Boynton/Cook, 1989.

Elbow, Peter. "The War between Reading and Writing—And How to End It." *Rhetoric Review* 12 (Fall 1993): 5–24.

"Four Comments on 'Two Views on the Use of Literature in Composition.'" *College English* 55 (October 1993): 673–79.

Lindemann, Erika. "Freshman Composition: No Place for Literature." *College English* 55 (March 1993): 311–16.

Reither, James A. "Writing and Knowing: Toward Redefining the Writing Process." *College English* 47 (October 1985): 620–28.

Tate, Gary. "A Place for Literature in Freshman Composition." *College English* 55 (March 1993): 317–21.

Wiener, Harvey S. "Collaborative Learning in the Classroom: A Guide to Evaluation." *College English* 48 (January 1986): 52–61.

Young, Richard E., Alton L. Becker, and Kenneth L. Pike. *Rhetoric: Discovery and Change.* New York: Harcourt, Brace & World, 1970.

Additional Sources

Berlin, James A. "Contemporary Composition: The Major Pedagogical Theories." *College English* 44 (December 1982): 765–77.

Divides approaches to composition into four categories: Aristotelian, current-traditional, expressionist, epistemic. Promotes the last as the most appropriate.

Hillocks, George Jr. *Research on Written Composition: New Directions for Teaching.* Urbana: NCRE, 1986.

Compiles and reviews qualitative and quantitative research on the teaching of written composition from 1963 on: the composing process, the writer's repertoire, experimental methods, modes of instruction, grammar and manipulation of syntax, criteria for better writing, invention.

Part I
Writing Processes and Audience Awareness

Chapter 2

The Writing Process

Given that the disparate, even mutually exclusive, approaches to the teaching of writing make persuasive claims for *their* benefits, instructors may find it extremely difficult to detect areas of common ground. Despite their differences, all sorts of theories, methodologies, and even qualitative and quantitative research agree that teaching writing as a process is most effective.

This rare amount of philosophical agreement is supported by almost thirty years of research. In the sixties, William Perry's studies of college students at Harvard suggested that extending Piaget's development model could explain what students really learn while at college. Perry argued that students learn the cognitive processes that enable them to move from a simple and highly authoritarian kind of dualism (that statements are true or false, and teachers should grade on that basis) to an informed skepticism (that there are many answers to most questions, and what matters is how well one makes one's case). Perry's research encouraged educators to think about teaching in terms of processes—the processes in which our students are engaged and the processes of how we teach.

This attention to process gained strength toward the end of the sixties and the beginning of the seventies when researchers began looking carefully at student writing processes. Janet Emig's (1971) groundbreaking study of twelfth grade students showed that many of the problems in students' products were connected to their processes. The research of Nancy Sommers, Sondra Perl, Carol Berkenkotter, Mike Rose, and Linda Flowers and Richard Hayes all confirmed this basic notion: Effective and successful writers have a flexible, complicated, and recursive writing process, whereas people with problems writing papers tend toward a more linear and rigid process that restricts revision to lexical editing.

This notion is most effectively conveyed in Flower and Hayes's metaphor of writing as problem-solving: Students need to see the writing task as solving a problem rather than simply as answering a question. It is interesting to speculate about why this conceptual shift seems so difficult for many students. As Rose notes, the answer to that question is almost certainly multivalent. For instance, my students often say that they do not know how to revise more substantially— their critical reading and analysis skills are not strong enough for them to identify what changes to make in their drafts. In addition, many students say that they were trained to write with a linear process, which limits opportunity for revision, and that they were punished for varying from a rigid outline or were required to follow a very narrow procedure. Because no one else has ever asked these students to make substantial revisions, they react to my suggestions for substantial revision with overt skepticism. Certainly, because few high school instructors have had the time to grade multiple drafts of their papers, few first-year college students have ever had the experience of revising at more than the sentence level.

Unfortunately, although the majority of research findings support the teaching of writing as a process, composition researchers do not agree about which teaching method is the best one for productively enhancing the intricacy of students' writing processes. For example, researchers disagree about whether students should be graded on the sorts of processes they use—assigning grades to their pieces of freewriting, clustering, and so on—or whether students should simply be graded according to a product, such as the completion of an effective final draft in a specific form. Nevertheless, composition research does indicate certain, more and less, productive approaches to influencing more intricate student writing processes. For instance, in "The Cognition of Discovery: Defining a Rhetorical Problem," Flower and Hayes have shown the importance of "problem-solving" in devising an effective writing process; that is, successful writers tend to shape an assignment, re-making it in important ways, whereas the novice writer tends to defer to the assignment, trying to infer clues to the correct answer. In "Rigid Rules, Inflexible Plans, and the Stifling of Language: A Cognitivist Analysis of Writer's Block," Rose has described this same quality, noting the importance of "some conflict, some stress, some gap or information" which "seems to trigger problem-solving behavior". This research indicates, then, that a good writing assignment will have some gap or conflict that will permit students to identify the problem they want to solve; hence, if we write assignments in which we are looking for a correct answer, we have stopped teaching writing.

Similarly, much of the research on writing process supports Rose's contention that writing blocks are closely associated with rigidity in the writing process. This research suggests that we help our students most when we teach them additional strategies for writing instead of replacing one rigid set of rules with another equally rigid set. Thus when we teach writing processes, we need to ensure that we are teaching what Rose calls "heuristics" rather than algorithms.

From experience, I can say that lecturing to students about the writing process is a waste of time. It is slightly more ambitious, but not overly so, to ask that students synthesize the research on writing process by attempting to apply it. For, although people like Sommers, Flower and Hayes, and Rose are not writing for a student audience, students are more than capable of reading and understanding those articles. They can then apply that research to their own writing processes, attempt protocol analysis of other students' writing, or read multiple submissions of papers from another section of composition students in order to apply the concepts and terms in the research on writing process. While such an approach does not immediately solve the problems in students' writing processes, I have found that it gives us a common vocabulary for talking about writing, and it does seem to make students productively reflective of their own strategies.

The Cognition of Discovery: Defining a Rhetorical Problem

Linda Flower and John R. Hayes

Metaphors give shape to mysteries, and traditionally we have used the metaphor of *discovery* to describe the writer's creative process. Its broad meaning has sheltered many intellectual styles ranging from classical invention to modern heuristics such as tagmemics to self-exploratory modes such as Pre-Writing. Furthermore, *discovery* carries an implicit suggestion that, somewhere in the mind's recesses or in data outside the mind, there is something waiting to be discovered, and that writing is a way to bring that something out. However, if we try to use this metaphor to teach or analyze the creative process itself, we discover its limitations.[1]

First of all, because *discovery* emphasizes the rather glamorous experience of "Eureka, now I see it," it obscures the fact that writers don't *find* meanings, they *make* them. A writer in the act of discovery is hard at work searching memory, forming concepts, and forging a new structure of ideas, while at the same time trying to juggle all the constraints imposed by his or her purpose, audience, and language itself.[2] Discovery, the event, and its product, new insights, are only the end result of a complicated intellectual process. And it is this process we need to understand more fully.

There is a second, practical reason for teachers to probe this metaphor. The notion of discovery is surrounded by a mythology which, like the popular myth of romantic inspiration, can lead writers to self-defeating writing strategies. The myth of discovery implies a method, and this method is based on the premise that hidden stores of insight and ready-made ideas exist, buried in the mind of the writer, waiting only to be "discovered." Or they are to be found in books and data if only the enterprising researcher knows where to look. What does one do when a ready-made answer can't be found in external sources? The myth says, "look to your own experience." But what happens when a writer on this internal voyage of discovery still can't "find" something to say because his or her "ideas" as such are not actually formed? What is there to "discover" if only confused experience and conflicting perceptions are stored in a writer's memory? The mythology of discovery doesn't warn the writer that he or she must often build

[1]This research was partially supported by a grant from the National Institute of Education, Department of Health, Education, and Welfare, Grant NIE G780195.

[2]Linda Flower and John R. Hayes, "The Dynamics of Composing: Making Plans and Juggling Constraints," in *Cognitive Processes in Writing,* ed. Lee Gregg and Erwin Steinberg (Hillsdale, NJ: Lawrence Erlbaum, in press); Linda Flower and John R. Hayes, "Problem Solving Strategies and the Writing Process," *College English,* 39 (Dec. 1977), 449–61.

or create new concepts out of the raw material of experience; nor does it tell the writer how to do it. And yet, this act of *creating* ideas, not finding them, is at the heart of significant writing.

When an attempt at this literal discovery fails, as it often must, it leads inexperienced writers to an unnecessary defeat. Fluent writers are affected by the myth of discovery in another way. As Nancy Sommers has shown, many seem to equate the successful discovery of something to say (i.e., the "flow" of stored ideas) with successful writing, whether that flow is appropriate to the rhetorical situation or not.[3] The myth of discovery, as many of us see it in students, leads the poor writer to give up too soon and the fluent writer to be satisfied with too little.

Discovery, then, is a perplexing notion. On the one hand, it metaphorically describes an intellectual process we want to teach. On the other hand, the metaphor and mythology of discovery itself often distort our vision of that process. This paper attempts to probe the cognition of discovery, the process itself, by studying the way writers initiate and guide themselves through the act of making meaning.

Our approach has been to study writing as a problem-solving, cognitive process. From a psychological point of view, people have a "problem" whenever they are at some point "A" and wish to be at another point "B"; for example, when they have a new insight into *Hamlet,* but have yet to write the paper that will explain it. Their problem-solving process is the thinking process they use to get to point "B," the completed paper. That process might involve many intellectual skills including open, exploratory procedures, such as free writing and day dreaming. But it is important to remember that this process is not a creative accident.

In this study we wanted to explore the problem-solving or discovery process that produces new insight and new ideas. So we started with what many feel to be the most crucial part of that process—the act of finding or defining the problem to be "solved." As Ann Berthoff says, "A shortcoming of most of our students [is] they do not easily recognize particular problems [that need to be solved] because they do not have a method for, that is, a means of formulating critical questions."[4]

This shortcoming turns out to be critical because people only solve the problem they give themselves to solve. The act of formulating questions is sometimes called "problem-finding," but is is more accurate to say that writers build or represent such a problem to themselves, rather than "find" it. A rhetorical problem in particular is never merely a given: it is an elaborate construction which the writer creates in the act of composing. We wanted to see how writers actually go about building this inner, private representation.

There are a number of reasons why this act of constructing an image of one's rhetorical problem is worth study. First, it helps explain why writing, like

[3]Nancy I. Sommers, "Revision Strategies of Student Writers and Experienced Writers," MLA Convention, New York, 28 Dec. 1978.

[4]Ann E. Berthoff, "Towards a Pedagogy of Knowing," *Freshman English News,* 7 (Spring 1978), 4.

other creative thinking, can be so utterly unpredictable. Even though a teacher gives 20 students the same assignment, *the writers themselves create the problem they solve.* The reader is not the writer's only "fiction." Furthermore, the act of problem-finding is a critical part of general creativity in both the arts and sciences. Because people only solve the problems they give themselves, the act of representing the problem has a dramatic impact on performance. James Britton saw this with bewildered or unmotivated children, with their strange notions of what the teacher wanted, as did Sondra Perl working with adult basic writers. People simply rewrite an assignment or a situation to make it commensurate with their own skills, habits, or fears.[5] Although writing texts generally ignore this part of the writing process,[6] our work suggests that it may be one of the most critical steps the average writer takes.

The first part of this paper, then, will describe our method for studying the cognitive process by which people represent the rhetorical problem. Then we will present a model of the rhetorical problem itself, that is, a description of the major elements writers could consider in building such an image. Finally, we will use this model of the possible as a basis for comparing what good and poor writers actually do.

Studying Cognitive Processes

The research question we posed for ourselves was this: if discovery is an act of making meaning, not finding it, in response to a *self-defined problem* or goal, how does this problem get defined? Specifically, we wanted to answer three questions:

1. What aspects of a rhetorical problem do people actively represent to themselves? For example, do writers actually spend much time analyzing their audience, and if so, how do they do it?
2. If writers do spend time developing a full representation of their problem, does it help them generate new ideas?
3. And finally, are there any significant differences in the way good and poor writers go about this task?

In order to describe the problem definition process itself, we collected thinking-aloud protocols from both expert and novice writers. A protocol is a detailed record of a subject's behavior. Our protocols include a transcript of a tape recording made by writers instructed to verbalize their thinking process as they write, as well as all written material the writer produced. A typical protocol from

---

[5]James Britton et al., *The Development of Writing Abilities* (11–18) (London: Macmillan, 1975); Sondra Perl, "Five Writers Writing: Case Studies of the Composing Process of Unskilled College Writers," Diss. New York University, 1978.

[6]Richard L. Larson, "The Rhetorical Act of Planning a Piece of Discourse." Beaver College Conference on Evaluation of Writing, Glenside, PA, October 1978.

The Rhetorical Problem	
Elements of the Problem	Examples
THE RHETORICAL SITUATION	
Exigency of Assignment	"Write for Seventeen magazine; this is impossible."
Audience	"Someone like myself, but adjusted for twenty years."
THE WRITER'S OWN GOALS involving the	
Reader	"I'll change their notion of English teachers . . . "
Persona or Self	"I'll look like an idiot if I say . . . "
Meaning	"So if I compare those two attitudes . . ."
Text	"First we'll want an introduction."

Figure 1 Elements of the rhetorical problem writers represent to themselves in composing

a one-hour session will include four to five pages of notes and writing and 15 pages of typed transcript. The novice writers were college students who had gone to the Communication Skills Center for general writing problems such as coherence and organization. The expert writers were teachers of writing and rhetoric who had received year-long NEH fellowships to study writing. Each writer was given the following problem: "write about your job for the readers of *Seventeen* magazine, 13–14 year-old girls," and was asked to compose out loud into a tape recorder as he or she worked. They were told to verbalize everything that went through their minds, including stray thoughts and crazy ideas, but not to try to analyze their thought process, just to express it.

A Model of the Rhetorical Problem

From these protocols, we pulled together a composite picture or model of the rhetorical problem itself. This composite is shown in Figure 1, with examples drawn from our writers' protocols. It is based on what the group of writers did and shows the basic elements of a writing problem which a given writer *could* actively consider in the process of composing, *if* he or she chose to. For example, the writer in the following excerpt is actively creating an image of himself or his *persona,* an image of what effect he might have on his reader, and an initial representation of a meaning or idea he might choose to develop, as the words in brackets indicate.

Ah, in fact, that might be a useful thing to focus on, how a professor differs from . . . how a teacher differs from a professor, [meaning], and I see myself as a teacher, [*persona*], that might help them, my audience, to reconsider their notion of what an English teacher does. [effect on audience]

Taken as a whole, the *rhetorical problem* breaks into two major units. The first is the rhetorical *situation*. This situation, which is the writer's given, includes the audience and assignment. The second unit is the set of *goals* the writer himself creates. The four dominant kinds of goals we observed involved affecting the *reader,* creating a *persona* or voice, building a *meaning,* and producing a formal *text.* As you see, these turned out to closely parallel the four terms of the communication triangle: reader, writer, world, word. This parallel between communication theory and our study is a happy one, since protocol analysis lets us describe what writers actually do as they write, not just what we, as theorists, think they should do. And, as we will see, one of the major differences between good and poor writers will be how many aspects of this total rhetorical problem they actually consider and how thoroughly they represent any aspect of it to themselves.

This model of the rhetorical problem reflects the elements writers actively consider as they write. It accounts for the conscious representation going on as writers compose. But is that enough? Protocols yield a wealth of information available in no other way, but they are limited to those aspects of the problem the writer is able in some way to articulate. But in understanding a writer's process we can't ignore that rich body of inarticulate information Polanyi would call our "tacit knowledge." We think that much of the information people have about rhetorical problems exists in the form of *stored problem representations.* Writers do no doubt have many such representations for familiar or conventional problems, such as writing a thank-you letter. Such a representation would contain not only a conventional definition of the situation, audience, and the writer's purpose, but might include quite detailed information about solutions, even down to appropriate tone and phrases. Experienced writers are likely to have stored representations of even quite complex rhetorical problems (e.g., writing a book review for readers of *The Daily Tribune*) if they have confronted them often before.

Naturally, if a writer has a stored representation that is fully adequate for the current situation, we wouldn't expect him to spend time building a new one. Achieving that kind of mental efficiency is what learning is all about. However, many writing problems, such as the one we gave our subjects, are unique and require a writer to build a *unique representation.* In such situations, we would expect a good writer to explore the problem afresh and to give conscious time and attention to building a unique representation. Therefore, in capturing the conscious representation of these unique problems, we feel we are likely to capture the critical part of the process. As it turned out, one of the most telling differences between our good and poor writers was the degree to which they created a unique, fully-developed representation of this unique rhetorical problem.

Our model or composite picture of the writer's rhetorical problem specifies two kinds of information writers represent to themselves: information about the rhetorical situation and information about the writer's own purpose and goals. We will discuss these two aspects of the rhetorical problem in order.

Representing a Rhetorical Situation

A *rhetorical situation* is the name we assign to the givens with which a writer must work, namely, the audience and assignment. Lloyd Bitzer's description of this situation as an exigency (e.g., assignment), an audience, and a set of constraints is a good description of what our subjects actually considered or represented to themselves.[7] (However, unlike Bitzer, we see this external situation as only part of a larger entity we call the rhetorical problem.)

The writer's initial analysis of the assignment and audience was usually brief. Most writers—both novice and expert—plunged quickly into generating ideas, but often returned to reconsider these givens later. For the novice writer, however, this re-examination of the *situation* often took the form of simply rereading the assignment, maybe two or three times, as if searching for a clue in it. A more intense form of this strategy was also observed by Perl, whose basic writers would read the assignment over and over until some key word struck an associative chord and reminded them of a topic on which they had something to say.[8] Although the novice writers in our study were actually analyzing the situation, they never moved beyond the sketchy, conventional representation of audience and assignment with which they started.

The good writers, by contrast, used their re-examination of the situation to add to their image of the audience or assignment. For example, this writer initially defined the audience as "someone like myself when I read—well, not like myself but adjusted for, well, twenty years later." Later in the protocol her image of the reader became significantly different:

> I feel a certain constraint knowing as I do the rather saccharine editorial policy. Perhaps I'm mistaken, but the last time I had my hair cut or something, I read it and they still seemed to be mostly looking at women as consumers of fashion and as consumers of men and really not as capable or interested in or likely to be drawn to an occupation like mine which is rather low paying and unglamorous and, ah, far from chic clothes.

As you can see, this writer is creating a sophisticated, complex image of a reader—half alter-ego, half fashion consumer—which she will have to deal with in the act of writing. No doubt it will be harder to write for such an audience than for a simple stereotype, but the final result is going to be more effective if

---

[7]Lloyd Bitzer, "The Rhetorical Situation," *Philosophy and Rhetoric,* 1 (Jan. 1968). 1–14.

[8]Perl, "Five Writers Writing."

she has indeed represented her audience accurately. We can imagine similar differences in two students' representations of an assignment such as "analyze *Hamlet*." Let us assume that both writers have roughly equal bodies of knowledge stored in memory. One writer might draw on that knowledge to give herself detailed instructions, e.g., 'analyze this play'; that means I should try to break it down into some kind of parts. Perhaps I could analyze the plot, or the issues in the play, or its theatrical conventions." This student is drawing on the experience and semantic knowledge which both students possess to create a highly developed image of how to analyze something (e.g., break it into parts) and how to analyze this play in particular (e.g., find the critical issues). Meanwhile, another writer might blithely represent the problem as "Write another theme and talk about *Hamlet* this time, in time for Tuesday's class. That probably means about two pages."

Representing One's Purpose and Goals

An audience and exigency can jolt a writer into action, but the force which drives composing is the writer's own set of goals, purposes, or intentions. A major part of defining the rhetorical problem then is representing one's own goals. As we might predict from the way writers progressively fill in their image of the audience, writers also build a progressive representation of their goals as they write.

We can break these goals into four groups. The first is focused on the effect the writer wants to have on the *reader*. These can range from quite ambitious global plans, such as "I'll change their image of English teachers," down to decisions about local effects, such as "make this sound plausible," or "make this seem immediate to their experience." At times the intention of the writer is to have a direct personal effect on the reader as a person. For example, one writer structured her paper in order to make her reader "remain in a state of suspension [about jobs] and remain in an attentive posture toward her own history, abilities, and sources of satisfaction." She wanted to make the reader "feel autonomous and optimistic and effective." At other times the goal is a more general one of making the reader simply see something or comprehend accurately a train of thought (e.g., "I've got to attract the attention of the reader," or "There needs to be a transition between those two ideas to be clear").

One of the hallmarks of the good writers was the time they spent thinking about how they wanted to affect a reader. They were clearly representing their rhetorical problem as a complex speech act. The poor writers, by contrast, often seemed tied to their topic. This difference matters because, in our study, one of the most powerful strategies we saw for producing new ideas throughout the composing process was planning what one wanted to do to or for one's reader.

A second kind of purpose writers represent to themselves involves the relationship they wish to establish with the reader. This relationship can also be described as the *persona,* projected self, or voice the writer wishes to create. This part of the problem representation is the least likely to appear in a protocol because writers are probably likely to draw on a stored representation of their *persona* even for unique problems. Furthermore, decisions about one's *persona* are often expressed by changes in word choice and tone, not by direct statements. Nevertheless, this is a part of a writer's goals or purpose which he or she must define in some way. In one writer this issue was directly broached three times. At the begining of composing, she saw her role as that of a free-lance writer writing to a formula. But unfortunately

> my sense is that it's a formula which I'm not sure I know, so I suppose what I have to do is invent what the formula might be, and then try to include events or occurrences or attitude or experiences in my own job that could be conveyed in formula. So let's see. . . .

Clearly, her sense of her role as formula writer affects how she will go about writing this paper. But later this same writer revised her relationship with the reader and in so doing radically changed the rhetorical problem. She accused herself of taking the hypocritical voice of adulthood and set a new goal:

> I feel enormously doubtful of my capacity to relate very effectively to the audience that is specified and in that case, I mean, all I can do is, is just, you know, present myself, present my concepts and my message or my utterance in a kind of simple and straightforward and unpretentious way, I hope.

A third goal writers develop involves the writer's attempt to build a coherent network of ideas, to create *meaning*. All writers start, we assume, with a stored goal that probably says something like, "Explore what you know about this topic and write it down; that is, generate and express relevant ideas." We see evidence of this goal when writers test or evaluate what they've just said to see if it is related to or consistent with other ideas. Many of our writers never appeared to develop goals much more sophisticated than this generate-and-express goal, which, in its most basic form, could produce simply an interior monologue. However, some writers defined their meaning-making problem in more complex and demanding ways, telling themselves to focus on an important difference, to pursue an idea because it seemed challenging, or to step back and decide "more generally, how do I want to characterize my job." Perhaps the difference here is one of degree. At one end of a spectrum, writers are merely trying to express a network of ideas already formed and available in memory; at the other, writers are consciously attempting to probe for analogues and contradictions, to form new concepts, and perhaps even to restructure their old knowledge of the subject.

Finally, a fourth goal which writers represent involves the formal or conventional features of a written text. Early in composing, writers appear to make many basic decisions about their genre and set up goals such as "write an introduction first." Most college students no doubt have a great deal of information in their stored representation of the problem "write a short essay." However, once into the text, writers often expand their image of possibilities by considering unique features the text might include. For example, writers tell themselves to "fictionalize it," to "use a direct question," "try a rhetorical question," or "try to add a little example or little story here to flesh it out." In doing so, they set up goals based primarily on their knowledge of the conventions of writing and the features of texts. This may be one way in which extensive reading affects a person's ability to write: a well-read person simply has a much larger and richer set of images of what a text can look like. Goals such as these often have plans for reaching the goal built right into them. For example, when one of the expert writers decided to use a problem/solution format for the paper, he was immediately able to tap a pocket of stored plans for creating such a format. The convention itself specified just what to include. Furthermore, once he set up this familiar format as a goal, he saw what to do with a whole body of previously unorganized ideas.

Differences among Writers

This six-part model of the rhetorical problem attempts to describe the major kinds of givens and goals writers could represent to themselves as they compose. As a model for comparison it allowed us to see patterns in what our good and poor writers actually did. The differences, which were striking, were these:

1. Good writers respond *to all* aspects of the rhetorical problem. As they compose they build a unique representation not only of their audience and assignment, but also of their goals involving the audience, their own *persona,* and the text. By contrast, the problem representations of the poor writers were concerned primarily with the features and conventions of a written text, such as number of pages or magazine format. For example, Figure 2 shows a vivid contrast between an expert and novice when we compare the way two writers represented their rhetorical problem in the first 60 lines of a protocol. The numbers are based on categorizing phrases and sentences within the protocol.

| | Analysis of rhetorical situation: Audience an Assignment | Analysis of goals | | | | |
		Audience	Self	Text	Meaning	Total
Novice	7	0	0	3	7	17
Expert	18	11	1	3	9	42

Figure 2   Number of times writer explicitly represented each aspect of the rhetorical problem in first 60 lines of protocol

As you can see, the expert made reference to his audience or assignment 18 times in the first seven to eight minutes of composing, whereas the novice considered the rhetorical situation less than half that often. The most striking difference, of course, is in their tendency to represent or create goals for dealing with the audience. Finally, the column marked "Total" shows our expert writer simply spending more time than the novice in thinking about and commenting on the rhetorical problem, as opposed to spending that time generating text.

2. In building their problem representation, good writers create a particularly rich network of goals for affecting their reader. Furthermore, these goals, based on affecting a reader, also helped the writer generate new ideas. In an earlier study we discovered that our experienced writers (a different group this time) generated up to 60 per cent of their new ideas in response to the larger rhetorical problem (that is, in response to the assignment, their audience, or their own goals). Only 30 per cent were in response to the topic alone. For example, a writer would say, "I'll want an introduction that pulls you in," instead of merely reciting facts about the topic, such as "As an engineer the first thing to do is . . ." In the poor writers the results were almost reversed: 70 per cent of their new ideas were statements about the topic alone without concern for the larger rhetorical problem.[9] All of this suggests that setting up goals to affect a reader is not only a reasonable act, but a powerful strategy for generating new ideas and exploring even a topic as personal as "my job."

As you might easily predict, plans for affecting a reader also give the final paper a more effective rhetorical focus. For example, one of the novice writers, whose only goals for affecting the audience were to "explain [his] job simply so it would appeal to a broad range of intellect," ended up writing a detailed technical analysis of steam turbulence in an electrical generator. The topic was of considerable importance to him as a future research engineer, but hardly well focused for the readers of *Seventeen.*

3. Good writers represent the problem not only in more breadth, but in depth. As they write, they continue to develop their image of the reader, the situation, and their own goals with increasing detail and specificity. We saw this in the writer who came back to revise and elaborate her image of her fashion-consuming reader. By contrast, poor writers often remain throughout the entire composing period with the flat, undeveloped, conventional representation of the problem with which they started.

The main conclusion of our study is this: good writers are simply solving a different problem than poor writers. Given the fluency we can expect from native speakers, this raises an important question. Would the performance of poor writers change if they too had a richer sense of what they were trying to do

[9]Linda Flower and John R. Hayes, "Process-Based Evaluation of Writing: Changing the Performance, Not the Product." American Educational Research Association Convention, San Francisco, 9 April 1979.

as they wrote, or if they had more of the goals for affecting the reader which were so stimulating to the good writers? People only solve the problems they represent to themselves. Our guess is that the poor writers we studied possess verbal and rhetorical skills which they fail to use because of their underdeveloped image of their rhetorical problem. Because they have narrowed a rhetorical act to a paper-writing problem, their representation of the problem doesn't call on abilities they may well have.

This study has, we think, two important implications, one for teaching and one for research. First, if we can describe how a person represents his or her own problem in the act of writing, we will be describing a part of what makes a writer "creative." A recent, long-range study of the development of creative skill in fine art showed some striking parallels between successful artists and our expert writers. This seven-year study, entitled *The Creative Vision: A Longitudinal Study of Problem-Finding in Art*, concluded that the critical ability which distinguished the successful artists was not technical skill, but what the authors called *problem-finding*—the ability to envision, pose, formulate, or create a new problematic situation.[10] Furthermore, in this experimental study of artists at work, the three behaviors which distinguished the successful artists were the breadth and depth of their exploration of the problem and their delay in reaching closure on the finished product. In this experiment the artists were given a studio equipped with materials and a collection of objects they might draw. The successful artists, like our expert writers, explored more of the materials before them and explored them in more depth, fingering, moving, touching, rearranging, and playing with alternatives, versus moving quickly to a rather conventional arrangement and sketch. Once drawing was begun, the artists' willingness to explore and reformulate the problem continued, often until the drawing was nearly completed. Similarly, our successful writers continued to develop and alter their representation of the problem throughout the writing process. This important study of creativity in fine art suggested that problem-finding is a talent, a cognitive skill which can lead to creativity. The parallels between these two studies suggest that problem-finding in both literature and art is related not only to success, but in some less well defined way to "creativity" itself.

Other studies in the psychology of creativity make this link between creative thinking and problem-solving processes more explicit.[11] Many "creative" breakthroughs in science and the arts are not the result of finding a better technical solution to an old problem (e.g., the disease-producing influence of evil spirits), but of seeing a new problem (e.g., the existence of germs). In many cases, the solution procedure is relatively straightforward once one has defined the

---

[10]Jacob W. Getzels and Mihaly Csikszentmihalyi, *The Creative Vision: A Longitudinal Study of Problem Finding in Art* (New York: John Wiley and Sons, 1976).

[11]John R. Hayes, *Cognitive Psychology: Thinking and Creating* (Homewood, IL: Dorsey Press, 1978); M. Wertheimer, *Productive Thinking* (New York: Harper and Row, 1945).

problem. For example, Virginia Woolf's *The Waves* or Van Gogh's impressionistic landscapes are less a technical feat than an act of imagining a new problem or set of goals for the artist.

We feel there are implications for exciting research in this area. This study has attempted to develop a model of the rhetorical problem as a guide to further research, and to describe three major differences between good and poor writers. But there is much we could learn about how people define their rhetorical problems as they write and why they make some of the choices they do.

The second implication we see in our own study is that the ability to explore a rhetorical problem is eminently teachable. Unlike a metaphoric "discovery," problem-finding is not a totally mysterious or magical act. Writers discover what they want to do by insistently, energetically exploring the entire problem before them and building for themselves a unique image of the problem they want to solve. A part of creative thinking is just plain thinking.

Exploring a topic alone isn't enough. As Donald Murray put it, "writers wait for signals" which tell them it is time to write, which "give a sense of closure, a way of handling a diffuse and overwhelming subject."[12] Many of the "signals" Murray described, such as having found a point of view, a voice, or a genre, parallel our description of the goals and plans we saw good writers making. If we can teach students to explore and define their own problems, even within the constraints of an assignment, we can help them to create inspiration instead of wait for it.

[12]Donald M. Murray, "Write Before Writing," *College Composition and Communication,* 29 (Dec. 1978), 375–81.

Rigid Rules, Inflexible Plans, and the Stifling of Language: A Cognitivist Analysis of Writer's Block
Mike Rose

Ruth will labor over the first paragraph of an essay for hours. She'll write a sentence, then erase it. Try another, then scratch part of it out. Finally, as the evening winds on toward ten o'clock and Ruth, anxious about tomorrow's deadline, begins to wind into herself, she'll compose that first paragraph only to sit back and level her favorite exasperated interdiction at herself and her page: "No. You can't say that. You'll bore them to death."

Ruth is one of ten UCLA undergraduates with whom I discussed writer's block, that frustrating, self-defeating inability to generate the next line, the right phrase, the sentence that will release the flow of words once again. These ten people represented a fair cross-section of the UCLA student community: lower-middle-class to upper-middle-class backgrounds and high schools, third-world and Caucasian origins, biology to fine arts majors, C+ to A− grade point averages, enthusiastic to blasé attitudes toward school. They were set off from the community by the twin facts that all ten could write competently, and all were currently enrolled in at least one course that required a significant amount of writing. They were set off among themselves by the fact that five of them wrote with relative to enviable ease while the other five experienced moderate to nearly immobilizing writer's block. This blocking usually resulted in rushed, often late papers and resultant grades that did not truly reflect these students' writing ability. And then, of course, there were other less measurable but probably more serious results: a growing distrust of their abilities and an aversion toward the composing process itself.

What separated the five students who blocked from those who didn't? It wasn't skill; that was held fairly constant. The answer could have rested in the emotional realm—anxiety, fear of evaluation, insecurity, etc. Or perhaps blocking in some way resulted from variation in cognitive style. Perhaps, too, blocking originated in and typified a melding of emotion and cognition not unlike the relationship posited by Shapiro between neurotic feeling and neurotic thinking.[1] Each of these was possible. Extended clinical interviews and testing could have teased out the answer. But there was one answer that surfaced readily in brief explorations of these students' writing processes. It was not profoundly emotional, nor was it embedded in that still unclear construct of cognitive style. It was constant, surprising, almost amusing if its results weren't so troublesome, and, in the final analysis, obvious: *the five students who experienced blocking were all operating*

[1] David Shapiro, *Neurotic Styles* (New York; Basic Books, 1965).

either with writing rules or with planning strategies that impeded rather than enhanced the composing process. The five students who were not hampered by writer's block also utilized rules, but they were less rigid ones, and thus more appropriate to a complex process like writing. Also, the plans these non-blockers brought to the writing process were more functional, more flexible, more open to information from the outside.

These observations are the result of one to three interviews with each student. I used recent notes, drafts, and finished compositions to direct and hone my questions. This procedure is admittedly non-experimental, certainly more clinical than scientific; still, it did lead to several inferences that lay the foundation for future, more rigorous investigation: (a) composing is a highly complex problem-solving process[2] and (b) certain disruptions of that process can be explained with cognitive psychology's problem-solving framework. Such investigation might include a study using "stimulated recall" techniques to validate or disconfirm these hunches. In such a study, blockers and non-blockers would write essays. Their activity would be videotaped and, immediately after writing, they would be shown their respective tapes and questioned about the rules, plans, and beliefs operating in their writing behavior. This procedure would bring us close to the composing process (the writers' recall is stimulated by their viewing the tape), yet would not interfere with actual composing.

In the next section I will introduce several key concepts in the problem-solving literature. In section three I will let the students speak for themselves. Fourth, I will offer a cognitivist analysis of blockers' and non-blockers' grace or torpor. I will close with a brief note on treatment.

Selected Concepts in Problem Solving: Rules and Plans

As diverse as theories of problem solving are, they share certain basic assumptions and characteristics. Each posits an *introductory period* during which a problem is presented, and all theorists, from Behaviorist to Gestalt to Information Processing, admit that certain aspects, stimuli, or "functions" of the problem must become or be made salient and attended to in certain ways if successful problem-solving processes are to be engaged. *Theorists also believe that some conflict, some stress, some gap in information in these perceived "aspects" seems to trigger problem-solving behavior.* Next comes a *processing period,* and for all the variance of opinion about this critical stage, theorists recognize the necessity of its existence—recognize that man, at the least, somehow "weighs" possible solutions as

---

[2]Barbara Hayes-Ruth, a Rand cognitive psychologist, and I are currently developing an information-processing model of the composing process. A good deal of work has already been done by Linda Flower and John Hayes (see p. 90 of this article) I have just received—and recommend—their "Writing as Problem Solving" (paper presented at American Educational Research Association, April, 1979).

they are stumbled upon and, at the most, goes through an elaborate and sophisticated information-processing routine to achieve problem solution. Furthermore, theorists believe—to varying degrees—that past learning and the particular "set," direction, or orientation that the problem solver takes in dealing with past experience and present stimuli have critical bearing on the efficacy of solution. Finally, all theorists admit to a *solution period,* an end-state of the process where "stress" and "search" terminate, an answer is attained, and a sense of completion or "closure" is experienced.

These are the gross similarities, and the framework they offer will be useful in understanding the problem-solving behavior of the students discussed in this paper. But since this paper is primarily concerned with the second stage of problem-solving operations, it would be most useful to focus this introduction on two critical constructs in the processing period: rules and plans.

Rules

Robert M. Gagné defines "rule" as "an inferred capability that enables the individual to respond to a class of stimulus situations with a class of performances."[3] Rules can be learned directly[4] or by inference through experience.[5] But, in either case, most problem-solving theorists would affirm Gagné's dictum that "rules are probably the major organizing factor, and quite possibly the primary one, in intellectual functioning."[6] As Gagné implies, we wouldn't be able to function without rules; they guide response to the myriad stimuli that confront us daily, and might even be the central element in complex problem-solving behavior.

Dunker, Polya, and Miller, Galanter, and Pribram offer a very useful distinction between two general kinds of rules: algorithms and heuristics.[7] *Algorithms are precise rules that will always result in a specific answer if applied to an appropri-*

---

[3] *The Conditions of Learning* (New York: Holt, Rinehart and Winston, 1970), p. 193.

[4] E. James Archer, "The Psychologieal Nature of Concepts," in H. J. Klausmeier and C. W. Harris, eds., *Analysis of Concept Learning* (New York: Academic Press, 1966), pp. 37–44; David P. Ausubel, *The Psychology of Meaningful Verbal Behavior* (New York: Grune and Stratton, 1963); Robert M. Gagné, "Problem Solving," in Arthur W. Melton, ed., *Categories of Human Learning* (New York: Academic Press, 1964), pp. 293–317; George A. Miller, *Language and Communication* (New York: McGraw-Hill, 1951).

[5] George Katona, *Organizing and Memorizing* (New York: Columbia Univ. Press, 1940); Roger N. Shepard, Carl I. Hovland, and Herbert M. Jenkins, "Learning and Memorization of Classifications," *Psychological Monographs,* 75, No. 13 (1961) (entire No. 517); Robert S. Woodworth, *Dynamics of Behavior* (New York: Henry Holt, 1958), chs. 10–12.

[6] *The Conditions of Learning,* pp. 190–91.

[7] Karl Dunker, "On Problem Solving," *Psychological Monographs,* 58, No. 5 (1945) (entire No. 270); George A. Polya, *How to Solve It* (Princeton: Princeton University Press, 1945); George A. Miller, Eugene Galanter, and Karl H. Pribram, *Plans and the Structure of Behavior* (New York: Henry Holt, 1960).

ate problem. Most mathematical rules, for example, are algorithms. Functions are constant (e.g., pi), procedures are routine (squaring the radius), and outcomes are completely predictable. However, few day-to-day situations are mathematically circumscribed enough to warrant the application of algorithms. Most often we function with the aid of fairly general heuristics or "rules of thumb," guidelines that allow varying degrees of flexibility when approaching problems. Rather than operating with algorithmic precision and certainty, we search, critically, through alternatives, using our heuristic as a divining rod—"if a math problem stumps you, try working backwards to solution"; "if the car won't start, check x, y, or z, and so forth. Heuristics won't allow the precision or the certitude afforded by algorithmic operations; heuristics can even be so "loose" as to be vague. But in a world where tasks and problems are rarely mathematically precise, heuristic rules become the most appropriate, the most functional rules available to us: "a heuristic does not guarantee the optimal solution or, indeed, any solution at all; rather, heuristics offer solutions that are good enough most of the time."[8]

Plans

People don't proceed through problem situations, in or out of a laboratory, without some set of internalized instructions to the self, some program, some course of action that, even roughly, takes goals and possible paths to that goal into consideration. Miller, Galanter, and Pribram have referred to this course of action as a plan: "A plan is any hierarchical process in the organism that can control the order in which a sequence of operations is to be performed". They name the fundamental plan in human problem-solving behavior the TOTE, with the initial T representing a *test* that matches a possible solution against the perceived end-goal of problem completion. O represents the clearance to *operate* if the comparison between solution and goal indicates that the solution is a sensible one. The second T represents a further, post-operation, *test* or comparison of solution with goal, and if the two mesh and problem solution is at hand the person *exits* (E) from problem-solving behavior. If the second test presents further discordance between solution and goal, a further solution is attempted in TOTE-fashion. Such plans can be both long-term and global and, as problem solving is underway, short-term and immediate.[9] Though the mechanicality of this information-processing model renders it simplistic and, possibly, unreal, the central notion of a plan and an operating procedure is an important one in problem-solving theory; it at least attempts to metaphorically explain what earlier cognitive psychologists could not—the mental procedures underlying problem-solving behavior.

[8]Lyle E. Bourne, Jr., Bruce R. Ekstrand, and Roger L. Dominowski, *The Psychology of Thinking* (Englewood Cliffs, NJ: Prentice-Hall, 1971).

[9]John R. Hayes, "Problem Topology and the Solution Process," in Carl P. Duncan, ed., *Thinking: Current Experimental Studies* (Philadelphia: Lippincott, 1967), pp. 167–81.

Before concluding this section, a distinction between heuristic rules and plans should be attempted; it is a distinction often blurred in the literature, blurred because, after all, we are very much in the area of gestating theory and preliminary models. Heuristic rules seem to function with the flexibility of plans. Is, for example, "If the car won't start, try x, y, or z" a heuristic or a plan? It could be either, though two qualifications will mark it as heuristic rather than plan. (A) Plans subsume and sequence heuristic and algorithmic rules. Rules are usually "smaller," more discrete cognitive capabilities; plans can become quite large and complex, composed of a series of ordered algorithms, heuristics, and further planning "sub-routines." (B) Plans, as was mentioned earlier, include criteria to determine successful goal-attainment and, as well, include "feedback" processes— ways to incorporate and use information gained from "tests" of potential solutions against desired goals.

One other distinction should be made: that is, between "set" and plan. Set, also called "determining tendency" or "readiness,"[10] refers to the fact that people often approach problems with habitual ways of reacting, a predisposition, a tendency to perceive or function in one way rather than another. Set, which can be established through instructions or, consciously or unconsciously, through experience, can assist performance if it is appropriate to a specific problem,[11] but much of the literature on set has shown its rigidifying, dysfunctional effects.[12] *Set differs from plan in that set represents a limiting and narrowing of response alternatives with no inherent process to shift alternatives.* It is a kind of cognitive habit that can limit perception, not a course of action with multiple paths that directs and sequences response possibilities.

The constructs of rules and plans advance the understanding of problem solving beyond that possible with earlier, less developed formulations. Still, critical problems remain. Though mathematical and computer models move one toward more complex (and thus more real) problems than the earlier research, they are still too neat, too rigidly sequenced to approximate the stunning complexity of day-to-day (not to mention highly creative) problem-solving behavior. Also, information-processing models of problem-solving are built on logic theorems, chess strategies, and simple planning tasks. Even Gagné seems to feel more comfortable with illustrations from mathematics and science rather than

[10]Hulda J. Rees and Harold E. Israel, "An Investigation of the Establishment and Operation of Mental Sets," *Psychological Monographs,* 46 (1925) (entire No. 210).

[11]Ibid.; Melvin H. Marx, Wilton W. Murphy, and Aaron J. Brownstein, "Recognition of Complex Visual Stimuli as a Function of Training with Abstracted Patterns," *Journal of Experimental Psychology,* 62 (1961), 456–60.

[12]James L. Adams, *Conceptual Blockbusting* (San Francisco: W. H. Freeman, 1974); Edward DeBono, *New Think* (New York: Basic Books, 1958); Ronald H. Forgus, *Perception* (New York: McGraw-Hill, 1966), ch. 13; Abraham Luchins and Edith Hirsch Luchins, *Rigidity of Behavior* (Eugene: Univ. of Oregon Books, 1959); N. R. F. Maier, "Reasoning in Humans. I. On Direction," *Journal of Comparative Psychology,* 10 (1920), 115–43.

with social science and humanities problems. So although these complex models and constructs tell us a good deal about problem-solving behavior, they are still laboratory simulations, still invoked from the outside rather than self-generated, and still founded on the mathematico-logical.

Two Carnegie-Mellon researchers, however, have recently extended the above into a truly real, amorphous, unmathematical problem-solving process—writing. Relying on protocol analysis (thinking aloud while solving problems), Linda Flower and John Hayes have attempted to tease out the role of heuristic rules and plans in writing behavior.[13] Their research pushes problem-solving investigations to the real and complex and pushes, from the other end, the often mysterious process of writing toward the explainable. The latter is important, for at least since Plotinus many have viewed the composing process as unexplainable, inspired, infused with the transcendent. But Flower and Hayes are beginning, anyway, to show how writing generates from a problem-solving process with rich heuristic rules and plans of its own. They show, as well, how many writing problems arise from a paucity of heuristics and suggest an intervention that provides such rules.

This paper, too, treats writing as a problem-solving process, focusing, however, on what happens when the process dead-ends in writer's block. It will further suggest that, as opposed to Flower and Hayes' students who need more rules and plans, blockers may well be stymied by possessing rigid or inappropriate rules, or inflexible or confused plans. Ironically enough, these are occasionally instilled by the composition teacher or gleaned from the writing textbook.

"Always Grab Your Audience"—The Blockers

In high school, *Ruth* was told and told again that a good essay always grabs a reader's attention immediately. Until you can make your essay do that, her teachers and textbooks putatively declaimed, there is no need to go on. For Ruth, this means that beginning bland and seeing what emerges as one generates prose is unacceptable. The beginning is everything. And what exactly is the audience seeking that reads this beginning? The rule, or Ruth's use of it, doesn't provide for such investigation. She has an edict with no determiners. Ruth operates with another rule that restricts her productions as well: if sentences aren't grammatically "correct," they aren't useful. This keeps Ruth from toying with ideas on paper, from the kind of linguistic play that often frees up the flow of prose. These two rules converge in a way that pretty effectively restricts Ruth's composing process.

The first two papers I received from *Laurel* were weeks overdue. Sections of

---

[13]"Plans and the Cognitive Process of Writing," paper presented at the National Institute of Education Writing Conference, June 1977; "Problem Solving Strategies and the Writing Process," *College English,* 39 (1977), 449–61. See also footnote 2.

them were well written; there were even moments of stylistic flair. But the papers were late and, overall, the prose seemed rushed. Furthermore, one paper included a paragraph on an issue that was never mentioned in the topic paragraph. This was the kind of mistake that someone with Laurel's apparent ability doesn't make. I asked her about this irrelevant passage. She knew very well that it didn't fit, but believed she had to include it to round out the paper. "You must always make three or more points in an essay. If the essay has less, then it's not strong." Laurel had been taught this rule both in high school and in her first college English class; no wonder, then, that she accepted its validity.

As opposed to Laurel, *Martha* possesses a whole arsenal of plans and rules with which to approach a humanities writing assignment, and, considering her background in biology, I wonder how many of them were formed out of the assumptions and procedures endemic to the physical sciences.[14] Martha will not put pen to first draft until she has spent up to two days generating an outline of remarkable complexity. I saw one of these outlines and it looked more like a diagram of protein synthesis or DNA structure than the timeworn pattern offered in composition textbooks. I must admit I was intrigued by the aura of process (vs. the static appearance of essay outlines) such diagrams offer, but for Martha these "outlines" only led to self-defeat: the outline would become so complex that all of its elements could never be included in a short essay. In other words, her plan locked her into the first stage of the composing process. Martha would struggle with the conversion of her outline into prose only to scrap the whole venture when deadlines passed and a paper had to be rushed together.

Martha's "rage for order" extends beyond the outlining process. She also believes that elements of a story or poem must evince a fairly linear structure and thematic clarity, or—perhaps bringing us closer to the issue—that analysis of a story or poem must provide the linearity or clarity that seems to be absent in the text. Martha, therefore, will bend the logic of her analysis to reason ambiguity out of existence. When I asked her about a strained paragraph in her paper on Camus' "The Guest," she said, "I didn't want to admit that it [the story's conclusion] was just hanging. I tried to force it into meaning."

Martha uses another rule, one that is not only problematical in itself, but one that often clashes directly with the elaborate plan and obsessive rule above. She believes that humanities papers must scintillate with insight, must present an array of images, ideas, ironies gleaned from the literature under examination. A problem arises, of course, when Martha tries to incorporate her myriad "neat little things," often inherently unrelated, into a tightly structured, carefully sequenced essay. Plans and rules that govern the construction of impressionistic,

[14]Jane, a student not discussed in this paper, was surprised to find out that a topic paragraph can be rewritten after a paper's conclusion to make that paragraph reflect what the essay truly contains. She had gotten so indoctrinated with Psychology's (her major) insistence that a hypothesis be formulated and then left untouched before an experiment begins that she thought revision of one's "major premise" was somehow illegal. She had formed a rule out of her exposure to social science methodology, and the rule was totally inappropriate for most writing situations.

associational prose would be appropriate to Martha's desire, but her composing process is heavily constrained by the non-impressionistic and non-associational. Put another way, the plans and rules that govern her exploration of text are not at all synchronous with the plans and rules she uses to discuss her exploration. It is interesting to note here, however, that as recently as three years ago Martha was absorbed in creative writing and was publishing poetry in high school magazines. Given what we know about the complex associational, often non-neatly-sequential nature of the poet's creative process, we can infer that Martha was either free of the plans and rules discussed earlier or they were not as intense. One wonders, as well, if the exposure to three years of university physical science either established or intensified Martha's concern with structure. Whatever the case, *she now is hamstrung by conflicting rules when composing papers for the humanities.*

Mike's difficulties, too, are rooted in a distortion of the problem-solving process. When the time of the week for the assignment of writing topics draws near, Mike begins to prepare material, strategies, and plans that he believes will be appropriate. If the assignment matches his expectations, he has done a good job of analyzing the professor's intentions. If the assignment *doesn't* match his expectations, however, he cannot easily shift approaches. He feels trapped inside his original plans, cannot generate alternatives, and blocks. As the deadline draws near, he will write something, forcing the assignment to fit his conceptual procrustian bed. Since Mike is a smart man, he will offer a good deal of information, but only some of it ends up being appropriate to the assignment. This entire situation is made all the worse when the time between assignment of topic and generation of product is attenuated further, as in an essay examination. Mike believes (correctly) that one must have a plan, a strategy of some sort in order to solve a problem. He further believes, however, that such a plan, once formulated, becomes an exact structural and substantive blueprint that cannot be violated. The plan offers no alternatives, no "sub-routines." So, whereas Ruth's, Laurel's, and some of Martha's difficulties seem to be rule-specific ("always catch your audience," "write grammatically"), Mike's troubles are more global. He may have strategies that are appropriate for various writing situations (e.g., "for this kind of political science assignment write a compare/contrast essay"), but his entire approach to formulating plans and carrying them through to problem solution is too mechanical. It is probable that Mike's behavior is governed by an explicitly learned or inferred rule: "Always try to 'psych out' a professor." But in this case this rule initiates a problem-solving procedure that is clearly dysfunctional.

While Ruth and Laurel use rules that impede their writing process and Mike utilizes a problem-solving procedure that hamstrings him, *Sylvia* has trouble deciding which of the many rules she possesses to use. Her problem can be characterized as cognitive perplexity: some of her rules are inappropriate, others are functional; some mesh nicely with her own definitions of good writing, others don't. She has multiple rules to invoke, multiple paths to follow, and that very complexity of choice virtually paralyzes her. More so than with the previous four students, there is probably a strong emotional dimension to Sylvia's blocking, but the cognitive difficulties are clear and perhaps modifiable.

Sylvia, somewhat like Ruth and Laurel, puts tremendous weight on the crafting of her first paragraph. If it is good, she believes the rest of the essay will be good. Therefore, she will spend up to five hours on the initial paragraph: "I won't go on until I get that first paragraph down." Clearly, this rule—or the strength of it—blocks Sylvia's production. This is one problem. Another is that Sylvia has other equally potent rules that she sees as separate, uncomplementary injunctions: one achieves "flow" in one's writing through the use of adquate transitions; one achieves substance to one's writing through the use of evidence. Sylvia perceives both rules to be "true," but several times followed one to the exclusion of the other. Furthermore, as I talked to Sylvia, many other rules, guidelines, definitions were offered, but none with conviction. While she is committed to one rule about initial paragraphs, and that rule is dysfunctional, she seems very uncertain about the weight and hierarchy of the remaining rules in her cognitive repertoire.

"If It Won't Fit My Work, I'll Change It" —The Non-blockers

Dale, Ellen, Debbie, Susan, and Miles all write with the aid of rules. But their rules differ from blockers' rules in significant ways. If similar in content, they are expressed less absolutely—e.g., "*Try* to keep audience in mind." If dissimilar, they are still expressed less absolutely, more heuristically—e.g., "I can use as many ideas in my thesis paragraph as I need and then develop paragraphs for each idea." Our non-blockers do express some rules with firm assurance, but these tend to be simple injunctions that free up rather than restrict the composing process, e.g., "When stuck, write!" or "I'll write what I can." And finally, at least three of the students openly shun the very textbook rules that some blockers adhere to: e.g., "Rules like 'write only what you know about' just aren't true. I ignore those." These three, in effect, have formulated a further rule that expresses something like: "If a rule conflicts with what is sensible or with experience, reject it."

On the broader level of plans and strategies, these five students also differ from at least three of the five blockers in that they all possess problem-solving plans that are quite functional. Interestingly, on first exploration these plans seem to be too broad or fluid to be useful and, in some cases, can barely be expressed with any precision. Ellen, for example, admits that she has a general "outline in [her] head about how a topic paragraph should look" but could not describe much about its structure. Susan also has a general plan to follow, but, if stymied, will quickly attempt to conceptualize the assignment in different ways: "If my original idea won't work, then I need to proceed differently." Whether or not these plans operate in TOTE-fashion, I can't say. But they do operate with the operate-test fluidity of TOTEs.

True, our non-blockers have their religiously adhered-to rules: e.g., "When stuck, write," and plans, "I couldn't imagine writing without this pattern," but as noted above, these are few and functional. Otherwise, these non-blockers operate with fluid, easily modified, even easily discarded rules and plans (Ellen: "I can throw things out") that are sometimes expressed with a vagueness that could almost be interpreted as ignorance. There lies the irony. *Students that offer the least precise rules and plans have the least trouble composing.* Perhaps this very lack of precision characterizes the functional composing plan. But perhaps this lack of precision simply masks habitually enacted alternatives and sub-routines. This is clearly an area that needs the illumination of further research.

And then there is feedback. At least three of the five non-blockers are an Information-Processor's dream. They get to know their audience, ask professors and T.A.s specific questions about assignments, bring half-finished products in for evaluation, etc. Like Ruth, they realize the importance of audience, but unlike her, they have specific strategies for obtaining and utilizing feedback. And this penchant for testing writing plans against the needs of the audience can lead to modification of rules and plans. Listen to Debbie:

> In high school I was given a formula that stated that you must write a thesis paragraph with *only* three points in it, and then develop each of those points. When I hit college I was given longer assignments. That stuck me for a bit, but then I realized that I could use as many ideas in my thesis paragraph as I needed and then develop paragraphs for each one. I asked someone about this and then tried it. I didn't get any negative feedback, so I figured it was o.k.

Debbie's statement brings one last difference between our blockers and non-blockers into focus; it has been implied above, but needs specific formulation: the goals these people have, and the plans they generate to attain these goals, are quite mutable. Part of the mutability comes from the fluid way the goals and plans are conceived, and part of it arises from the effective impact of feedback on these goals and plans.

Analyzing Writer's Block

Algorithms Rather Than Heuristics

In most cases, the rules our blockers use are not "wrong" or "incorrect"—it is good practice, for example, to "grab your audience with a catchy opening" or "craft a solid first paragraph before going on." *The problem is that these rules seem to be followed as though they were algorithms, absolute dicta, rather than the loose heuristics that they were intended to be.* Either through instruction, or the power of the textbook, or the predilections of some of our blockers for absolutes, or all three, these useful rules of thumb have been transformed into near-algorithmic urgencies. The result, to paraphrase Karl Dunker, is that these rules do not allow a flexible penetration into the nature of the problem. It is this transformation of heuristic into algorithm that contributes to the writer's block of Ruth and Laurel.

Questionable Heuristics Made Algorithmic

Whereas "grab your audience" could be a useful heuristic, "always make three or more points in an essay" is a pretty questionable one. Any such rule, though probably taught to aid the writer who needs structure, ultimately transforms a highly fluid process like writing into a mechanical lockstep. As heuristics, such rules can be troublesome. As algorithms, they are simply incorrect.

Set

As with any problem-solving task, students approach writing assignments with a variety of orientations or sets. Some are functional, others are not. Martha and Jane (see footnote 14), coming out of the life sciences and social sciences respectively, bring certain methodological orientations with them—certain sets or "directions" that make composing for the humanities a difficult, sometimes confusing, task. In fact, this orientation may cause them to misperceive the task. Martha has formulated a planning strategy from her predisposition to see processes in terms of linear, interrelated steps in a system. Jane doesn't realize that she can revise the statement that "committed" her to the direction her essay has taken. Both of these students are stymied because of formative experiences associated with their majors—experiences, perhaps, that nicely reinforce our very strong tendency to organize experiences temporally.

The Plan That Is Not a Plan

If fluidity and multi-directionality are central to the nature of plans, then the plans that Mike formulates are not true plans at all but, rather, inflexible and static cognitive blueprints.[15] Put another way, Mike's "plans" represent a restricted "closed system" (vs. "open system") kind of thinking, where closed system thinking is defined as focusing on "a limited number of units or items, or members, and those properties of the members which are to be used are known to begin with and do not change as the thinking proceeds," and open system thinking is characterized by an "adventurous exploration of multiple alterna-

---

[15]Cf. "A plan is flexible if the order of execution of its parts can be easily interchanged without affecting the feasibility of the plan . . . the flexible planner might tend to think of lists of things he had to do; the inflexible planner would have his time planned like a sequence of cause-effect relations. The former could rearrange his lists to suit his opportunities, but the latter would be unable to strike while the iron was hot and would generally require considerable 'lead-time' before he could incorporate any alternative sub-plans" (Miller, Galanter, and Pribram, p. 120).

tives with strategies that allow redirection once 'dead ends' are encountered."[16] Composing calls for open, even adventurous thinking, not for constrained, no-exit cognition.

Feedback

The above difficulties are made all the more problematic by the fact that they seem resistant to or isolated from corrective feedback. One of the most striking things about Dale, Debbie, and Miles is the ease with which they seek out, interpret, and apply feedback on their rules, plans, and productions. They "operate" and then they "test," and the testing is not only against some internalized goal, but against the requirements of external audience as well.

Too Many Rules—"Conceptual Conflict"

According to D. E. Berlyne, one of the primary forces that motivate problem-solving behavior is a curiosity that arises from conceptual conflict—the convergence of incompatible beliefs or ideas. In *Structure and Direction in Thinking*,[17] Berlyne presents six major types of conceptual conflict, the second of which he terms "perplexity":

> This kind of conflict occurs when there are factors inclining the subject toward each of a set of mutually exclusive beliefs. (p. 257)

If one substitutes "rules" for "beliefs" in the above definition, perplexity becomes a useful notion here. Because perplexity is unpleasant, people are motivated to reduce it by problem-solving behavior that can result in "disequalization":

> Degree of conflict will be reduced if either the number of competing . . . [rules] or their nearness to equality of strength is reduced. (p. 259)

But "disequalization" is not automatic. As I have suggested, Martha and Sylvia hold to rules that conflict, but their perplexity does *not* lead to curiosity and resultant problem-solving behavior. Their perplexity, contra Berlyne, leads to immobilization. Thus "disequalization" will have to be effected from without. The importance of each of, particularly, Sylvia's rules needs an evaluation that will aid her in rejecting some rules and balancing and sequencing others.

A Note On Treatment

Rather than get embroiled in a blocker's misery, the teacher or tutor might interview the student in order to build a writing history and profile: How much and what kind of writing was done in high school? What is the student's major? What kind of writing does it require? How does the student compose? Are there

[16]Frederic Bartlett, *Thinking* (New York: Basic Books, 1958), pp. 74–76.

[17]*Structure and Direction in Thinking* (New York: John Wiley, 1965). p. 255.

rough drafts or outlines available? By what rules does the student operate? How would he or she define "good" writing? etc. This sort of interview reveals an incredible amount of information about individual composing processes. Furthermore, it often reveals the rigid rule or the inflexible plan that may lie at the base of the student's writing problem. That was precisely what happened with the five blockers. And with Ruth, Laurel, and Martha (and Jane) what was revealed made virtually immediate remedy possible. Dysfunctional rules are easily replaced with or counter-balanced by functional ones if there is no emotional reason to hold onto that which simply doesn't work. Furthermore, students can be trained to select, to "know which rules are appropriate for which problems."[18] Mike's difficulties, perhaps because plans are more complex and pervasive than rules, took longer to correct. But inflexible plans, too, can be remedied by pointing out their dysfunctional qualities and by assisting the student in developing appropriate and flexible alternatives. Operating this way, I was successful with Mike. Sylvia's story, however, did not end as smoothly. Though I had three forty-five minute contacts with her, I was not able to appreciably alter her behavior. Berlyne's theory bore results with Martha but not with Sylvia. Her rules were in conflict, and perhaps that conflict was not exclusively cognitive. Her case keeps analyses like these honest; it reminds us that the cognitive often melds with, and can be overpowered by, the affective. So while Ruth, Laurel, Martha, and Mike could profit from tutorials that explore the rules and plans in their writing behavior, students like Sylvia may need more extended, more affectively oriented counseling sessions that blend the instructional with the psychodynamic.

Additional Sources

Faigley, Lester. "Competing Theories of Process: A Critique and a Proposal." *College English* 48 (October 1986): 527–42.

Describes and criticizes three dominant views of the composing process: expressive, cognitive, and social.

Hatch, Gary Layne. "Reviving the Rodential Model for Composition: Robert Zoellner's Alternative to Flower and Hayes." *Rhetoric Review* Vol. 10, 2 (Spring 1992): 244–49.

Criticizes much research in the composing process for relying on instrumental metaphors; promotes Zoellner's work.

LeFevre, Karen Burke. *Invention as a Social Act.* Carbondale: Southern Illinois UP, 1987.

Argues that the neo-Platonic view of invention (as a solitary act dependent upon inspiration) should be replaced by a more accurate social view of the invention process.

[18]Flower and Hayes, "Plans and the Cognitive Process of Writing." p. 26.

Murray, Donald M. "All Writing Is Autobiography." *College Composition and Communication* Vol. 42, 1 (February 1991): 66–74.

Based largely on personal experience, explores the autobiographical impulse behind all genres of writing.

Perl, Sondra. "The Composing Process of Unskilled College Writers." *Research in the Teaching of English* Vol. 13, 4(December 1979): 317–36.

Uses cognitive approach on five writers' writing processes in order to suggest better ways of teaching unskilled writers.

Chapter 3
Audience

One of the best writing teachers I ever had insisted that almost all writing blocks were caused by a muddled notion of audience. It is certainly easy to get the concept of audience muddled, given the very different relationships described by the term "audience." In an extremely useful footnote, Peter Elbow lists these different relationships in terms of different "entities": the actual audience, the writer's intended audience, the audience implied by the text, the discourse community indicated by formal conventions, and what Elbow calls "ghost" readers.

These "entities" can be seen in the following situation: If, when standing in line at a grocery store with a friend, I begin to talk about Kevin Costner in loud tones, there is likely to be an actual audience that includes other people near us. That audience would include my intended audience (my friend), but it would not be limited to her. I might, however, make assumptions about my friend that are not true (for example, that she has seen *Dances with Wolves*); therefore, my intended and my implied audience would not be the same. I might also appeal to certain conventions of film analysis (indicating an audience of film critics) or include comments that have more to do with someone else than with whom I have discussed: Costner. Interestingly, the more that I am aware of conflicts among those various audiences, the more likely I am to be completely paralyzed and unable to say anything.

Some instructors will specify the audience in the assignment itself. Telling students, for example, to write the paper for publication in a certain magazine (or kind of magazine) can help students identify what Lindemann calls "the systems and conventions characterizing particular discourse communities". As Lindemann notes in "Three Views of English 101," assignments like this (often, but not necessarily, connected to a writing in the disciplines program) "treat invention, arrangement, and style as conventional, as practices admitting considerable variability". In other words, there are not the sorts of rigid rules about format that Rose argued can contribute to writing blocks, but an understanding of the conventions which a student might choose to violate for a specific intention.

The advantage of specifying the class as the audience is that students can literally see their audience reactions. The vividness of that reaction can help the teacher reshape some unhelpful advice that students may have been given about writing. For instance, students have sometimes been told that research or informative papers do not have a thesis, which is a recipe for a boring paper. They may not have the same kind of thesis as some other papers, but there must be a point, and the paper must not only explain that point but give the reader a sense as to why it is an important point. If students write their thesis (by which I mean a one- or two-sentence summary of their point) on the chalkboard, they can find out if any class member would choose to read the paper. They can get useful advice from their prospective audience about what parts of the point should be gone into at length and what parts should be dealt with briefly.

There are disadvantages to papers being written for other class members. For example, argumentative writing requires an audience that is knowledgeable, and writing to fellow class members normally limits just how knowledgeable a rhetor can assume his or her audience to be. Hence, many programs ask that students not write to fellow class members, but to experts in the field. Clearly, such a program makes strategies like peer review and group work much less important.

But, there is always the option of writing about one kind of audience while talking to another. Students can try to produce an analysis on another topic—doing careful analysis of audience expectations in the field of engineering, for instance—and write that analysis to fellow class members. They would then present their analysis of an expert audience to an audience which is itself expert on audience analysis.

In "Closing My Eyes as I Speak: An Argument for Ignoring Audience," the first article in this chapter, Elbow makes the argument that there are benefits to ignoring audience, at least at certain moments in the writing process. What Elbow does not fully acknowledge is that I am likely to irritate and alienate my friend if I don't pay attention to her signals—if I don't notice that she looks confused when I mention *Dances with Wolves,* she may conclude I am a self-absorbed fool. Nevertheless, as Elbow argues, it is not the sort of audience that matters, but the sort of relationship we have with that audience.

There are some audiences whom we can imagine wanting to hear what we have to say or with whom we want to communicate, whereas other audiences intimidate and inhibit us. Elbow discusses the various sorts of feelings we might have for those audiences, and how those feelings might improve or impede the writing process, but he does not discuss the relationship in terms of intentions. That is, when Elbow says "It's often difficult to work out new meaning while thinking about readers," what he means is that it is difficult to work out new meaning when we are thinking about how to please an imagined reader. It is not thinking about audience that causes the problems but thinking about how to gratify them.

This distinction may seem pedantic, but it is central to the point that Ede and Lunsford discuss in the second article in this chapter, "Audience Addressed/Audience Invoked: The Role of Audience in Composition Theory and Pedagogy." In this article, Ede and Lunsford claim that there is an ethical component to how we teach audience. Teaching what they call "audience addressed" seems to make writing a form of pandering, and it seems to place all responsibility for accommodation on the writer. Teaching "audience invoked" is, however, unrealistic, as it seems to place all responsibility on the reader to accommodate to the writer. As Ede and Lunsford argue, either view seems to present the reading/writing act as a relationship in which one person is fixed and the other must move—it seems to suggest that either the writer or reader must submit to the views of the other.

Ede and Lunsford's solution to this problem is that theorists of audience "must balance the creativity of the writer with the different, but equally important, creativity of the reader." This solution models the reader-writer relationship as a complicated and dynamic one, and it is a solution endorsed by many theorists of argument. For instance, in *Modern Dogma and the Rhetoric of Assent* and elsewhere, Wayne Booth has argued that the central responsibility of audiences is "in-dwelling"—a kind of empathy with the author. Obviously, not all actual audiences are willing to in-dwell, and many enter the reading experience desiring nothing more than being pandered to. Keeping this distinction between actual and intended audiences (with the concomitant difference in models of responsibilities) helps define what Elbow means by an "inviting" versus an "inhibiting" audience. As Elbow says, "we can get relief from an inhibiting audience by writing to a more inviting one"—specifically, we can imagine someone who is willing to enter a reciprocal relationship with the text. This does not necessarily mean someone who already agrees with everything we have to say, nor someone with high boots of patience for wading through horrible prose, but someone who is willing to listen.

Simply defining an audience as willing to listen will not help an author invent or revise a paper, however, because there are other variations in audience that are equally important. For instance, a student writing a paper about *Dances with Wolves* would have to decide whether or not the intended audience had seen the movie in order to decide how much time to spend summarizing it. If the student intended to apply certain theories of film criticism, she or he would have to decide if the intended audience knew those methods in order to decide how much time to spend explicating those theories.

Closing My Eyes as I Speak:
An Argument for Ignoring Audience
Peter Elbow

*Very often people don't listen to you when you speak to them. It's only when
you talk to yourself that they prick up their ears.*

—John Ashberry

When I am talking to a person or a group and struggling to find words or
thoughts, I often find myself involuntarily closing my eyes as I speak. I realize now
that this behavior is an instinctive attempt to blot out awareness of audience when
I need all my concentration for just trying to figure out or express what I want to
say. Because the audience is so imperiously *present* in a speaking situation, my
instinct reacts with this active attempt to avoid audience awareness. This behavior—in a sense impolite or antisocial—is not so uncommon. Even when we write,
alone in a room to an absent audience, there are occasions when we are struggling to figure something out and need to push aside awareness of those absent
readers. As Donald Murray puts it, "My sense of audience is so strong that I have
to suppress my conscious awareness of audience to hear what the text demands"
(Berkenkotter and Murray, 171). In recognition of how pervasive the role of audience is in writing, I write to celebrate the benefits of ignoring audience.[1]

It will be clear that my argument for writing without audience awareness is
not meant to undermine the many good reasons for writing *with* audience awareness some of the time. (For example, that we are liable to neglect audience
because we write in solitude; that young people often need more practice in tak-

I benefited from much help from audiences in writing various drafts of this piece. I am
grateful to Jennifer Clarke, with whom I wrote a collaborative piece containing a case
study on this subject. I am also grateful for extensive feedback from Pat Belanoff, Paul
Connolly, Sheryl Fontaine, John Trimbur, and members of the Martha's Vineyard Summer Writing Seminar.

[1]There are many different entities called audience: (a) The actual readers to whom
the text will be given; (b) the writer's conception of those readers—which may be mistak-
en (see Ong; Park; Ede and Lunsford); (c) the audience that the text implies—which may
be different still (see Booth); (d) the discourse community or even genre addressed or
implied by the text (see Walzer); (e) ghost or phantom "readers in the head" that the
writer may unconsciously address or try to please (see Elbow, *Writing with Power* 186ff.
Classically, this is a powerful former teacher. Often such an audience is so ghostly as not
to show up as actually "implied" by the text). For the essay I am writing here, these differences don't much matter: I'm celebrating the ability to put aside the needs or demands of
any or all of these audiences. I recognize, however, that we sometimes cannot fight our
way free of unconscious or tacit audiences (as in b or e above) unless we bring them to
greater conscious awareness.

ing into account points of view different from their own; and that students often have an impoverished sense of writing as communication because they have only written in a school setting to teachers.) Indeed I would claim some part in these arguments for audience awareness—which now seem to be getting out of hand.

I start with a limited claim: even though ignoring audience will usually lead to weak writing at first—to what Linda Flower calls "writer-based prose"—this weak writing can help us in the end to better writing than we would have written if we'd kept readers in mind from the start. Then I will make a more ambitious claim: writer-based prose is sometimes better than reader-based prose. Finally I will explore some of the theory underlying these issues of audience.

A Limited Claim

It's not that writers should never think about their audience. It's a question of when. An audience is a field of force. The closer we come—the more we think about these readers—the stronger the pull they exert on the contents of our minds. The practical question, then, is always whether a particular audience functions as a helpful field of force or one that confuses or inhibits us.

Some audiences, for example, are *inviting* or *enabling*. When we think about them as we write, we think of more and better things to say—and what we think somehow arrives more coherently structured than usual. It's like talking to the perfect listener: we feel smart and come up with ideas we didn't know we had. Such audiences are helpful to keep in mind right from the start.

Other audiences, however, are powerfully *inhibiting*—so much so, in certain cases, that awareness of them as we write blocks writing altogether. There are certain people who always make us feel dumb when we try to speak to them: we can't find words or thoughts. As soon as we get out of their presence, all the things we wanted to say pop back into our minds. Here is a student telling what happens when she tries to follow the traditional advice about audience:

> You know _____ [author of a text] tells us to pay attention to the audi-
> ence that will be reading our papers, and I gave that a try. I ended up
> without putting a word on paper until I decided the hell with _____ ;
> I'm going to write to who I damn well want to; otherwise I can hardly
> write at all.

Admittedly, there are some occasions when we benefit from keeping a threatening audience in mind from the start. We've been putting off writing that letter to that person who intimidates us. When we finally sit down and write *to* them—walk right up to them, as it were, and look them in the eye—we may manage to stand up to the threat and grasp the nettle and thereby find just what we need to write.

Most commonly, however, the effect of audience awareness is somewhere between the two extremes: the awareness disturbs or disrupts our writing and thinking without completely blocking it. For example, when we have to write to someone we find intimidating (and of course students often perceive teachers as intimidating), we often start thinking wholly defensively. As we write down each thought or sentence, our mind fills with thoughts of how the intended reader will criticize or object to it. So we try to qualify or soften what we've just written—or write out some answer to a possible objection. Our writing becomes tangled. Sometimes we get so tied in knots that we cannot even figure out what we *think*. We may not realize how often audience awareness has this effect on our students when we don't see the writing processes behind their papers: we just see texts that are either tangled or empty.

Another example. When we have to write to readers with whom we have an awkward relationship, we often start beating around the bush and feeling shy or scared, or start to write in a stilted, overly careful style or voice. (Think about the cute, too-clever style of many memos we get in our departmental mailboxes—the awkward self-consciousness academics experience when writing to other academics.) When students are asked to write to readers they have not met or cannot imagine, such as "the general reader" or "the educated public," they often find nothing to say except cliches they know *they* don't even quite believe.

When we realize that an audience is somehow confusing or inhibiting us, the solution is fairly obvious. We can ignore that audience altogether during the *early* stages of writing and direct our words only to ourselves or to no one in particular—or even to the "wrong" audience, that is, to an *inviting* audience of trusted friends or allies. This strategy often dissipates the confusion; the clenched, defensive discourse starts to run clear. Putting audience out of mind is of course a traditional practice: serious writers have long used private journals for early explorations of feeling, thinking, or language. But many writing teachers seem to think that students can get along without the private writing serious writers find so crucial—or even that students will *benefit* from keeping their audience in mind for the whole time. Things often don't work out that way.

After we have figured out our thinking in copious exploratory or draft writing—perhaps finding the right voice or stance as well—*then* we can follow the traditional rhetorical advice: think about readers and revise carefully to adjust our words and thoughts to our intended audience. For a particular audience it may even turn out that we need to *disguise* our point of view. But it's hard to disguise something while engaged in trying to figure it out. As writers, then, we need to learn when to think about audience and when to put readers out of mind.

Many people are too quick to see Flower's "writer-based prose" as an analysis of what's wrong with this type of writing and miss the substantial degree to which she was celebrating a natural, and indeed developmentally enabling, response to cognitive overload. What she doesn't say, however, despite her emphasis on planning and conscious control in the writing process, is that we can *teach* students to notice when audience awareness is getting in their way—and when this happens, consciously to put aside the needs of readers for a while. She seems to assume that when an overload occurs, the writer-based gear will, as it were, automatically kick into action to relieve it. In truth, of course, writers often persist in using a malfunctioning *reader*-based gear despite the overload—

thereby mangling their language or thinking. Though Flower likes to rap the knuckles of people who suggest a "correct" or "natural" order for steps in the writing process, she implies such an order here: when attention to audience causes an overload, start out by ignoring them while you attend to your thinking; after you work out your thinking, turn your attention to audience.

Thus if we ignore audience while writing on a topic about which we are not expert or about which our thinking is still evolving, we are likely to produce exploratory writing that is unclear to anyone else—perhaps even inconsistent or a complete mess. Yet by doing this exploratory "swamp work" in conditions of safety, we can often coax our thinking through a process of new discovery and development. In this way we can end up with something better than we could have produced if we'd tried to write to our audience all along. In short, ignoring audience can lead to worse drafts but better revisions. (Because we are professionals and adults, we often write in the role of expert: we may know what we think without new exploratory writing; we may even be able to speak confidently to critical readers. But students seldom experience this confident professional stance in their writing. And think how much richer *our* writing would be if we defined ourselves as *in*expert and allowed ourselves private writing for new explorations of those views we are allegedly sure of.)

Notice then that two pieties of composition theory are often in conflict:

1. Think about audience as you write (this stemming from the classical rhetorical tradition).
2. Use writing for *making new meaning,* not just transmitting old meanings already worked out (this stemming from the newer epistemic tradition I associate with Ann Berthoff's classic explorations).

It's often difficult to work out new meaning while thinking about readers.

A More Ambitious Claim

I go further now and argue that ignoring audience can lead to better writing—immediately. In effect, writer-based prose can be *better* than reader-based prose. This might seem a more controversial claim, but is there a teacher who has not had the experience of struggling and struggling to no avail to help a student untangle his writing, only to discover that the student's casual journal writing or freewriting is untangled and strong? Sometimes freewriting is stronger than the essays we get only because it is expressive, narrative, or descriptive writing and the student was not constrained by a topic. But teachers who collect drafts with completed assignments often see passages of freewriting that are strikingly stronger *even* when they are expository and constrained by the assigned topic. In some of these passages we can sense that the strength derives from the student's unawareness of readers.

It's not just unskilled, tangled writers, though, who sometimes write better by forgetting about readers. Many competent and even professional writers produce mediocre pieces *because* they are thinking too much about how their readers will receive their words. They are acting too much like a salesman trained to look the customer in the eye and to think at all times about the characteristics of the "target audience." There is something too staged or planned or self-aware about such writing. We see this quality in much second-rate newspaper or magazine or business writing: "good-student writing" in the awful sense of the term. Writing produced this way reminds us of the ineffective actor whose consciousness of self distracts us: he makes us too aware of his own awareness of us. When we read such prose, we wish the writer would stop thinking about us—would stop trying to "adjust" or "fit" what he is saying to our frame of reference. "Damn it, put all your attention on what you are saying," we want to say, "and forget about us and how we are reacting."

When we examine really good student or professional writing, we can often see that its goodness comes from the writer's having gotten sufficiently wrapped up in her meaning and her language as to forget all about audience needs: the writer manages to "break through." The Earl of Shaftesbury talked about writers needing to escape their audience in order to find their own ideas (Cooper 1:109; see also Griffin). It is characteristic of much truly good writing to be, as it were, on fire with its meaning. Consciousness of readers is burned away; involvement in subject determines all. Such writing is analogous to the performance of the actor who has managed to stop attracting attention to her awareness of the audience watching her.

The arresting power in some writing by small children comes from their obliviousness to audience. As readers, we are somehow sucked into a more-than-usual connection with the meaning itself because of the child's gift for more-than-usual concentration on what she is saying. In short, we can feel some pieces of children's writing as being very writer-based. Yet it's precisely that quality which makes it powerful for us as readers. After all, why should we settle for a writer's entering our point of view, if we can have the more powerful experience of being sucked out of our point of view and into her world? This is just the experience that children are peculiarly capable of giving because they are so expert at total absorption in their world as they are writing. It's not just a matter of whether the writer "decenters," but of whether the writer has a sufficiently strong focus of attention to make the *reader* decenter. This quality of concentration is what D. H. Lawrence so admires in Melville:

> [Melville] was a real American in that he always felt his audience in front of him. But when he ceases to be American, when he forgets all audience, and gives us his sheer apprehension of the world, then he is wonderful, his book [*Moby Dick*] commands a stillness in the soul, an awe. (158)

What most readers value in really excellent writing is not prose that is right for readers but prose that is right for thinking, right for language, or right for the subject being written about. If, in addition, it is clear and well suited to readers, we appreciate that. Indeed we feel insulted if the writer did not somehow try to make the writing *available* to us before delivering it. But if it succeeds at being really true to language and thinking and "things," we are willing to put up with much difficulty as readers:

> [G]ood writing is not always or necessarily an adaptation to communal norms (in the Fish/Bruffee sense) but may be an attempt to construct (and instruct) a reader capable of reading the text in question. The literary history of the "difficult" work—from Mallarme to Pound, Zukofsky, Olson, etc.—seems to say that much of what we value in writing we've had to learn to value by learning how to read it. (Trimbur)

The effect of audience awareness on *voice* is particularly striking—if paradoxical. Even though we often develop our voice by finally "speaking up" to an audience or "speaking out" to others, and even though much dead student writing comes from students' not really treating their writing as a communication with real readers, nevertheless, the opposite effect is also common: we often do not really develop a strong, authentic voice in our writing till we find important occasions for *ignoring* audience—saying, in effect, "To hell with whether they like it or not. I've got to say this the way *I* want to say it." Admittedly, the voice that emerges when we ignore audience is sometimes odd or idiosyncratic in some way, but usually it is stronger. Indeed, teachers sometimes complain that student writing is "writer-based" when the problem is simply the idiosyncracy—and sometimes in fact the *power*—of the voice. They would value this odd but resonant voice if they found it in a published writer (see "Real Voice," Elbow, *Writing with Power*). Usually we cannot *trust* a voice unless it is unaware of us and our needs and speaks out in its own terms (see the Ashberry epigraph). To celebrate writer-based prose is to risk the charge of *romanticism:* just warbling one's woodnotes wild. But my position also contains the austere *classic* view that we must nevertheless *revise* with conscious awareness of audience in order to figure out which pieces of writer-based prose are good as they are—and how to discard or revise the rest.

To point out that writer-based prose can be *better* for readers than reader-based prose is to reveal problems in these two terms. Does *writer-based* mean:

1. That the text doesn't work for readers because it is too much oriented to the writer's point of view?
2. Or that the writer was not thinking about readers as she wrote, although the text *may* work for readers?

Does *reader-based* mean:

3. That the text works for readers—meets their needs?
4. Or that the writer was attending to readers as she wrote although her text may *not* work for readers?

In order to do justice to the reality and complexity of what actually happens in both writers and readers, I was going to suggest four terms for the four conditions listed above, but I gradually realized that things are even too complex for that. We really need to ask about what's going on in three dimensions—in the *writer,* in the *reader,* and in the *text*—and realize that the answers can occur in virtually any combination:

- —Was the *writer* thinking about readers or oblivious to them?
- —Is the *text* oriented toward the writer's frame of reference or point of view, or oriented toward that of readers? (A writer may be thinking about readers and still write a text that is largely oriented toward her own frame of reference.)
- —Are the readers' needs being met? (The text may meet the needs of readers whether the writer was thinking about them or not, and whether the text is oriented toward them or not.)

Two Models of Cognitive Development

Some of the current emphasis on audience awareness probably derives from a model of cognitive development that needs to be questioned. According to this model, if you keep your readers in mind as your write, you are operating at a higher level of psychological development than if you ignore readers. Directing words to readers is "more mature" than directing them to no one in particular or to yourself. Flower relates writer-based prose to the inability to "decenter" which is characteristic of Piaget's early stages of development, and she relates reader-based prose to later more mature stages of development.

On the one hand, of course this view must be right. Children do decenter as they develop. As they mature they get better at suiting their discourse to the needs of listeners, particularly to listeners very different from themselves. Especially, they get better at doing so *consciously*—thinking *awarely* about how things appear to people with different viewpoints. Thus much unskilled writing is unclear or awkward *because* the writer was doing what it is so easy to do—unthinkingly taking her own frame of reference for granted and not attending to the needs of readers who might have a different frame of reference. And of course this failure is more common in younger, immature, "egocentric" students (and also more common in writing than in speaking since we have no audience present when we write).

But on the other hand, we need the contrary model that affirms what is also obvious once we reflect on it, namely that the ability to *turn off* audience awareness—especially when it confuses thinking or blocks discourse—is also a "higher" skill. I am talking about an ability to use language in "the desert island mode," an ability that tends to require learning, growth, and psychological development. Children, and even adults who have not learned the art of quiet, thoughtful, inner reflection, are often unable to get much cognitive action going in their heads unless there are other people present to have action *with.* They are dependent on live audience and the social dimension to get their discourse rolling or to get their thinking off the ground.

For in contrast to a roughly Piagetian model of cognitive development that says we start out as private, egocentric little monads and grow up to be public and social, it is important to invoke the opposite model that derives variously from Vygotsky, Bakhtin, and Meade. According to this model, we *start out* social and plugged into others and only gradually, through learning and development, come to "unplug" to any significant degree so as to function in a more private, individual and differentiated fashion: "Development in thinking is not from the individual to the socialized, but from the social to the individual" (Vygotsky 20). The important general principle in this model is that we tend to *develop* our important cognitive capacities by means of social interaction with others, and having done so we gradually learn to perform them alone. We fold the "simple" back-and-forth of dialogue into the "complexity" (literally, "foldedness") of individual, private reflection.

Where the Piagetian (individual psychology) model calls our attention to the obvious need to learn to enter into viewpoints other than our own, the Vygotskian (social psychology) model calls our attention to the equally important need to learn to produce good thinking and discourse *while alone.* A rich and enfolded mental life is something that people achieve only gradually through growth, learning, and practice. We tend to associate this achievement with the fruits of higher education.

Thus we see plenty of students who lack this skill, who have nothing to say when asked to freewrite or to write in a journal. They can dutifully "reply" to a question or a topic, but they cannot seem to *initiate* or *sustain* a train of thought on their own. Because so many adolescent students have this difficulty, many teachers chime in: "Adolescents have nothing to write about. They are too young. They haven't had significant experience." In truth, adolescents don't lack experience or material, no matter how "sheltered" their lives. What they lack is practice and help. Desert island discourse is a learned cognitive process. It's a mistake to think of private writing (journal writing and freewriting) as merely "easy"—merely a relief from trying to write right. It's also hard. Some exercises and strategies that help are Ira Progoff's "Intensive Journal" process, Sondra Perl's "Composing Guidelines," or Elbow's "Loop Writing" and "Open Ended Writing" processes (*Writing with Power* 50–77).

The Piagetian and Vygotskian developmental models (language-begins-as-private vs. language-begins-as-social) give us two different lenses through which to look at a common weakness in student writing, a certain kind of "thin" writing where the thought is insufficiently developed or where the language doesn't really explain what the writing implies or gestures toward. Using the Piagetian model, as Flower does, one can specify the problem as a weakness in audience orientation. Perhaps the writer has immaturely taken too much for granted and unthinkingly assumed that her limited explanations carry as much meaning for readers as they do for herself. The cure or treatment is for the writer to think more about readers.

Through the Vygotskian lens, however, the problem and the "immaturity" look altogether different. Yes, the writing isn't particularly clear or satisfying for readers, but this alternative diagnosis suggests a failure of the private desert island dimension: the writer's explanation is too thin because she didn't work out her train of thought fully enough *for herself.* The suggested cure or treatment is *not* to think more about readers but to think more for herself, to practice exploratory writing in order to learn to engage in that reflective discourse so central to mastery of the writing process. How can she engage readers more till she has engaged herself more?

The current emphasis on audience awareness may be particularly strong now for being fueled by *both* psychological models. From one side, the Piagetians say, in effect, "The egocentric little critters, we've got to *socialize* 'em! Ergo, make them think about audience when they write!" From the other side, the Vygotskians say, in effect, "No wonder they're having trouble writing. They've been bamboozled by the Piagetian heresy. They think they're solitary individuals with private selves when really they're just congeries of voices that derive from their discourse community. Ergo, let's intensify the social context—use peer groups and publication: make them think about audience when they write! (And while we're at it, let's hook them up with a better class of discourse community.)" To advocate ignoring audience is to risk getting caught in the crossfire from two opposed camps.

Two Models of Discourse: Discourse as Communication and Discourse as Poesis or Play

We cannot talk about writing without at least implying a psychological or developmental model. But we'd better make sure it's a complex, paradoxical, or spiral model. Better yet, we should be deft enough to use two contrary models or lenses. (Bruner pictures the developmental process as a complex movement in an upward reiterative spiral—not a simple movement in one direction.)

According to one model, it is characteristic of the youngest children to direct their discourse to an audience. They learn discourse *because* they have an audience; without an audience they remain mute, like "the wild child." Language is social from the start. But we need the other model to show us what is also true, namely that it is characteristic of the youngest children to use language in a *non-social* way. They use language not only because people talk to them but also because they have such a strong propensity to play and to build—often in a *non-*social or non-audience-oriented fashion. Thus although one paradigm for discourse is social communication, another is private exploration or solitary play. Babies and toddlers tend to babble in an exploratory and reflective way—to themselves and not to an audience—often even with no one else near. This archetypally private use of discourse is strikingly illustrated when we see a pair of toddlers in "parallel play" alongside each other—each busily talking but not at all trying to communicate with the other.

Therefore, when we choose paradigms for discourse, we should think not only about children using language to communicate, but also about children building sandcastles or drawing pictures. Though children characteristically show their castles or pictures to others, they just as characteristically trample or crumple them before anyone else can see them. Of course sculptures and pictures are different from words. Yet discourse implies more media than words; and even if you restrict discourse to words, one of our most mature uses of language is for building verbal pictures and structures for their own sake—not just for communicating with others.

Consider this same kind of behavior at the other end of the life cycle: Brahms staggering from his deathbed to his study to rip up a dozen or more completed but unpublished and unheard string quartets that dissatisfied him. How was he relating to audience here—worrying too much about audience or not giving a damn? It's not easy to say. Consider Glenn Gould deciding to renounce performances before an audience. He used his private studio to produce recorded performances for an audience, but to produce ones that satisfied *himself* he clearly needed to suppress audience awareness. Consider the more extreme example of Kerouac typing page after page—burning each as soon as he completed it. The language behavior of humans is slippery. Surely we are well advised to avoid positions that say it is "always X" or "essentially Y."

James Britton makes a powerful argument that the "making" or poesis function of language grows out of the expressive function. Expressive language is often for the sake of communication with an audience, but just as often it is only for the sake of the speaker—working something out for herself (66–67, 74ff). Note also that "writing to learn," which writing-across-the-curriculum programs are discovering to be so important, tends to be writing for the self or even for no one at all rather than for an outside reader. You throw away the writing, often unread, and keep the mental changes it has engendered.

I hope this emphasis on the complexity of the developmental process—the limits of our models and of our understanding of it—will serve as a rebuke to the tendency to label students as being at a lower stage of cognitive development just because they don't yet write well. (Occasionally they *do* write well—in a way—but not in the way that the labeler finds appropriate.) Obviously the psychologistic labeling impulse started out charitably. Shaughnessy was fighting those who called basic writers *stupid* by saying they weren't dumb, just at an earlier developmental stage. Flower was arguing that writer-based prose is a natural response to a cognitive overload and indeed developmentally enabling. But this kind of talk can be dangerous since it labels students as literally "retarded" and makes teachers and administrators start to think of them as such. Instead of calling poor writers *either* dumb or slow (two forms of blaming the victim), why not simply call them poor writers? If years of schooling haven't yet made them good writers, perhaps they haven't gotten the kind of teaching and support they need. Poor students are often deprived of the very thing they need most to write well (which is given to good students): lots of extended and adventuresome writing for self and for audience. Poor students are often asked to write *only* answers to fill-in exercises.

As children get older, the developmental story remains complex or spiral. Though the first model makes us notice that babies start out with a natural gift for using language in a social and communicative fashion, the second model makes us notice that children and adolescents must continually learn to relate their discourse better to an audience—must struggle to decenter better. And though the second model makes us notice that babies also start out with a natural gift for using language in a *private,* exploratory and playful way, the first model makes us notice that children and adolescents must continually learn to master this solitary, desert island, poesis mode better. Thus we mustn't think of language only as communication—nor allow communication to claim dominance either as the earliest or as the most "mature" form of discourse. It's true that language is inherently communicative (and without communication we don't develop language), yet language is just as inherently the stringing together of exploratory discourse for the self—or for the creation of objects (play, poesis, making) for their own sake.

In considering this important poesis function of language, we need not discount (as Berkenkotter does) the striking testimony of so many witnesses who think and care most about language: professional poets, writers, and philosophers. Many of them maintain that their most serious work is *making,* not *communicating,* and that their commitment is to language, reality, logic, experience, not to readers. Only in their willingness to cut loose from the demands or needs of readers, they insist, can they do their best work. Here is William Stafford on this matter:

> I don't want to overstate this . . . but . . . my impulse is to say I don't think of an audience at all. When I'm writing, the satisfactions in the process of writing are my satisfactions in dealing with the language, in being surprised by phrasings that occur to me, in finding that this miraculous kind of convergent focus begins to happen. That's my satisfaction, and to think about an audience would be a distraction. I try to keep from thinking about an audience. (Cicotello 176)

And Chomsky:

> I can be using language in the strictest sense with no intention of communicating. . . . As a graduate student, I spent two years writing a lengthy manuscript, assuming throughout that it would never be published or read by anyone. I meant everything I wrote, intending nothing as to what anyone would [understand], in fact taking it for granted that there would be no audience. . . . [C]ommunication is only one function of language, and by no means an essential one. (Quoted in Feldman 5–6).

It's interesting to see how poets come together with philosophers on this point—and even with mathematicians. All are emphasizing the "poetic" function of language in its literal sense—"poesis" as "making." They describe their writing process as more like "getting something right" or even "solving a problem" for its own sake than as communicating with readers or addressing an audience. The task is not to satisfy readers but to satisfy the rules of the system: "[T]he writer is not thinking of a reader at all; he makes it 'clear' as a contract with *language*" (Goodman 164).

Shall we conclude, then, that solving an equation or working out a piece of symbolic logic is at the opposite end of the spectrum from communicating with readers or addressing an audience? No. To draw that conclusion would be to fall again into a onesided position. Sometimes people write mathematics *for* an audience, sometimes not. The central point in this essay is that we cannot answer audience questions in an *a priori* fashion based on the "nature" of discourse or of language or of cognition—only in terms of the different *uses* or *purposes* to which humans put discourse, language, or cognition on different occasions. If most people have a restricted repertoire of uses for writing—if most people use writing-only to send messages to readers, that's no argument for constricting the *definition* of writing. It's an argument for helping people expand their repertoire of uses.

The value of learning to ignore audience while writing, then, is the value of learning to cultivate the private dimension: the value of writing in order to make meaning to oneself, not just to others. This involves learning to free oneself (to some extent, anyway) from the enormous power exerted by society and others, to unhook oneself from external prompts and social stimuli. We've grown accustomed to theorists and writing teachers puritanically stressing the *problem* of writing: the tendency to neglect the needs of readers because we usually write in solitude. But let's also celebrate this same feature of writing as one of its glories: writing *invites* disengagement too, the inward turn of mind, and the dialogue with self. Though writing is deeply social and though we usually help things by enhancing its social dimension, writing is also the mode of discourse best suited to helping us develop the reflective and private dimension of our mental lives.

"But Wait a Minute, ALL Discourse Is Social"

Some readers who see *all* discourse as social will object to my opposition between public and private writing (the "trap of oppositional thinking") and insist that *there is no such thing as private discourse*. What looks like private, solitary mental work, they would say, is really social. Even on the desert island I am in a crowd.

> [B]y ignoring audience in the conventional sense, we return to it in another sense. What I get from Vygotsky and Bakhtin is the notion that audience is not really out there at all but is in fact "always already" (to use that poststructuralist mannerism . . .) inside, interiorized in the conflicting languages of others—parents, former teachers, peers, prospective readers, whomever—that writers have to negotiate to write, and that we do negotiate when we write whether we're aware of it or not. The audience we've got to satisfy in order to feel good about our writing is as much in the past as in the present or future. But we experience it (it's so internalized) as *ourselves*. (Trimbur)

(Ken Bruffee likes to quote from Frost: "'Men work together, . . . //Whether they work together or apart'" ["The Tuft of Flowers"].) Or—putting it slightly differently—when I engage in what seems like private non-audience-directed writing, I am really engaged in communication with the "audience of self." For the self is multiple, not single, and discourse to self is communication from one entity to another. As Feldman argues, "The self functions as audience in much the same way that others do" (290).

Suppose I accept this theory that all discourse is really social—including what I've been calling "private writing" or writing I don't intend to show to any reader. Suppose I agree that all language is essentially communication directed toward an audience—whether some past internalized voice or (what may be the same thing) some aspect of the self. What would this theory say to my interest in "private writing"?

The theory would seem to destroy my main argument. It would tell me that there's no such thing as "private writing"; it's impossible *not* to address audience; there are no vacations from audience. But the theory might try to console me by saying not to worry, because we don't *need* vacations from audience. Addressing audience is as easy, natural, and unaware as breathing—and we've been at it since the cradle. Even young, unskilled writers are already expert at addressing audiences.

But if we look closely we can see that in fact this theory doesn't touch my central practical argument. For even if all discourse is naturally addressed to *some* audience, it's not naturally addressed to the *right* audience—the living readers we are actually trying to reach. Indeed the pervasiveness of past audiences in our heads is one more reason for the difficulty of reaching present audiences with our texts. Thus even if I concede the theoretical point, there still remains an enormous practical and phenomenological difference between writing "public" words for others to read and writing "private" words for no one to read.

Even if "private writing" is "deep down" social, the fact remains that, as we engage in it, we don't have to worry about whether it works on readers or even makes sense. We can refrain from doing all the things that audience-awareness advocates advise us to do ("keeping our audience in mind as we write" and trying to "decenter"). Therefore this social-discourse theory doesn't undermine the benefits of "private writing" and thus provides no support at all for the traditional rhetorical advice that we should "always try to think about (intended) audience as we write."

In fact this social-discourse theory reinforces two subsidiary arguments I have been making. First, even if there is no getting away from *some* audience, we can get relief from an inhibiting audience by writing to a more inviting one. Second, audience problems don't come only from *actual* audiences but also from phantom "audiences in the head" (Elbow, *Writing with Power* 186ff). Once we learn how to be more aware of the effects of both external and internal readers and how to direct our words elsewhere, we can get out of the shadow even of a troublesome phantom reader.

And even if all our discourse is *directed to* or *shaped by* past audiences or voices, it doesn't follow that our discourse is *well directed to* or *successfully shaped for* those audiences or voices. Small children *direct* much talk to others, but that doesn't mean they always *suit* their talk to others. They often fail. When adults discover that a piece of their writing has been "heavily shaped" by some audience, this is bad news as much as good: often the writing is crippled by defensive moves that try to fend off criticism from this reader.

As teachers, particularly, we need to distinguish and emphasize "private writing" in order to teach it, to teach that crucial cognitive capacity to engage in extended and productive thinking that doesn't depend on audience prompts or social stimuli. It's sad to see so many students who can reply to live voices but cannot engage in productive dialogue with voices in their heads. Such students often lose interest in an issue that had intrigued them—just because they don't find other people who are interested in talking about it and haven't learned to talk reflectively to *themselves* about it.

For these reasons, then, I believe my main argument holds force even if I accept the theory that all discourse is social. But, perhaps more tentatively, I resist this theory. I don't know all the data from developmental linguistics, but I cannot help suspecting that babies engage in *some* private poesis—or "play-language"—some private babbling in addition to social babbling. Of course Vygotsky must be right when he points to so much social language in children, but can we really trust him when he denies *all* private or nonsocial language (which Piaget and Chomsky see)? I am always suspicious when someone argues for the total nonexistence of a certain kind of behavior or event. Such an argument is almost invariably an act of definitional aggrandizement, not empirical searching. To say that *all* language is social is to flop over into the opposite onesidedness that we need Vygotsky's model to save us from.

And even if all language is *originally* social, Vygotsky himself emphasizes how "inner speech" becomes more individuated and private as the child matures. "[E]gocentric speech is relatively accessible in three-year-olds but quite inscrutable in seven-year-olds: the older the child, the more thoroughly has his thought become inner speech" (Emerson 254; see also Vygotsky 134). "The inner speech of the adult represents his 'thinking for himself' rather than social adaptation. . . . Out of context, it would be incomprehensible to others because it omits to mention what is obvious to the 'speaker'" (Vygotsky 18).

I also resist the theory that all private writing is really communication with the *"audience of self."* ("When we represent the objects of our thought in language, we intend to make use of these representations at a later time. . . . [T]he speaker-self must have audience directed intentions toward a listener-self" [Feldman 289].) Of course private language often *is* a communication with the audience of self:

—When we make a shopping list. (It's obvious when we can't decipher that third item that we're confronting *failed* communication with the self.)
—When we make a rough draft for ourselves but not for others' eyes. Here

we are seeking to clarify our thinking with the leverage that comes from standing outside and reading our own utterance as audience—experiencing our discourse as receiver instead of as sender.

—When we experience ourselves as slightly split. Sometimes we experience ourselves as witness to ourselves and hear our own words from the outside—sometimes with great detachment, as on some occasions of pressure or stress.

But there are other times when private language is *not* communication with audience of self:

—Freewriting to no one: for the *sake* of self but not *to* the self. The goal is not to communicate but to follow a train of thinking or feeling to see where it leads. In doing this kind of freewriting (and many people have not learned it), you don't particularly plan to come back and read what you've written. You just write along and the written product falls away to be ignored, while only the "real product"—any new perceptions, thoughts, or feelings produced in the mind by the freewriting—is saved and looked at again. (It's not that you don't experience your words *at all* but you experience them only as speaker, sender, or emitter—not as receiver or audience. To say that's the same as being audience is denying the very distinction between 'speaker' and 'audience.')

As this kind of freewriting actually works, it often *leads* to writing we look at. That is, we freewrite along to no one, following discourse in hopes of getting somewhere, and then at a certain point we often sense that we have *gotten* somewhere: we can tell (but not because we stop and read) that what we are now writing seems new or intriguing or important. At this point we may stop writing; or we may keep on writing, but in a new audience-relationship, realizing that we *will* come back to this passage and read it as audience. Or we may take a new sheet (symbolizing the new audience-relationship) and try to write out for ourselves what's interesting.

—Writing as exorcism is a more extreme example of private writing *not* for the audience of self. Some people have learned to write in order to get rid of thoughts or feelings. By freewriting what's obsessively going round and round in our head we can finally let it go and move on.

I am suggesting that some people (and especially poets and freewriters) engage in a kind of discourse that Feldman, defending what she calls a "communication-intention" view, has never learned and thus has a hard time imagining and understanding. Instead of always using language in an audience-directed fashion for the sake of communication, these writers unleash language for its own sake and let *it* function a bit on its own, without much *intention* and without much need for *communication,* to see where it leads—and thereby end up with some intentions and potential communications they didn't have before.

It's hard to turn off the audience-of-self in writing—and thus hard to imagine writing to no one (just as it's hard to turn off the audience of *outside* readers when writing an audience-directed piece). Consider "invisible writing" as an intriguing technique that helps you become less of an audience-of-self for your writing. Invisible writing prevents you from seeing what you have written: you write on a computer with the screen turned down, or you write with a spent ball-point pen on paper with carbon paper and another sheet underneath. Invisible writing tends to get people not only to write faster than they normally do, but often better (see Blau). I mean to be tentative about this slippery issue of whether we can really stop being audience to our own discourse, but I cannot help drawing the following conclusion: just as in freewriting, suppressing the *other* as audience tends to enhance quantity and sometimes even quality of writing; so in invisible writing, suppressing the *self* as audience tends to enhance quantity and sometimes even quality.

Contraries in Teaching

So what does all this mean for teaching? It means that we are stuck with two contrary tasks. On the one hand, we need to help our students enhance the social dimension of writing: to learn to be *more* aware of audience, to decenter better and learn to fit their discourse better to the needs of readers. Yet it is every bit as important to help them learn the private dimension of writing: to learn to be *less* aware of audience, to put audience needs aside, to use discourse in the desert island mode. And if we are trying to advance contraries, we must be prepared for paradoxes.

For instance if we emphasize the social dimension in our teaching (for example, by getting students to write to each other, to read and comment on each others' writing in pairs and groups, and by staging public discussions and even debates on the topics they are to write about), we will obviously help the social, public, communicative dimension of writing—help students experience writing not just as jumping through hoops for a grade but rather as taking part in the life of a community of discourse. But "social discourse" can also help private writing by getting students sufficiently involved or invested in an issue so that they finally want to carry on producing discourse alone and in private—and for themselves.

Correlatively, if we emphasize the private dimension in our teaching (for example, by using lots of private exploratory writing, freewriting, and journal writing and by helping students realize that of course they may need practice with this "easy" mode of discourse before they can use it fruitfully), we will obviously help students learn to write better reflectively for themselves without the need for others to interact with. Yet this private discourse can also help public, social writing—help students finally feel full enough of their *own* thoughts to have some genuine desire to *tell* them to others. Students often feel they "don't have anything to say" until they finally succeed in engaging themselves in private desert island writing for themselves alone.

Another paradox: whether we want to teach greater audience awareness or the ability to ignore audience, we must help students learn not only to "try harder" but also to "just relax." That is, sometimes students fail to produce reader-based prose because they don't *try* hard enough to think about audience needs. But sometimes the problem is cured if they just relax and write *to* people—as though in a letter or in talking to a trusted adult. By unclenching, they effortlessly call on social discourse skills of immense sophistication. Sometimes, indeed, the problem is cured if the student simply writes in a more social *setting*—in a classroom where it is habitual to share lots of writing. Similarly, sometimes students can't produce sustained private discourse because they don't try hard enough to keep the pen moving and forget about readers. They must persist and doggedly push aside those feelings of, "My head is empty, I have run out of anything to say." But sometimes what they need to learn through all that persistence is how to relax and let go—to unclench.

As teachers, we need to think about what it means to *be an audience* rather than just be a teacher, critic, assessor, or editor. If our only response is to tell students what's strong, what's weak, and how to improve it (diagnosis, assessment, and advice), we actually *undermine* their sense of writing as a social act. We reinforce their sense that writing means doing school exercises, producing for authorities what they already know—*not* actually trying to say things to readers. To help students experience us as *audience* rather than as assessment machines, it helps to respond by "replying" (as in a letter) rather than always "giving feedback."

Paradoxically enough, one of the best ways teachers can help students learn to turn off audience awareness and write in the desert island mode—to turn off the babble of outside voices in the head and listen better to quiet inner voices— is to be a special kind of private audience to them, to be a reader who nurtures by trusting and believing in the writer. Britton has drawn attention to the importance of teacher as "trusted adult" for school children (67–68). No one can be good at private, reflective writing without some *confidence and trust in self.* A nurturing reader can give a writer a kind of permission to forget about other readers or to be one's own reader. I have benefitted from this special kind of audience and have seen it prove useful to others. When I had a teacher who believed in me, who was interested in me and interested in what I had to say, I wrote well. When I had a teacher who thought I was naive, dumb, silly, and in need of being "straightened out," I wrote badly and sometimes couldn't write at all. Here is an interestingly paradoxical instance of the social-to-private principle from Vygotsky and Meade: we learn to listen better and more trustingly to *ourselves* through interaction with trusting *others.*

Look for a moment at lyric poets as paradigm writers (instead of seeing them as aberrant), and see how they heighten *both* the public and private dimensions of writing. Bakhtin says that lyric poetry implies "the absolute certainty of the listener's sympathy" (113). I think it's more helpful to say that lyric poets learn to create more than usual privacy in which to write *for themselves*—and then they turn around and let *others overhear*. Notice how poets tend to argue for the importance of no-audience writing, yet they are especially gifted at being public about what they produce in private. Poets are revealers—sometimes even grandstanders or showoffs. Poets illustrate the need for opposite or paradoxical or double audience skills: on the one hand, the ability to be private and solitary and tune out others—to write only for oneself and not give a damn about readers, yet on the other hand, the ability to be more than usually interested in audience and even to be a ham.

If writers really need these two audience skills, notice how bad most conventional schooling is on both counts. Schools offer virtually no privacy for writing: everything students write is collected and read by a teacher, a situation so ingrained students will tend to complain if you don't collect and read every word they write. Yet on the other hand, schools characteristically offer little or no social dimension for writing. It is *only* the teacher who reads, and students seldom feel that in giving their writing to a teacher they are actually communicating something they really want to say to a real person. Notice how often they are happy to turn in to teachers something perfunctory and fake that they would be embarrassed to show to classmates. Often they feel shocked and insulted if we want to distribute to classmates the assigned writing they hand in to us. (I think of Richard Wright's realization that the naked white prostitutes didn't bother to cover themselves when he brought them coffee as a black bellboy because they didn't really think of him as a man or even a person.) Thus the conventional school setting for writing tends to be the least private and the least public—when what students need, like all of us, is practice in writing that is the most private and also the most public.

Practical Guidelines About Audience

The theoretical relationships between discourse and audience are complex and paradoxical, but the practical morals are simple:

1. Seek ways to heighten both the *public* and *private* dimensions of writing. (For activities, see the previous section.)

2. When working on important audience-directed writing, we must try to emphasize audience awareness *sometimes*. A useful rule of thumb is to start by putting the readers in mind and carry on as long as things go well. If difficulties arise, try putting readers out of mind and write either to no audience, to self, or to an inviting audience. Finally, always *revise* with readers in mind. (Here's another occasion when orthodox advice about writing is wrong—but turns out right if applied to revising.)

3. Seek ways to heighten awareness of one's writing process (through process writing and discussion) to get better at taking control and deciding when to keep readers in mind and when to ignore them. Learn to discriminate factors like these:

(a) The writing task. Is this piece of writing *really* for an audience? More often than we realize, it is not. It is a draft that only we will see, though the final version will be for an audience; or exploratory writing for figuring something out; or some kind of personal private writing meant only for ourselves.

(b) Actual readers. When we put them in mind, are we helped or hindered?

(c) One's own temperament. Am I the sort of person who tends to think of what to say and how to say it when I keep readers in mind? Or someone (as I am) who needs long stretches of forgetting all about readers?

(d) Has some powerful "audience-in-the-head" tricked me into talking to it when I'm really trying to talk to someone else—distorting new business into old business? (I may be an inviting teacher-audience to my students, but they may not be able to pick up a pen without falling under the spell of a former, intimidating teacher.)

(e) Is *double audience* getting in my way? When I write a memo or report, I probably have to suit it not only to my "target audience" but also to some colleagues or supervisor. When I write something for publication, it must be right for readers but it won't be published unless it is also right for the editors—and if it's a book it won't be much read unless it's right for reviewers. Children's stories won't be bought unless they are right for editors and reviewers *and* parents. We often tell students to write to a particular "real-life" audience—or to peers in the class—but of course they are also writing for us as graders. (This problem is more common as more teachers get interested in audience and suggest "second" audiences.)

(f) Is *teacher-audience* getting in the way of my students' writing? As teachers we must often read in an odd fashion: in stacks of 25 or 50 pieces all on the same topic; on topics we know better than the writer; not for pleasure or learning but to grade or find problems (see Elbow, *Writing with Power* 216–236).

To list all these audience pitfalls is to show again the need for thinking about audience needs—yet also the need for vacations from readers to think in peace.

Works Cited

Bakhtin, Mikhail. "Discourse in Life and Discourse in Poetry." Appendix. *Freudianism: A Marxist Critique.* By V. N. Volosinov. Trans. I. R. Titunik. Ed. Neal H. Bruss. New York: Academic, 1976. (Holquist's attribution of this work to Bakhtin is generally accepted.)

Berkenkotter, Carol, and Donald Murray. "Decisions and Revisions: The Planning Strategies of a Publishing Writer and the Response of Being a Rat—or

Being Protocoled." *College Composition and Communication* 34 (1983): 156–172.

Blau, Sheridan. "Invisible Writing." *College Composition and Communication* 34 (1983): 297–312.

Booth, Wayne. *The Rhetoric of Fiction.* Chicago: U of Chicago P, 1961.

Britton, James. *The Development of Writing Abilities*, 11–18. Urbana: NCTE, 1977.

Bruffee, Kenneth A. "Liberal Education and the Social Justification of Belief." *Liberal Education* 68 (1982): 95–114.

Bruner, Jerome. *Beyond the Information Given: Studies in the Psychology of Knowing.* Ed. Jeremy Anglin. New York: Norton, 1973.

———. *On Knowing: Essays for the Left Hand.* Expanded ed. Cambridge: Harvard UP, 1979.

Chomsky, Noam. *Reflections on Language.* New York: Random, 1975.

Cicotello, David M. "The Art of Writing: An Interview with William Stafford." *College Composition and Communication* 34 (1983): 173–177.

Clarke, Jennifer, and Peter Elbow. "Desert Island Discourse: On the Benefits of Ignoring Audience." *The Journal Book.* Ed. Toby Fulwiler. Montclair, NJ: Boynton, 1987.

Cooper, Anthony Ashley, 3rd Earl of Shaftesbury. *Characteristics of Men, Manners, Opinions, Times, Etc.* Ed. John M. Robertson. 2 vols. Gloucester, MA: Smith, 1963.

Ede, Lisa, and Andrea Lunsford. "Audience Addressed/Audience Invoked: The Role of Audience in Composition Theory and Pedagogy." *College Composition and Communication* 35 (1984): 140–154.

Elbow, Peter. *Writing with Power.* New York: Oxford UP, 1981.

———. *Writing Without Teachers.* New York: Oxford UP, 1973.

Emerson, Caryl. "The Outer Word and Inner Speech: Bakhtin, Vygotsky, and the Internalization of Language." *Critical Inquiry* 10 (1983): 245–264.

Feldman, Carol Fleisher. "Two Functions of Language." *Harvard Education Review* 47 (1977): 282–293.

Flower, Linda. "Writer-Based Prose: A Cognitive Basis for Problems in Writing." *College English* 41 (1979): 19–37.

Goodman, Paul. *Speaking and Language: Defense of Poetry.* New York: Random, 1972.

Griffin, Susan. "The Internal Voices of Invention: Shaftesbury's Soliloquy." Unpublished. 1986.

Lawrence, D. H. *Studies in Classic American Literature.* Garden City: Doubleday, 1951.

Ong, Walter. "The Writer's Audience Is Always a Fiction." *PMLA* 90 (1975): 9–21.

Park, Douglas B. "The Meanings of 'Audience.'" *College English* 44 (1982): 247–257.

Perl, Sondra. "Guidelines for Composing." Appendix A. *Through Teachers' Eyes: Portraits of Writing Teachers at Work.* By Sondra Perl and Nancy Wilson. Portsmouth, NH: Heinemann, 1986.

Progoff, Ira. *At a Journal Workshop.* New York: Dialogue, 1975.

Shaughnessy, Mina. *Errors and Expectations: A Guide for the Teacher of Basic Writing.* New York: Oxford UP, 1977.

Trimbur John. Letter to the author. September 1985.

——. "Beyond Cognition: Voices in Inner Speech." *Rhetoric Review* 5 (1987): 211–221.

Vygotsky, L. S. *Thought and Language.* Trans. and ed. E. Hanfmann and G. Vakar. 1934. Cambridge: MIT P, 1962.

Walzer, Arthur E. "Articles from the 'California Divorce Project': A Case Study of the Concept of Audience." *College Composition and Communication* 36 (1985): 150–159.

Wright, Richard. *Black Boy.* New York: Harper, 1945

Audience Addressed/Audience Invoked: The Role of Audience in Composition Theory and Pedagogy
Lisa Ede and Andrea Lunsford

One important controversy currently engaging scholars and teachers of writing involves the role of audience in composition theory and pedagogy. How can we best define the audience of a written discourse? What does it mean to address an audience? To what degree should teachers stress audience in their assignments and discussions? What *is* the best way to help students recognize the significance of this critical element in any rhetorical situation?

Teachers of writing may find recent efforts to answer these questions more confusing than illuminating. Should they agree with Ruth Mitchell and Mary Taylor, who so emphasize the significance of the audience that they argue for abandoning conventional composition courses and instituting a "cooperative effort by writing and subject instructors in adjunct courses. The cooperation and courses take two main forms. Either writing instructors can be attached to subject courses where writing is required, an organization which disperses the instructors throughout the departments participating; or the composition courses can teach students how to write the papers assigned in other concurrent courses, thus centralizing instruction for diversifying topics."[1] Or should teachers side with Russell Long, who asserts that those advocating greater attention to audience overemphasize the role of "observable physical or occupational characteristics" while ignoring the fact that most writers actually create their audiences. Long argues against the usefulness of such methods as developing hypothetical rhetorical situations as writing assignments, urging instead a more traditional emphasis on "the analysis of texts in the classroom with a very detailed examination given to the signals provided by the writer for his audience."[2]

To many teachers, the choice seems limited to a single option—to be for or against an emphasis on audience in composition courses. In the following essay, we wish to expand our understanding of the role audience plays in composition theory and pedagogy by demonstrating that the arguments advocated by each side of the current debate oversimplify the act of making meaning through written discourse. Each side, we will argue, has failed adequately to recognize 1) the fluid, dynamic character of rhetorical situations; and 2) the integrated, interdependent nature of reading and writing. After discussing the strengths and weaknesses of the two central perspectives on audience in composition—which we group under the rubrics of *audience addressed* and *audience invoked*[3]—we will

[1]Ruth Mitchell and Mary Taylor, "The Integrating Perspective: An Audience-Response Model for Writing," *CE,* 41 (November, 1979), 267. Subsequent references to this article will be cited in the text.

[2]Russell C. Long, "Writer-Audience Relationships: Analysis or Invention," *CCC,* 31 (May, 1980), 223 and 225. Subsequent references to this article will be cited in the text.

propose an alternative formulation, one which we believe more accurately reflects the richness of "audience" as a concept.[4]

Audience Addressed

Those who envision audience as addressed emphasize the concrete reality of the writer's audience; they also share the assumption that knowledge of this audience's attitudes, beliefs, and expectations is not only possible (via observation and analysis) but essential. Questions concerning the degree to which this audience is "real" or imagined, and the ways it differs from the speaker's audience, are generally ignored or subordinated to a sense of the audience's powerfulness. In their discussion of "A Heuristic Model for Creating a Writer's Audience," for example, Fred Pfister and Joanne Petrik attempt to recognize the ontological complexity of the writer-audience relationship by noting that "students, like all writers, must fictionalize their audience."[5] Even so, by encouraging students to "construct in their imagination an audience that is as nearly a replica as is possible of *those many readers who actually exist in the world of reality*," Pfister and Petrik implicitly privilege the concept of audience as addressed.[6]

Many of those who envision audience as addressed have been influenced by the strong tradition of audience analysis in speech communication and by current research in cognitive psychology on the composing process.[7] They often see themselves as reacting against the current-traditional paradigm of composition, with its a-rhetorical, product-oriented emphasis.[8] And they also frequently encourage what is called "real-world" writing.[9]

---

[3]For these terms we are indebted to Henry W. Johnstone, Jr., who refers to them in his analysis of Chaim Perelman's universal audience in *Validity and Rhetoric in Philosophical Argument: An Outlook in Transition* (University Park, PA: The Dialogue Press of Man & World, 1978), p. 105.

[4]A number of terms might be used to characterize the two approaches to audience which dominate current theory and practice. Such pairs as identified/envisaged, "real"/fictional, or analyzed/created all point to the same general distinction as do our terms. We chose "addressed/invoked" because these terms most precisely represent our intended meaning. Our discussion will, we hope, clarify their significance; for the present, the following definitions must serve. The "addressed" audience refers to those actual or real-life people who read a discourse, while the "invoked" audience refers to the audience called up or imagined by the writer.

[5]Fred R. Pfister and Joanne F. Petrik, "A Heuristic Model for Creating a Writer's Audience," *CCC*, 31 (May, 1980), 213.

[6]Pfister and Petrik, 214; our emphasis.

[7]See, for example, Lisa S. Ede. "On Audience and Composition," *CCC*, 30 (October, 1979), 291–295.

[8]See, for example, David Tedlock, "The Case Approach to Composition," *CCC*, 32 (October, 1981), 253–261.

[9]See, for example, Linda Flower's *Problem-Solving Strategies for Writers* (New York: Harcourt Brace Jovanovich, 1981) and John P. Field and Robert H. Weiss' *Cases for Composition* (Boston: Little Brown, 1979).

Our purpose here is not to draw up a list of those who share this view of audience but to suggest the general outline of what most readers will recognize as a central tendency in the teaching of writing today. We would, however, like to focus on one particularly ambitious attempt to formulate a theory and pedagogy for composition based on the concept of audience as addressed: Ruth Mitchell and May Taylor's "The Integrating Perspective: An Audience-Response Model for Writing." We choose Mitchell and Taylor's work because of its rhetorical richness and practical specificity. Despite these strengths, we wish to note several potentially significant limitations in their approach, limitations which obtain to varying degress in much of the current work of those who envision audience as addressed.

In their article, Mitchell and Taylor analyze what they consider to be the two major existing composition models: one focusing on the writer and the other on the written product. Their evaluation of these two models seems essentially accurate. The "writer" model is limited because it defines writing as either self-expression or "fidelity to fact" (p. 255)—epistemologically naive assumptions which result in troubling pedagogical inconsistencies. And the "written product" model, which is characterized by an emphasis on "certain intrinsic features [such as a] lack of comma splices and fragments" (p. 258), is challenged by the continued inability of teachers of writing (not to mention those in other professions) to agree upon the precise intrinsic features which characterize "good" writing.

Most interesting, however, is what Mitchell and Taylor *omit* in their criticism of these models. Neither the writer model nor the written product model pays serious attention to invention, the term used to describe those "methods designed to aid in retrieving information, forming concepts, analyzing complex events, and solving certain kinds of problems."[10] Mitchell and Taylor's lapse in not noting this omission is understandable, however, for the same can be said of their own model. When these authors discuss the writing process, they stress that "our first priority for writing instruction at every level ought to be certain major tactics for structuring material because these structures are the most important in guiding the reader's comprehension and memory" (p. 271). They do not concern themselves with where "the material" comes from—its sophistication, complexity, accuracy, or rigor.

Mitchell and Taylor also fail to note another omission, one which might be best described in reference to their own model (Figure 1). This model has four components. Mitchell and Taylor use two of these, "writer" and "written product," as labels for the models they condemn. The third and fourth components, "audience" and "response," provide the title for their own "audience-response model for writing" (p. 249).

---

[10]Richard E. Young, "Paradigms and Problems: Needed Research in Rhetorical Invention," in *Research on Composing: Points of Departure*, ed. Charles R. Cooper and Lee Odell (Urbana, IL: National Council of Teachers of English, 1978), p. 32 (footnote #3).

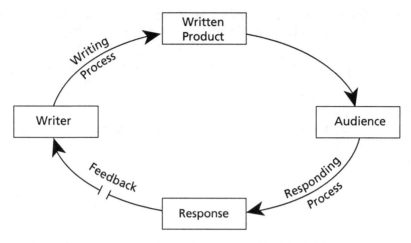

Figure 1 Mitchell and Taylor's "general model of writing" (p. 250)

Mitchell and Taylor stress that the components in their model interact. Yet, despite their emphasis on interaction, it never seems to occur to them to note that the two other models may fail in large part because they overemphasize and isolate one of the four elements—wrenching it too greatly from its context and thus inevitably distorting the composing process. Mitchell and Taylor do not consider this possibility, we suggest, because their own model has the same weakness.

Mitchell and Taylor argue that a major limitation of the "writer" model is its emphasis on the self, the person writing, as the only potential judge of effective discourse. Ironically, however, their own emphasis on audience leads to a similar distortion. In their model, the audience has the sole power of evaluating writing, the success of which "will be judged by the audience's reaction: 'good' translates into 'effective,' 'bad' into 'ineffective.'" Mitchell and Taylor go on to note that "the audience not only judges writing; it also motivates it" (p. 250),[11] thus suggesting that the writer has less control than the audience over both evaluation and motivation.

Despite the fact that Mitchell and Taylor describe writing as "an interaction, a dynamic relationship" (p. 250), their model puts far more emphasis on the role of the audience than on that of the writer. One way to pinpoint the source of imbalance in Mitchell and Taylor's formulation is to note that they are right in emphasizing the creative role of readers who, they observe, "actively contribute to the meaning of what they read and will respond according to a complex set of expectations, preconceptions, and provocations" (p. 251), but wrong in failing to

[11]Mitchell and Taylor do recognize that internal psychological needs ("unconscious challenges") may play a role in the writing process, but they cite such instances as an "extreme case (often that of the creative writer)" (p. 251). For a discussion of the importance of self-evaluation in the composing process see Susan Miller, "How Writers Evaluate Their Own Writing," *CCC,* 33 (May, 1982), 176–183.

recognize the equally essential role writers play throughout the composing process not only as creators but also as *readers* of their own writing.

As Susan Wall observes in "In the Writer's Eye: Learning to Teach the Rereading/Revising Process," when writers read their own writing, as they do continuously while they compose, "there are really not one but two contexts for rereading: there is the writer-as-reader's sense of what the established text is actually saying, as of this reading; and there is the reader-as-writer's judgment of what the text might say or should say. . . ."[12] What is missing from Mitchell and Taylor's model, and from much work done from the perspective of audience as addressed, is a recognition of the crucial importance of this internal dialogue, through which writers analyze inventional problems and conceptualize patterns of discourse. Also missing is an adequate awareness that, no matter how much feedback writers may receive after they have written something (or in breaks while they write), as they compose *writers must rely in large part upon their own vision of the reader, which they create, as readers do their vision of writers, according to their own experiences and expectations.*

Another major problem with Mitchell and Taylor's analysis is their apparent lack of concern for the ethics of language use. At one point, the authors ask the following important question: "Have we painted ourselves into a corner, so that the audience-response model must defend sociologese and its related styles?" (p. 265). Note first the ambiguity of their answer, which seems to us to say no and yes at the same time, and the way they try to deflect its impact:

> No. We defend only the right of audiences to set their own standards and we repudiate the ambitions of English departments to monopolize that standard-setting. If bureaucrats and scientists are happy with the way they write, then no one should interfere.
>
> But evidence is accumulating that they are not happy. (p. 265)

Here Mitchell and Taylor surely underestimate the relationship between style and substance. As those concerned with Doublespeak can attest, for example, the problem with sociologese is not simply its (to our ears) awkward, convoluted, highly nominalized style, but the way writers have in certain instances used this style to make statements otherwise unacceptable to lay persons, to "gloss over" potentially controversial facts about programs and their consequences, and thus violate the ethics of language use. Hence, although we support Mitchell and Taylor when they insist that we must better understand and respect the linguistic traditions of other disciplines and professions, we object to their assumption that style is somehow value free.

As we noted earlier, an analysis of Mitchell and Taylor's discussion clarifies weaknesses, inherent in much of the theoretical and pedagogical research based on the concept of audience as addressed. One major weakness of this research lies in its narrow focus on helping students learn how to "continually modify their work with reference to their audience" (p. 251). Such a focus, which in its

---

[12]Susan Wall, "In the Writer's Eye: Learning to Teach the Rereading/Revising Process," *English Education,* 14 (February, 1982), 12.

extreme form becomes pandering to the crowd, tends to undervalue the responsibility a writer has to a subject and to what Wayne Booth in *Modern Dogma and the Rhetoric of Assent* calls "the art of discovering good reasons."[13] The resulting imbalance has clear ethical consequences, for rhetoric has traditionally been concerned not only with the effectiveness of a discourse, but with truthfulness as well. Much of our difficulty with the language of advertising, for example, arises out of the ad writer's powerful concept of audience as addressed divorced from a corollary ethical concept. The toothpaste ad that promises improved personality, for instance, knows too well how to address the audience. But such ads ignore ethical questions completely.

Another weakness in research done by those who envision audience as addressed suggests an oversimplified view of language. As Paul Kameen observes in "Rewording the Rhetoric of Composition," "discourse is not grounded in forms or experience or audience; it engages all of these elements simultaneously."[14] Ann Berthoff has persistently criticized our obsession with one or another of the elements of discourse, insisting that meaning arises out of their synthesis. Writing is more, then, than "a means of acting upon a receiver" (Mitchell and Taylor, p. 250); it is a means of making meaning for writer *and* reader.[15] Without such a unifying, balanced understanding of language use, it is easy to overemphasize one aspect of discourse, such as audience. It is also easy to forget, as Anthony Petrosky cautions us, that "reading, responding, and composing are aspects of understanding, and theories that attempt to account for them outside of their interaction with each other run the serious risk of building reductive models of human understanding."[16]

Audience Invoked

Those who envision audience as invoked stress that the audience of a written discourse is a construction of the writer, a "created fiction" (Long, p. 225). They do not, of course, deny the physical reality of readers, but they argue that writers simply cannot know this reality in the way that speakers can. The central task of the writer, then, is not to analyze an audience and adapt discourse to meet its needs. Rather, the writer uses the semantic and syntactic resources of language to provide cues for the reader—cues which help to define the role or roles the writer wishes the reader to adopt in responding to the text. Little scholarship in composition takes this perspective; only Russell Long's article

[13]Wayne Booth, *Modern Dogma and the Rhetoric of Assent* (Chicago: The University of Chicago Press, 1974), p. xiv.

[14]Paul Kameen, "Rewording the Rhetoric of Composition," *Pre/Text,* 1 (Spring–Fall, 1980), 82.

[15]Mitchell and Taylor's arguments in favor of adjunct classes seem to indicate that they see writing instruction, wherever it occurs, as a skills course, one instructing students in the proper use of a tool.

[16]Anthony R. Petrosky. "From Story to Essay: Reading and Writing," *CCC.* 33 (February, 1982), 20.

and Walter Ong's "The Writer's Audience Is Always a Fiction" focus centrally on this issue.[17] If recent conferences are any indication, however, a growing number of teachers and scholars are becoming concerned with what they see as the possible distortions and oversimplifications of the approach typified by Mitchell and Taylor's model.[18]

Russell Long's response to current efforts to teach students analysis of audience and adaptation of text to audience is typical: "I have become increasingly disturbed not only about the superficiality of the advice itself, but about the philosophy which seems to lie beneath it" (p. 211). Rather than detailing Long's argument, we wish to turn to Walter Ong's well-known study. Published in *PMLA* in 1975, "The Writer's Audience Is Always a Fiction" has had a significant impact on composition studies, despite the fact that its major emphasis is on fictional narrative rather than expository writing. An analysis of Ong's argument suggests that teachers of writing may err if they uncritically accept Ong's statement that "what has been said about fictional narrative applies ceteris paribus to all writing" (p. 17).

Ong's thesis includes two central assertions: "What do we mean by saying the audience is a fiction? Two things at least. First, that the writer must construct in his imagination, clearly or vaguely, an audience cast in some sort of role. . . . Second, we mean that the audience must correspondingly fictionalize itself" (p. 12). Ong emphasizes the creative power of the adept writer, who can both project and alter audiences, as well as the complexity of the reader's role. Readers, Ong observes, must learn or "know how to play the game of being a member of an audience that 'really' does not exist" (p. 12).

On the most abstract and general level, Ong is accurate. For a writer, the audience is not *there* in the sense that the speaker's audience, whether a single person or a large group, is present. But Ong's representative situations—the orator addressing a mass audience versus a writer alone in a room—oversimplify the potential range and diversity of both oral and written communication situations.

Ong's model of the paradigmatic act of speech communication derives from traditional rhetoric. In distinguishing the terms audience and reader, he notes that "the orator has before him an audience which is a true audience, a collectivity. . . . Readers do not form a collectivity, acting here and now on one another and on the speaker as members of an audience do" (p. 11). As this quotation indicates, Ong also stresses the potential for interaction among members of an audience, and between an audience and a speaker.

But how many audiences are actually collectives, with ample opportunity for interaction? In *Persuasion: Understanding, Practice, and Analysis,* Herbert Simons

[17]Walter J. Ong, S. J., "The Writer's Audience Is Always a Fiction," *PMLA.* 90 (January, 1975), 9–21. Subsequent references to this article will be cited in the text.

[18]See, for example, William Irmscher, "Sense of Audience: An Intuitive Concept," unpublished paper delivered at the CCCC in 1981; Douglas B. Park, "The Meanings of Audience: Pedagogical Implications," unpublished paper delivered at the CCCC in 1981; and Luke M. Reinsma, "Writing to an Audience: Scheme or Strategy?" unpublished paper delivered at the CCCC in 1982.

establishes a continuum of audiences based on opportunities for interaction.[19] Simons contrasts commercial mass media publics, which "have little or no contact with each other and certainly have no reciprocal awareness of each other as members of the same audience" with "face-to-face work groups that meet and interact continuously over an extended period of time." He goes on to note that: "Between these two extremes are such groups as the following: (1) the *pedestrian audience,* persons who happen to pass a soap box orator . . . ; (2) the *passive, occasional audience,* persons who come to hear a noted lecturer in a large auditorium . . . ; (3) the *active, occasional audience,* persons who meet only on specific occasions but actively interact when they do meet" (pp. 97–98).

Simons' discussion, in effect, questions the rigidity of Ong's distinctions between a speaker's and a writer's audience. Indeed, when one surveys a broad range of situations inviting oral communication, Ong's paradigmatic situation, in which the speaker's audience constitutes a "collectivity, acting here and now on one another and on the speaker" (p. 11), seems somewhat atypical. It is certainly possible, at any rate, to think of a number of instances where speakers confront a problem very similar to that of writers: lacking intimate knowledge of their audience, which comprises not a collectivity but a disparate, and possibly even divided, group of individuals, speakers, like writers, must construct in their imaginations "an audience cast in some sort of role."[20] When President Carter announced to Americans during a speech broadcast on television, for instance, that his program against inflation was "the moral equivalent of warfare," he was doing more than merely characterizing his economic policies. He was providing an important cue to his audience concerning the role he wished them to adopt as listeners—that of a people braced for a painful but necessary and justifiable battle. Were we to examine his speech in detail, we would find other more subtle, but equally important, semantic and syntactic signals to the audience.

We do not wish here to collapse all distinctions between oral and written communication, but rather to emphasize that speaking and writing are, after all, both rhetorical acts. There are important differences between speech and writing. And the broad distinction between speech and writing that Ong makes is both commonsensical and particularly relevant to his subject, fictional narrative. As our illustration demonstrates, however, when one turns to precise, concrete situations, the relationship between speech and writing can become far more complex than even Ong represents.

Just as Ong's distinction between speech and writing is accurate on a highly general level but breaks down (or at least becomes less clear-cut) when examined closely, so too does his dictum about writers and their audiences. Every

[19]Herbert W. Simons, *Persuasion: Understanding, Practice, and Analysis* (Reading, MA: Addison-Wesley, 1976).

[20]Ong, p. 12. Ong recognizes that oral communication also involves role-playing, but he stresses that it "has within it a momentum that works for the removal of masks" (p. 20). This may be true in certain instances, such as dialogue, but does not, we believe, obtain broadly.

writer must indeed create a role for the reader, but the constraints on the writer and the potential sources of and possibilities for the reader's role are both more complex and diverse than Ong suggests. Ong stresses the importance of literary tradition in the creation of audience: "If the writer succeeds in writing, it is generally because he can fictionalize in his imagination an audience he has learned to know not from daily life but from earlier writers who were fictionalizing in their imagination audiences they had learned to know in still earlier writers, and so on back to the dawn of written narrative" (p. 11). And he cites a particularly (for us) germane example, a student "asked to write on the subject to which schoolteachers, jaded by summer, return compulsively every autumn: 'How I Spent My Summer Vacation'" (p. 11). In order to negotiate such an assignment successfully, the student must turn his real audience, the teacher, into someone else. He or she must, for instance, "make like Samuel Clemens and write for whomever Samuel Clemens was writing for" (p. 11).

Ong's example is, for his purposes, well-chosen. For such an assignment does indeed require the successful student to "fictionalize" his or her audience. But why is the student's decision to turn to a literary model in this instance particularly appropriate? Could one reason be that the student knows (consciously or unconsciously) that his English teacher, who is still the literal audience of his essay; appreciates literature and hence would be entertained (and here the student may intuit the assignment's actual aim as well), by such a strategy? In Ong's example the audience—the "jaded" schoolteacher—is not only willing to accept another role but, perhaps, actually yearns for it. How else to escape the tedium of reading 25, 50, 75 student papers on the same topic? As Walter Minot notes, however, not all readers are so malleable:

> In reading a work of fiction or poetry, a reader is far more willing to suspend his beliefs and values than in a rhetorical work dealing with some current social, moral, or economic issue. The effectiveness of the created audience in a rhetorical situation is likely to depend on such constraints as the actual identity of the reader, the subject of the discourse, the identity and purpose of the writer, and many other factors in the real world.[21]

An example might help make Minot's point concrete.

Imagine another composition student faced, like Ong's, with an assignment. This student, who has been given considerably more latitude in her choice of a topic, has decided to write on an issue of concern to her at the moment, the possibility that a home for mentally-retarded adults will be built in her neighborhood. She is alarmed by the strongly negative, highly emotional reaction of most of her neighbors and wishes in her essay to persuade them that such a residence might not be the disaster they anticipate.

This student faces a different task from that described by Ong. If she is to succeed, she must think seriously about her actual readers, the neighbors to

[21]Walter S. Minot, "Response to Russell C. Long," *CCC*, 32 (October, 1981), 337.

whom she wishes to send her letter. She knows the obvious demographic factors—age, race, class—so well that she probably hardly needs to consider them consciously. But other issues are more complex. How much do her neighbors know about mental retardation, intellectually or experientially? What is their image of a retarded adult? What fears does this project raise in them? What civic and religious values do they most respect? Based on this analysis—and the process may be much less sequential than we describe here—she must, of course, define a role for her audience, one congruent with her persona, arguments, the facts as she knows them, etc. She must, as Minot argues, *both* analyze and invent an audience.[22] In this instance, after detailed analysis of her audience and her arguments, the student decided to begin her essay by emphasizing what she felt to be the genuinely admirable qualities of her neighbors, particularly their kindness, understanding, and concern for others. In so doing, she invited her audience to see themselves as *she* saw them: as thoughtful, intelligent people who, if they were adequately informed, would certainly not act in a harsh manner to those less fortunate than they. In accepting this role, her readers did not have to "play the game of being a member of an audience that 'really' does not exist" (Ong, "The Writer's Audience," p. 12). But they did have to recognize in themselves the strengths the student described and to accept her implicit linking of these strengths to what she hoped would be their response to the proposed "home."

When this student enters her history class to write an examination she faces a different set of constraints. Unlike the historian who does indeed have a broad range of options in establishing the reader's role, our student has much less freedom. This is because her reader's role has already been established and formalized in a series of related academic conventions. If she is a successful student, she has so effectively internalized these conventions that she can subordinate a concern for her complex and multiple audiences to focus on the material on which she is being tested and on the single audience, the teacher, who will respond to her performance on the test.[23]

[22]We are aware that the student actually has two audiences, her neighbors and her teacher, and that this situation poses an extra constraint for the writer. Not all students can manage such a complex series of audience constraints, but it is important to note that writers in a variety of situations often write for more than a single audience.

[23]In their paper on "Student and Professional Syntax in Four Disciplines" (unpublished paper delivered at the CCCC in 1981), Ian Pringle and Aviva Freedman provide a good example of what can happen when a student creates an aberrant role for an academic reader. They cite an excerpt from a third year history assignment, the tone of which "is essentially the tone of the opening of a television travelogue commentary" and which thus asks the reader, a history professor, to assume the role of the viewer of such a show. The result is as might be expected: "Although the content of the paper does not seem significantly more abysmal than other papers in the same set, this one was awarded a disproportionately low grade" (p. 2).

We could multiply examples. In each instance the student writing—to friend, employer, neighbor, teacher, fellow readers of her daily newspaper—would need, as one of the many conscious and unconscious decisions required in composing, to envision and define a role for the reader. But *how* she defines that role—whether she relies mainly upon academic or technical writing conventions, literary models, intimate knowledge of friends or neighbors, analysis of a particular group, or some combination thereof—will vary tremendously. At times the reader may establish a role for the reader which indeed does not "coincide[s] with his role in the rest of actual life" (Ong, p. 12). At other times, however, one of the writer's primary tasks may be that of analyzing the "real life" audience and adapting the discourse to it. One of the factors that makes writing so difficult, as we know, is that we have no recipes: each rhetorical situation is unique and thus requires the writer, catalyzed and guided by a strong sense of purpose, to reanalyze and reinvent solutions.

Despite their helpful corrective approach, then, theories which assert that the audience of a written discourse is a construction of the writer present their own dangers.[24] One of these is the tendency to overemphasize the distinction between speech and writing while undervaluing the insights of discourse theorists, such as James Moffett and James Britton, who remind us of the importance of such additional factors as distance between speaker or writer and audience and levels of abstraction in the subject. In *Teaching the Universe of Discourse*, Moffett establishes the following spectrum of discourse: recording ("the drama of what is happening"), reporting ("the narrative of what happened"), generalizing ("the exposition of what happens") and theorizing ("the argumentation of what will, may happen").[25] In an extended example, Moffett demonstrates the important points of connection between communication acts at any one level of the spectrum, whether oral or written:

> Suppose next that I tell the cafeteria experience to a friend some time later in conversation. . . . Of course, instead of recounting the cafeteria scene to my friend in person I could write it in a letter to an audience more removed in time and space. Informal writing is usually still rather spontaneous, directed at an audience known to the writer, and reflects the transient mood and circumstances in which the writing occurs. Feedback and audience influence, however, are delayed and weakened. . . .

[24]One danger which should be noted is a tendency to foster a questionable image of classical rhetoric. The agonistic speaker-audience relationship which Long cites as an essential characteristic of classical rhetoric is actually a central point of debate among those involved in historical and theoretical research in rhetoric. For further discussion, see: Lisa Ede and Andrea Lunsford, "On Distinctions Between Classical and Modern Rhetoric," in *Classical Rhetoric and Modern Discourse: Essays in Honor of Edward P. J. Corbett,* ed. Robert Connors, Lisa Ede, and Andrea Lunsford (Carbondale, IL: Southern Illinois University Press, 1984).

[25]James Moffett, *Teaching the Universe of Discourse* (Boston: Houghton Mifflin, 1968), p. 47. Subsequent references will be mentioned in the text.

Compare in turn now the changes that must occur all down the line when I
write about this cafeteria experience in a discourse destined for publication
and distribution to a mass, anonymous audience of present and perhaps,
unborn people. I cannot allude to things and ideas that only my friends
know about. I must use a vocabulary, style, logic, and rhetoric that any-
body in that mass audience can understand and respond to. I must
name and organize what happened during those moments in the cafeteria that day in such a way that this mythical average reader can
relate what I say to some primary moments of experience of his own.
(pp. 37–38; our emphasis)

Though Moffett does not say so, many of these same constraints would obtain if he
decided to describe his experience in a speech to a mass audience—the viewers of
a television show, for example, or the members of a graduating class. As Moffett's
example illustrates, the distinction between speech and writing is important; it is,
however, only one of several constraints influencing any particular discourse.

Another weakness of research based on the concept of audience as invoked
is that it distorts the processes of writing and reading by overemphasizing the
power of the writer and undervaluing that of the reader. Unlike Mitchell and
Taylor, Ong recognizes the creative role the writer plays as reader of his or her
own writing, the way the writer uses language to provide cues for the reader and
tests the effectiveness of these cues during his or her own rereading of the text.
But Ong fails adequately to recognize the constraints placed on the writer, in
certain situations, by the audience. He fails, in other words, to acknowledge that
readers' own experiences, expectations, and beliefs do play a central role in their
reading of a text, and that the writer who does not consider the needs and interests of his audience risks losing that audience. To argue that the audience is a
"created fiction" (Long, p. 225), to stress that the reader's role "seldom coincides
with his role in the rest of actual life" (Ong, p. 12), is just as much an oversimplification, then, as to insist, as Mitchell and Taylor do, that "the audience not only
judges writing, it also motivates it" (p. 250). The former view overemphasizes
the writer's independence and power; the latter, that of the reader.

Rhetoric and Its Situations[26]

If the perspectives we have described as audience addressed and audience
invoked represent incomplete conceptions of the role of audience in written discourse, do we have an alternative? How can we most accurately conceive of this
essential rhetorical element? In what follows we will sketch a tentative model
and present several defining or constraining statements about this apparently

[26]We have taken the title of this section from Scott Consigny's article of the same
title, *Philosophy and Rhetoric,* 7 (Summer, 1974), 175–186. Consigny's effort to mediate
between two opposing views of rhetoric provided a stimulating model for our own efforts.

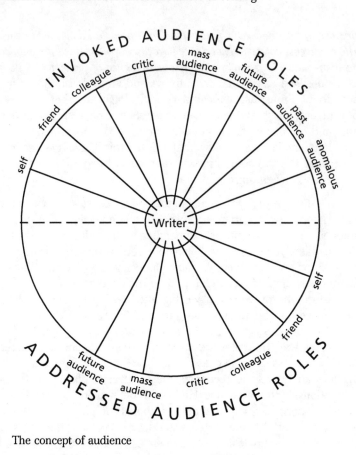

Figure 2 The concept of audience

slippery concept, "audience." The result will, we hope, move us closer to a full understanding of the role audience plays in written discourse.

Figure 2 represents our attempts to indicate the complex series of obligations, resources, needs, and constraints embodied in the writer's concept of audience. (We emphasize that our goal here is *not* to depict the writing process as a whole—a much more complex task—but to focus on the writer's relation to audience.) As our model indicates, we do not see the two perspectives on audience described earlier as necessarily dichotomous or contradictory. Except for past and anomalous audiences, special cases which we describe paragraphs hence, all of the audience roles we specify—self, friend, colleague, critic, mass audience, and future audience—may be invoked or addressed.[27] It is the writer who, as writer

---

[27]Although we believe that the range of audience roles cited in our model covers the general spectrum of options, we do not claim to have specified all possibilities. This is particularly the case since, in certain instances, these roles may merge and blend—shifting subtly in character. We might also note that other terms for the same roles might be used. In a business setting, for instance, colleague might be better termed coworker, critic, supervisor.

and reader of his or her own text, one guided by a sense of purpose and by the particularities of a specific rhetorical situation, establishes the range of potential roles an audience may play. (Readers may, of course, accept or reject the role or roles the writer wishes them to adopt in responding to a text.)

Writers who wish to be read must often adapt their discourse to meet the needs and expectations of an addressed audience. They may rely on past experience in addressing audiences to guide their writing, or they may engage a representative of that audience in the writing process. The latter occurs, for instance, when we ask a colleague to read an article intended for scholarly publication. Writers may also be required to respond to the intervention of others—a teacher's comments on an essay, a supervisor's suggestions for improving a report, or the insistent, catalyzing questions of an editor. Such intervention may in certain cases represent a powerful stimulus to the writer, but it is the writer who interprets the suggestions—or even commands—of others, choosing what to accept or reject. Even the conscious decision to accede to the expectations of a particular addressed audience may not always be carried out; unconscious psychological resistance, incomplete understanding, or inadequately developed ability may prevent the writer from following through with the decision—a reality confirmed by composition teachers with each new set of essays.

The addressed audience, the actual or intended readers of a discourse, exists outside of the text. Writers may analyze these readers' needs, anticipate their biases, even defer to their wishes. But it is only through the text, through language, that writers embody or give life to their conception of the reader. In so doing, they do not so much create a role for the reader—a phrase which implies that the writer somehow creates a mold to which the reader adapts—as invoke it. Rather than relying on incantations, however, writers conjure their vision—a vision which they hope readers will actively come to share as they read the text—by using all the resources of language available to them to establish a broad, and ideally coherent, range of cues for the reader. Technical writing conventions, for instance, quickly formalize any of several writer-reader relationships, such as colleague to colleague or expert to lay reader. But even comparatively local semantic decisions may play an equally essential role. In "The Writer's Audience Is Always a Fiction," Ong demonstrates how Hemingway's use of definite articles in *A Farewell to Arms* subtly cues readers that their role is to be that of a "companion in arms . . . a confidant" (p. 13).

Any of the roles of the addressed audience cited in our model may be invoked via the text. Writers may also invoke a past audience, as did, for instance, Ong's student writing to those Mark Twain would have been writing for. And writers can also invoke anomalous audiences, such as a fictional character—Hercule Poirot perhaps. Our model, then, confirms Douglas Park's observation that the meanings of audience, though multiple and complex, "tend to diverge in two general directions: one toward actual people external to a text, the audience whom the writer must accommodate; the other toward the text itself and the audience implied there: a set of suggested or evoked attitudes, interests, reactions, conditions of knowledge which may or may not fit with the qualities of actual readers or listeners."[28] The most complete understanding of audience thus involves a synthesis of the perspectives we have termed audience addressed, with its focus on the reader, and audience invoked, with its focus on the writer.

One illustration of this constantly shifting complex of meanings for "audience" lies in our own experiences writing this essay. One of us became interested in the concept of audience during an NEH Seminar, and her first audience was a small, close-knit seminar group to whom she addressed her work. The other came to contemplate a multiplicity of audiences while working on a textbook; the first audience in this case was herself, as she debated the ideas she was struggling to present to a group of invoked students. Following a lengthy series of conversations, our interests began to merge: we shared notes and discussed articles written by others on audience, and eventually one of us began a draft. Our long distance telephone bills and the miles we travelled up and down I-5 from Oregon to British Columbia attest most concretely to the power of a coauthor's expectations and criticisms and also illustrate that one person can take on the role of several different audiences: friend, colleague, and critic.

As we began to write and re-write the essay, now for a particular scholarly journal, the change in purpose and medium (no longer a seminar paper or a textbook) led us to new audiences. For us, the major "invoked audience" during this period was Richard Larson, editor of this journal, whose questions and criticisms we imagined and tried to anticipate. (Once this essay was accepted by *CCC*, Richard Larson became for us an addressed audience: he responded in writing with questions, criticisms, and suggestions, some of which we had, of course, failed to anticipate.) We also thought of the readers of *CCC* and those who attend the annual CCCC, most often picturing you as members of our own departments, a diverse group of individuals with widely varying degrees of interest in and knowledge of composition. Because of the generic constraints of academic writing, which limit the range of roles we may define for our readers, the audience represented by the readers of *CCC* seemed most vivid to us in two situations: 1) when we were concerned about the degree to which we needed to explain concepts or terms; and 2) when we considered central organizational decisions, such as the most effective way to introduce a discussion. Another, and for us extremely potent, audience was the authors—Mitchell and Taylor, Long, Ong, Park, and others—with whom we have seen ourselves in silent dialogue. As we read and reread their analyses and developed our responses to them, we felt a responsibility to try to understand their formulations as fully as possible, to play fair with their ideas, to make our own efforts continue to meet their high standards.

Our experience provides just one example, and even it is far from complete. (Once we finished a rough draft, one particular colleague became a potent but demanding addressed audience, listening to revision upon revision and challenging us with harder and harder questions. And after this essay is published, we may revise our understanding of audiences we thought we knew or recognize

[28]Douglas B. Park, "The Meanings of 'Audience,'" *CE,* 44 (March, 1982), 249.

the existence of an entirely new audience. The latter would happen, for instance, if teachers of speech communication for some reason found our discussion useful.) But even this single case demonstrates that the term *audience* refers not just to the intended, actual, or eventual readers of a discourse, but to *all* those whose image, ideas, or actions influence a writer during the process of composition. One way to conceive of "audience," then, is as an overdetermined or unusually rich concept, one which may perhaps be best specified through the analysis of precise, concrete situations.

We hope that this partial example of our own experience will illustrate how the elements represented in Figure 3 will shift and merge, depending on the particular rhetorical situation, the writer's aim, and the genre chosen. Such an understanding is critical: because of the complex reality to which the term audience refers and because of its fluid, shifting role in the composing process, any discussion of audience which isolates it from the rest of the rhetorical situation or which radically overemphasizes or underemphasizes its function in relation to other rhetorical constraints is likely to oversimplify. Note the unilateral direction of Mitchell and Taylor's model (p. 5), which is unable to represent the diverse and complex role(s) audience(s) can play in the actual writing process—in the creation of meaning. In contrast, consider the model used by Edward P. J. Corbett in his *Little Rhetoric and Handbook.*[29] This representation, which allows for interaction among all the elements of rhetoric, may at first appear less elegant and predictive than Mitchell and Taylor's. But it is finally more useful since it accurately represents the diverse range of potential interrelationships in any written discourse.

We hope that our model also suggests the integrated, interdependent nature of reading and writing. Two assertions emerge from this relationship. One involves the writer as reader of his or her own work. As Donald Murray notes in "Teaching the Other Self: The Writer's First Reader," this role is critical, for "the reading writer—the map-maker and map-reader—reads the word, the line, the sentence, the paragraph, the page, the entire text. This constant back-and-forth reading monitors the multiple complex relationships between all the elements in writing."[30] To ignore or devalue such a central function is to risk distorting the writing process as a whole. But unless the writer is composing a diary or journal entry, intended only for the writer's own eyes, the writing process is not complete unless another person, someone other than the writer, reads the text also. The second assertion thus emphasizes the creative, dynamic duality of the process of reading and writing, whereby writers create readers and readers create writers. In the meeting of these two lies meaning, lies communication.

A fully elaborated view of audience, then, must balance the creativity of the writer with the different, but equally important, creativity of the reader. It must account for a wide and shifting range of roles for both addressed and invoked

[29]Edward P. J. Corbett, *The Little Rhetoric & Handbook,* 2nd edition (Glenview, IL: Scott, Foresman, 1982), p. 5.

[30]Donald M. Murray. "Teaching the Other Self: The Writer's First Reader," *CCC,* 33 (May, 1982), 142.

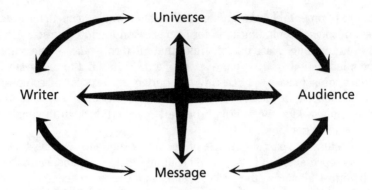

Figure 3   Corbett's model of "The Rhetorical Interrelationships" (p. 5)

audiences. And, finally, it must relate the matrix created by the intricate relationship of writer and audience to all elements in the rhetorical situation. Such an enriched conception of audience can help us better understand the complex act we call composing.

Audience: Additional Readings

Lisa Ede. "Audience: An Introduction to Research." *College Composition and Communication* 35 (May 1984): 140–54.

Peter Elbow. "Closing My Eyes as I Speak: An Argument for Ignoring Audience." *College English* 49 (January 1987): 50–69.

Barry M. Kroll. "Writing for Readers: Three Perspectives on Audience." *College Composition and Communication* 35 (May 1984): 172–85.

Douglas B. Park. "Analyzing Audiences." *College Composition and Communication* 37 (December 1986): 478–88.

James E. Porter. "Intertextuality and the Discourse Community." *Rhetoric Review* 5 (Fall 1986): 34–45.

Robert G. Roth. "The Evolving Audience: Alternatives to Audience Accommodation." *College Composition and Communication* 38 (February 1987): 47–55.

Additional Sources

Booth, Wayne. *The Rhetoric of Fiction.* Chicago: University of Chicago Press, 1963.

Groundbreaking analysis of narrative strategies that emphasizes the importance of implied author. Investigates the ways in which literature is persuasive.

Clark, Gregory. "Rescuing the Discourse of Community." *College Composition & Communication* Vol. 45, 1 (February 1994); 61–74.

Discusses the issue of difference in discourse communities and argues for a model of community that permits participants to include difference.

Flower, Linda. "Writer-Based Prose: A Cognitive Basis for Problems in Writing." *College English* 41 (September 1979): 19–37.

Argues that many problems in experienced writers has to do with a kind of egocentrism, causing them to write writer-based, rather than reader-based, prose.

Ong, Walter J., S. J. "The Writer's Audience Is Always a Fiction." *PMLA* 90 (January 1975): 9–21.

Discusses the role that the fictionalized audience has for both the author and reader in fiction.

Park, Douglas B. "The Meanings of 'Audience.'" *College English* 44 (1982): 247–57.

Argues that much teaching of audience awareness is ineffective because writing assignments implicitly demand considerable deftness in handling audience without making the various possible rhetorical contexts clear.

Part II

Pedagogical Issues
and Trends

Chapter 4

Group Work

My first experience with group peer review was as a student in freshman composition. On the days we turned in our papers, we were put into groups and traded papers. We were then asked to comment on one another's papers. My main sensation was guilt—if I noticed a major problem in a paper, I felt guilty if I didn't remark on it; if I did remark on it, I also felt guilty, since there was nothing the person could do to change the paper. If another student noted anything more than typos in my paper, I spent the next week wondering if the teacher would notice the same problems. All in all, it seemed a way to waste a class period. In high school, I had often been assigned group projects, and my experience was equally negative. Sometimes I was the responsible student who resented the slacker student for procrastinating, and sometimes I was the slacker who resented the nagging of the responsible one. Either way, I did not like it, and I saw it as a cynical attempt on the part of teachers to reduce grading.

When I reflect back on these experiences, I am most struck by any lack of explanation as to why we were engaging in group work. It was not clear to me what we were supposed to learn. The main lessons seemed to be negative. In high school, I learned to avoid group assignments, and in college I learned not to pay attention to the peer reviews. These were harmful lessons. Like many others with unpleasant experiences with group work, I began to rethink my position when I began seeing the importance of audience in writing. As a teacher, I was dependent upon class discussions—I could see students reflect more deeply the more they were exposed to the ways that other students saw the same topics. It made the course more than a simple exercise if the students became engaged in persuading other students in class—students whose reactions on the same topics they had heard. If they did not know what other students thought, then they were unlikely to take seriously the task of persuading other students, and they were more likely to write papers whose only purpose was to get a grade from me. In other words, I had adopted a teaching strategy which made the class itself a peer group.

This strategy worked because students learned what they thought about something by having to explain it to someone else. They also learned by listening to other points of view—sometimes other students articulated their own vague ideas, and sometimes other students inspired reflection by saying something with which they disagreed.

In "A New Perspective on Why Small Groups Do and Don't Work," Peter Smagorinsky and Pamela Fly emphasize the importance of "prompts" for whole-class discussion. Some of these prompts are explicitly problems (questions that emphasize why, questions that ask students to define their terms) and some are better described as gaps. For instance, when the teacher used the "method of repeating student statements in the form of a question" it pointed to the gap in the student's initial assertion (57). Probably the most helpful aspect of Smagorinsky and Fly's research is that it points to the connection between small and whole group activities. Small group dynamics, they argue, replicate the whole group ones. The conclusion they reach—"teachers need to attend to the total environment they create in their classrooms and to look at particular instructional methods and classroom episodes as they relate to learning and instruction as a whole" (58)—emphasizes the importance of *kairos,* or the rhetorical situation, in rhetoric. Any single teaching strategy will work only to the extent that it is appropriate to the context. The context for small groups remains the larger.

Of course, students will tend to ask one another questions the teacher asked them. What writing instructors have learned about groups is that they take time to set up effectively. This does not necessarily mean that the teacher must determine the membership of the group—Brooke et al.'s *Small Groups in Writing Workshops: Invitations to a Writer's Life* contains reports from some people who do and some people who do not try to place students in particular groups—but it does mean that the group work must be planned carefully. Hillocks has suggested that student learning improves when classroom tasks contribute to the goal, and the same is true of group activities. While nothing will make all groups work well, ensuring that the students understand the relevance of their group tasks will help them work more effectively within them.

Effectively run peer groups do not save the instructor very much (if any) time. In my experience, students will rarely take the group work any more or less seriously than the instructor. So, putting students into groups with vague tasks that appear to make no difference to the quality of student work will usually ensure that students will be as unhappy about group work as I was. For this reason, some instructors grade the group work, some instructors will quote peer reviews in their own paper comments, and some instructors will ask that students assign grades to one another's contributions to the groups.

There is a similar variety of strategy in ensuring that group projects are effective. Some instructors recommend shepherding the groups (meeting frequently with the groups to discuss the progress they are making) while other instructors rely on assigning carefully thought through projects. Even with careful thought before or during the group project, something will go wrong. Hence, it is always a good idea to have plans for dealing with irresponsible students, groups that fail to thrive, groups whose schedules preclude their being able to meet outside of class, and groups that turn into open warfare. In other words, like any other pedagogical practice, it will not always work perfectly, and instructors should be prepared for the glitches.

A New Perspective on Why Small Groups Do and Don't Work
Peter Smagorinsky and Pamela K. Fly

Since we began teaching, we both have been great proponents of using small groups in the English class. In our own teaching, students have worked in small groups for a variety of purposes: to work on many aspects of writing, to analyze short stories, to play vocabulary games, to produce plays, and to engage in other activities with the support of their peers. Like many language-arts educators at all levels, we have found that small-group activities increase levels of interaction among students, enable students to teach and learn from each other, and promote a healthy social climate in the classroom.

We have also found, however, that small groups "just don't seem to work" for some teachers. We all know of colleagues who say, "I tried that once, and it was a disaster," or "Small groups only give kids a license to goof off." Upon hearing these comments, we would always think, "The problem isn't with small groups; it's with the way you run them." These teachers could have more success, we believed, if only they would allow kids to work on more challenging and appropriate tasks, if they would provide better incentives for working harmoniously, or if they would supervise the group work more effectively. We have spent many hours developing ideas on how to set up and manage small groups in order to make them work well. Like many educators who have advocated small groups, we have believed that managerial considerations strongly affect the ways in which small groups operate.

Yet, we also knew that no matter how effectively some teachers set up small groups, the groups floundered or got hopelessly off task. Management, it became clear, was only part of the story. As Anne DiPardo and Sarah Freedman have pointed out, "We know little about precisely why groups work when they do, or perhaps more importantly, what accounts for their failures" (1987, 2).

Our uncertainty about the factors that affect small-group success led us to undertake a classroom investigation that tried to answer some of our questions about effective small-group process. The research, which examined the talk of students engaged in small-group discussions of literature, has given us a better understanding of "why groups work when they do." (See Marshall, Smagorinsky, and Smith [in press] and Smagorinsky and Fly [1993] for detailed reports on the research.) We examined tape recordings of high-school sophomores discussing "coming-of-age" stories in two settings: first in a teacher-led discussion of one story from a course anthology, and then in small-group discussions of a second story from the same anthology. Our purpose was to examine the extent to which the patterns of talk established by the teachers in the initial discussions affected the ways in which students talked when discussing the story with each other.

The study involved a limited number of teachers and students, so we must be cautious in generalizing from the results. From our analysis of the transcripts, however, it seems that the behavior of teachers in class discussions has a great deal to do with the success of students working independently. In other words, assuming that the groups are set up and managed in more or less the same ways, the patterns of discussion established by teachers *leading up to* small-group sessions seem to influence the ability of students to talk on their own. The following discussion-leading techniques seemed to facilitate successful small-group interactions: (1) prompting students to generate a contextual framework to guide interpretation; (2) prompting students to elaborate their responses; (3) building on student contributions to generate questions; and (4) making the process of analysis explicit. The following sections illustrate each of these techniques with segments from classroom discussions.

Prompting Students to Generate a Contextual Framework to Guide Interpretation

In their whole-class discussions, all of the teachers strove to provide a broad context through which to interpret the story. One teacher provided that context himself, sharing with his students lengthy personal experiences that illustrated the plight of the literary characters. Often these personal connections were riveting and relevant to the literary dilemma. Teachers who provided this context for the students, however, did not appear to help students learn how to generate relevant personal examples themselves. Here, for instance, a teacher posed questions about the behavior of a character and then elaborated a student response into a hypothetical situation that helped illuminate the character's situation.

> Teacher: Rachel, what happens after he jumps into the water?
> Rachel: He saves the girl.
> Teacher: Is it an easy saving?
> Rachel: No, because the current pulls them under.
> Teacher: That is described in great detail. Why do you suppose the author describes the saving in such great detail?
> Student: [inaudible]
> Teacher: It has to be arduous for anything to be important. It has to be difficult. For example, if it were easy to play the guitar, we would all be Eric Clapton. But all of us probably have sat down with either our guitar or somebody else's guitar. The first thing you find out is that it sort of hurts and it is hard to keep the frets down. So you get one chord and you struggle for a while, like row, row your boat. You got to change it, and it is difficult. Now, if it is a matter of just hopping off a two foot bridge into three feet of water and saying, don't be silly, you're all right honey, that is not going to be something that changes him very much. But in the act of saving itself, one particular thing happens between the two people. Can you remember what that is?

Presumably, the reference to a rock-and-roll icon will build on students' interests and help them see the connection between their own worlds and those of the characters in the story. Yet when teachers generated an appropriate context without engaging students in the process, they did not appear to help their students gain the ability to produce such contexts for themselves. Here, for instance, is a complete episode in the small-group discussion of this teacher's students:

Ellen: [Reads from assignment sheet] "What characteristics does the protagonist have at the beginning of the story that you would call immature? Give examples and explain why they are immature."

Betty: I don't know.

Judy: Wait, I forgot the story. Let me get my book right here.

Ellen: I think that at the beginning of the story, he thinks that to be mature, he's going to be six feet tall, he's going to have arms of steel, and he thinks he's going to be in control.

Judy: He watches TV too much.

Ellen: And he thinks he's rebelling by eating grape seeds just because his mother is not there.

Ginny: Good answer.

Ellen: Somebody else talk. (pause) Does anyone else have any more reasons why he is immature?

Betty: Nope.

Episodes of this length and depth were typical in the discussions of the students whose teachers provided the broad context of interpretation. Their interpretations appeared to serve the purpose of generating an acceptable answer and then moving on to the next question. Although the teacher made a great effort to provide a model for how to generate a context from personal experience, when left on their own students did not appear to know how to do so.

When teachers used questioning techniques that *prompted the students* to generate a context to frame the story, the students were far more capable of producing a relevant framework in their small-group discussions. In the following excerpt from one whole-class discussion, the teacher pushed students to provide a conceptual context through which to interpret the literary character's experience:

Patsy: He thought it was so mature to, well, he was eating grapes and staying up late with, he was eating grapes and grape seeds and staying up late and watching TV without his mother's approval.

Teacher: OK, eating grapes and seeds and a couple of other examples. He was staying up late.

Patsy: Yeah.

Teacher: And he was also . . .

Patsy: Watching TV.

Teacher: And watching TV when told not to. And these fall into the category of what?

Patsy: Huh?

Teacher: These all have something in common.

Patsy: Well, disobeying.

Teacher: OK. He was disobeying his mother. All right. Now what can you do with this? In other words, what are you trying to tell us by bringing up these points?

Patsy: That he thought he was mature by disobeying his mother. He thought it made him a more mature person and older by doing things he wasn't supposed to do.

Teacher: Thought he was mature through these acts. OK, and what does Patsy think? Do you agree with it?

Patsy: What? No.

Teacher: Why not?

Patsy: He was just showing how immature he is by doing that.

Teacher: And what criterion of a definition of maturity are you using to make this judgment? Why is this, you are saying that this is, in fact, immature even though he thought he was mature. That is what you are saying, right?

Patsy: Yes.

Teacher: Why? You are saying he is immature because of something and that *because* is your definition. And what is it about your definition that allows you to make this judgment?

In their small-group discussions, students of this teacher worked to establish a similar sort of conceptual interpretive framework:

Veronica: The protagonist was very insecure.

Kay: Why is he insecure?

Hope: Why is he insecure? Because he stayed home all the time and didn't want to go on this trip.

Kay: So that was immature?

Tammy: That was insecure.

Hope: Insecure which is immature.

Tammy: Yeah.

Kay: Why is immaturity insecurity?

Tammy: [reads from assignment sheet] ". . . that you would call immature?"

Kay: Why is insecure immature? By staying home, is that immature?

Tammy: No, he had no friends.

Kay: No friends is insecure?

Hope: No, he's insecure and insecurity is immaturity.

Kay: The second question asks, "Explain why . . ."

Tammy: You have to know yourself and he doesn't; therefore he's insecure.

Hope: Insecure means no self-knowledge.

Tammy: Yeah.

Kay: OK, he had no self-knowledge. Now, why is that immature?

Tammy: Because he was too protected.

Hope: It's immature because . . .

Kay: He was protected.

Hope: Yeah. He was 17, he was afraid to go out. Well, actually . . .

Kay: He was old enough to know . . .

Hope: Right.

Kay: He spent his life at home.

Hope: He was never really out.

Veronica: Maybe he was a hermit. I don't know why. He just like stayed at home with his family. I feel sorry for him.

Hope: He's one of those people you don't want to know. How is no self-knowledge immature?

Tammy: Let me explain this one. You see like, no self-knowledge, that leads to . . . I don't know.

Kay: He has no idea what the outside world is.

Tammy: You have to know yourself, and by knowing yourself, you know your limits.

Hope: Yeah.

Simply *modeling* an interpretive strategy, then, does not appear to be effective in teaching students how to apply it; teachers must saturate the classroom with prompts for students to generate their own interpretive framework for analyzing literature in order to get them to do so on their own. The teacher in the excerpt just given never explicitly told students that he was teaching them a strategy, yet they seem to have picked it up through routine participation in such exchanges.

Prompting Students to Elaborate Their Responses

A second effective discussion-leading technique was for teachers to prompt their students to develop insufficient responses. One teacher, for instance, had a method of repeating student statements in the form of a question in order to prompt them to elaborate:

Jane: . . . it seems like she is just this mother figure. He is kind of scared of her.

Teacher: He is kind of scared of his grandmother?

Jane: Yeah. Like she is kind of turning against him.

Teacher: She is turning against him?

A method such as this appeared quite effective in getting students to develop their own self-prompts for elaborating; students of teachers who demonstrated some method of prompting elaboration engaged in longer, more detailed analysis of the literature in their small groups than did students of teachers who elaborated student responses themselves. Each teacher had a unique way of providing such prompts; no particular method seemed more effective than others. The point that stood out was that teachers who prompted students to elaborate, rather than taking over the responsibility of elaboration themselves, seemed to provide students with procedures for discussing literature independent of the teacher's influence.

Building on Student Contributions to Generate Questions

Another effective discussion-leading technique was for teachers to engage in what Martin Nystrand and Adam Gamoran (1991) have called *uptake;* that is, to pose questions that build on student interpretations and serve as elaboration prompts. Teachers whose preconceived questions guided and structured their discussions did not appear to empower students to guide their own discussions well. "Uptake" sequences such as reported in the following excerpt appeared to help students generate longer episodes in their small-group discussions:

> Larry: You don't have a male figure if you are a man, and you don't have a reference because you see things a little differently because men and women have different . . .
> Teacher: Yeah, he has just got a grandmother and an aunt in the house, and he has just lost his mother. It doesn't seem like he ever had a father around. So you are saying you wouldn't call it immaturity? You would call it . . .
> Fred: Innocence.
> Larry: No. I think it is more what is going on in the house.
> Teacher: Just a reflection of the life, the way he has been growing up?

In this sequence the teacher is going with the flow of the discussion. Rather than setting the direction of the discussion through posing predetermined questions, he is basing his questions on student interpretations in order to get them to elaborate on or defend their ideas. Such a questioning method appeared highly effective in getting students to engage in extensive discussion in their small-group sessions.

Making the Process of Analysis Explicit

A final effective discussion-leading strategy was for the teacher to make the process of analysis explicit by calling attention to procedures for interpreting literature, as in the following sequence:

> Teacher: I think we assume they must [have four children] because she is supporting them, right?
> Chorus: Yeah.
> Teacher: There is something else that we need to ask.
> Sally: What happened to the uncle?
> Teacher: We don't get any information about the boy's father or the grand-

father, for that matter. Any of the men, we don't learn anything about in the story. But there is another question from the beginning, at least about his behavior.

Students of teachers who made the process of interpretation explicit by pointing out the need to pose questions, to make generalizations, to search for evidence, to refer to a broader conceptual framework had longer, more detailed small-group discussions than did students of teachers who simply modeled the interpretive behavior.

Conclusion

This research relies on a limited number of teachers and students, and so we cannot regard it as conclusive. It does help generate hypotheses, however, about why small groups work when they do, and what accounts for their failure. It appears from the discussions analyzed here that the success of small groups is related to the overall discussion patterns that govern the classrooms in which they take place. This hypothesis finds support in the work of Lev Vygotsky (1978, 1986), whose theories centered on the importance of social and cultural influences on learning. Drawing on Vygotsky's work, Jerome Bruner (1975) coined the term "scaffolding" to describe the manner in which a teacher (who can be an adult or peer) supports a person's early learning experiences and gradually withdraws support as the learner becomes more independent. In the research we've reported, all of the teachers were *attempting* to provide a scaffold of support for student learning. Effective instructional scaffolding, however, appears to involve a dynamic interaction between students and teacher and not simply the modeling of a learning process or the presentation of information. Teachers whose students engaged in fruitful small-group activities *cultivated student expertise,* rather than issuing expert opinions.

Since conducting this research, we have come to regard small groups quite differently than we did for many years. We now see them as an extension of the continuum of discussions enacted during the school year. Their success seems dependent on the prevailing language of the classroom, which makes it unlikely that a teacher whose talk dominates the classroom can use them effectively. Teachers who have struggled with small groups might benefit from examining their own discussion-leading styles in order to make their classes more flexible and interactive; teachers who have had success with small groups might be more cautious in recommending them to others. In all cases, the research suggests that teachers need to attend to the total environment they create in their classrooms and to look at particular instructional methods and classroom episodes as they relate to learning and instruction as a whole.

The University of Oklahoma
Norman, Oklahoma 73019

Works Cited

Bruner, Jerome. 1975. "From Communication to Language: A Psychological Perspective." *Cognition* 3.3: 255–87.

DiPardo, Anne, and Sarah W. Freedman. 1987. "Historical Overview: Groups in the Writing Classroom." Technical Report No. 4. Berkeley, CA: Center for the Study of Writing.

Marshall, James, Peter Smagorinsky, and Michael W. Smith. In press. *The Language of Interpretation: Patterns of Discourse in Discussions of Literature.* Urbana: NCTE.

Nystrand, Martin, and Adam Gamoran. 1991. "Instructional Discourse, Student Engagement, and Literature Achievement." *Research in the Teaching of English* 25.3 (Nov.): 261–90.

Smagorinsky, Peter, and Pamela K. Fly. 1993. "The Social Climate of the Classroom: A Vygotskian Perspective on Small Group Process." *Communication Education* 42.2 (Apr.): 159–71.

Vygotsky, Lev. 1978. *Mind in Society: The Development of Higher Psychological Processes.* Ed. Michael Cole, et al. Cambridge: Harvard UP.

——. 1986. *Thought and Language.* Cambridge: MIT P.

Additional Sources

Brooke, Robert, et al. *Small Groups in Writing Workshops: Invitations to a Writer's Life.* Urbana, IL: National Council of Teachers of English, 1994.

Describes the approaches and experiences of several teachers with group work in composition courses, ranges from theoretical discussion to pedagogical recommendations.

George, Diana. "Working with Peer Groups in the Composition Classroom." *College Composition and Communication* 35 (October 1984): 320–26.

Discusses problems of three types of peer groups, with recommendations for improving less functional groups.

Gere, Anne Ruggles. *Writing Groups: History, Theory, and Implications.* Carbondale: Southern Illinois UP, 1987.

Discusses history, theory, and implications of writing groups in America, ending with practical recommendations.

Trimbur, John. "Consensus and Difference in Collaborative Learning." *College English* 51 (1989): 602–16.

Defends collaborative learning against two common criticisms regarding the pressure of consensus.

Chapter 5
Writing in Communities

In the Platonic dialogue named after him, the character Gorgias brags that he would be more persuasive than the experts when talking to a popular audience. Socrates points out that this could easily lead a large community into rather serious errors; they might buy a bunch of donkeys when they really need horses. As mentioned earlier, this is the way in which the issue of audience is an ethical one. There are ethical reasons for having writing evaluated by people who know something about the subject matter. In a sense, the movement toward writing across the curriculum is partly the result of facing this problem: It presumes that writing is not merely a question of value-free rules which can be applied in all circumstances. The recognition of *kairos* in writing means that we have recognized that "good" writing in an agriculture course might be very different from "good" writing in a poetry course.

It is partly a question of stylistic conventions—that some disciplines forbid the passive voice while others require it—and partly a question of priorities—that some disciplines put tremendous emphasis on format while others do not. But the differences in disciplines go much deeper. There are different sorts of relationships to reality in different disciplines, or, as Bazerman says, different ways of knowing the world.

The principle behind writing across the curriculum is essentially that, as Cooper says, "One does not begin to write about bird behavior, say, without observing birds, talking with other observers, and reading widely in the literature of animal behavior in general". In other words, writing is *about* something and happens within the context of a particular community. Marie Secor and Jeanne Fahnestock have defined the goal of their writing course as enabling students to: "write clear, orderly, convincing arguments which show respect for evidence, build in refutation, and accommodate their audience". Such a goal necessitates defining a community, for quality of evidence, legitimacy of refutation, and audience needs are not qualities that exist separate from the discourse on the topic. Different communities accord different kinds of respect for various kinds of evidence.

There is some indication that writing instruction which is free of community does little long-term good for students. This was the conclusion of the Harvard Assessment Program, which indicated that student writing improved over the long-term only if students continued writing in their courses. They especially need courses in their disciplines which teach the conventions, priorities, and ways of knowing within those communities.

There are numerous benefits for students and teachers of such an approach. In informal surveys I have conducted, it seems that students are more likely to get a lot out of my writing courses if they believe that they will be writing for their entire lives. The students who describe themselves as doing very little writing once they finish my course are also the ones who describe their writing have changed very little in the course. Simply knowing that there are writing intensive courses in their fields helps students understand that experts in their own disciplines see writing as a life-long professional activity.

Writing in the disciplines is one form of placing writing within communities, and there are other forms. For instance, some programs have begun to introduce service-learning in writing courses, in which students engage in some form of community service for their writing assignments. This might take the form of a single assignment (one friend has students write a paper based largely on interviews with community volunteers) or an entire course (some instructors of writing intensive courses will have students take on substantial community projects). The idea is simply that, as Cooper argues, writing purposes do not "arise solely out of individual desires, but rather arise out of the interaction between their needs and the needs of the various groups that structure their society". Community-based writing, whether it is the community of experts in a particular discipline, or the community of the polis, means trying to get students to understand how those needs and desire interact.

There are numerous different models for such courses, just as there are different models for how they should relate to first-year composition courses. For instance, many WAC programs are based on the lecture-discussion model, in which the students hear lectures on the subject matter and then writing is handled in discussion sections. Other programs have the writing assignments more integrated into the whole coursework, usually with lower enrollment in the writing intensive versions of large lecture classes. Some programs rely on major written projects for students, and some programs use microthemes, journals, lab reports, or other short forms of writing.

Whether or not it is explicitly part of the program design, first-year composition courses generally function as a gateway to writing in a student's discipline. Some departments choose to make that function explicit, and they have writing assignments which reflect that function. For instance, students might examine how the same topic is handled by different disciplines, or the changes that the same author makes when talking about the same topic for a popular versus scholarly journal, or they might read reviews of the same book in journals from different disciplines.

In addition, certain kinds of assignments effectively prepare students for such courses because they typify the assignments students will get. Fahnestock and Secor note that what they call "the content/problem-solving approach effectively approximates real-life writing situations." This approach relies on giving students a casebook, or a group of related readings, or a real-world problem to resolve. (Obviously, this sort of assignment is particularly easy to devise in a service-learning based composition course.) Similarly, the theory-practice assignment is a very common writing assignment in which students read a theory and apply it to a specific situation that the theory does not mention. Writing intensive courses often ask that students perform a rhetorical analysis of a variety of texts that take opposite sides on the same topic—that is, to evaluate the merits of the cases that the various authors present.

The Ecology of Writing
Marilyn M. Cooper

The idea that writing is a process and that the writing process is a recursive cognitive activity involving certain universal stages (prewriting, writing, revising seemed quite revolutionary not so many years ago. In 1982, Maxine Hairston hailed "the move to a process-centered theory of teaching writing" as the first sign of a paradigm shift in composition theory (77). But even by then "process, not product" was the slogan of numerous college textbooks, large and small, validated by enclosure within brightly-colored covers with the imprimatur of Harper & Row, Macmillan, Harcourt Brace Jovanovich, Scott, Foresman. So revolution dwindles to dogma. Now, perhaps, the time has come for some assessment of the benefits and limitations of thinking of writing as essentially—and simply—a cognitive process.

Motivation for the paradigm shift in writing theory perhaps came first from writing teachers increasingly disenchanted with red-inking errors, delivering lectures on comma splices or on the two ways to organize a comparison-contrast essay, and reading alienated and alienating essays written from a list of topic sentences or in the five-paragraph format. Reacting against pedagogy that now seemed completely ineffective, we developed methods that required students to concentrate less on form and more on content, that required them to think. We decided to talk about ideas rather than forms in the classroom and sent students off to do various kinds of free writing and writing using heuristics in order to find out what they thought about a topic—best of all, we found we didn't have to read any of this essential but private and exploratory "prewriting." We told students they had primary responsibility for the purpose of their writing: only they could decide what was important to them to write about, only they could tell whether what they intended was actually fulfilled in the writing they produced. We decided to be friendly readers rather than crabby Miss Fidditches; we said things like, "You have lots of ideas," and, with Pirsig's Phaedrus, "You know quality in thought and statement when you see it," instead of "Your essay does not clearly develop a point," and "You have made many usage errors here."

These ideas were in the air—and in print. We developed them in talking with colleagues, in reading the advice of fellow teachers Peter Elbow and Donald Murray. We found further support for them in similar ideas being developed by literary theorists, educational psychologists, and linguists—some of whom were also writing teachers. In literary theory the shift from a New Critical emphasis on the text to a post-structural emphasis on the reader paralleled the shift from product to process in writing theory. As Jonathan Culler and Stanley Fish adapted the nouvelle French notions to American tastes, the complementarity between reading and writing in terms of their both being mental processes became clear. Culler states that readers possess "literary competence," that they make sense of texts by applying various conventions that explain how one is to interpret the cues on the page. Writers, ideally, possess the same literary competence. Fish states that readers are guided by interpretive strategies, that these strategies are constitutive of interpretive communities, and that the strategies originate with writers. Culler's conventions, Fish's strategies, are not present in the text; rather, they are part of the mental equipment of writers and readers, and only by examining this mental equipment can we explain how writers and readers communicate.

In the fields of educational psychology and linguistics, research on how readers process texts also revealed an active reader who used strategies to recreate meaning from the cues on the page. These strategies implied certain expected structures in texts. When adopted by writing teachers, readers' expectations became a new way of explaining "errors" in student writing and a new rationale for instruction on matters of form. George Dillon, expanding David Olson's analysis, attributes much of the incomprehensibility of his students' writing to their inability to shift from the conventions of utterance to the conventions of text, conventions that enjoin explicitness, correctness, novelty, logical consistency, and so forth. Linda Flower and Joseph Williams explain how readers link new information to old information in order to comprehend texts, and they advise students, consequently, to supply context and to clearly mark old and new information in sentence structure.

Gradually, as interest in writing theory increased, a model of writing as a cognitive process was codified, and the unified perspective the model offered in turn allowed us to redefine other vexing problems: the relation between grammar and writing, the function of revision. These were all undoubtedly beneficial changes. But theoretical models even as they stimulate new insights blind us to some aspects of the phenomena we are studying. The problem with the cognitive process model of writing has nothing to do with its specifics: it describes something of what writers do and goes some way toward explaining how writers, texts, and readers are related. But the belief on which it is based—that writing is thinking and, thus, essentially a cognitive process—obscures many aspects of writing we have come to see as not peripheral.

Like all theoretical models, the cognitive process model projects an ideal image, in this case an image of a writer that, transmitted through writing pedagogy, influences our attitudes and the attitudes of our students toward writing. The ideal writer the cognitive process model projects is isolated from the social world, a writer I will call the solitary author. The solitary author works alone, within the privacy of his own mind. He uses free writing exercises and heuristics to find out what he knows about a subject and to find something he wants to say to others; he uses his analytic skills to discover a purpose, to imagine an audience, to decide on strategies, to organize content; and he simulates how his text will be read by reading it over himself, making the final revisions necessary to assure its success when he abandons it to the world of which he is not a part. The isolation of the solitary author from the social world leads him to see ideas and goals as originating primarily within himself and directed at an unknown and largely hostile other. Writing becomes a form of parthenogenesis, the author producing propositional and pragmatic structures, Athena-like, full grown and complete, out of his brow. Thus, the solitary author perceives the functions that writing might serve in limited and abstract terms. All four of the major pedagogical theories James Berlin describes assume that the function of writing is solely cognitive, a matter of discovering the truth and communicating it: the solitary author can express his feelings, pass on information, persuade others to believe as he does, or charm others with his exquisite phrases (cf. Kinneavy's taxonomy of the aims of writing). Finally, the solitary author sees his writing as a goal-directed piece of work, the process of producing a text.

Such images of the solitary author inspire a great deal of what goes on in writing classes today—and more of what is recommended in composition textbooks, especially those that depend on the latest theory. But many classes still escape its tyranny, classes in which students engage in group work, activities such as collaborative brainstorming on a topic, discussions and debates of topics or readings, writers reading their texts aloud to others, writers editing other writers' texts. Some teachers eschew setting writing assignments (even writing assignments that are "rhetorically based") in favor of letting writing emerge from the life-situations of their students, whether this writing takes the form of papers that fulfill requirements for other courses, letters written for employment or business purposes, journals kept as personal records, reports of projects completed or in progress. And in some classes, students even use writing to interact with one another: they write suggestions to their teacher and to other students; they produce class newspapers full of interviews, jokes, personal stories, advice, information.

Such changes in writing pedagogy indicate that the perspective allowed by the dominant model has again become too confining. I suggest that what goes on in these classes signals a growing awareness that language and texts are not simply the means by which individuals discover and communicate information, but are essentially social activities, dependent on social structures and processes not only in their interpretive but also in their constructive phases. I am not, of course, the only—or even the first—writing theorist to notice this. In 1981, for example, Kenneth Bruffee argued that "writing is not an inherently private act but is a displaced social act we perform in private for the sake of convenience" (745). And, more recently, James A. Reither, summarizing the work of four other prominent theorists, comes to the same conclusions I have as the beginning point of his attempt to redefine the writing process:

> the issues [Larson, Odell, Bizzell, and Gage] raise should lead us to wonder if our thinking is not being severely limited by a concept of process that explains only the cognitive processes that occur as people write. Their questions and observations remind us that writing is not merely a process that occurs within contexts. That is, writing and what writers do during writing cannot be artificially separated from the social-rhetorical situations in which writing gets done, from the conditions that enable writers to do what they do, and from the motives writers have for doing what they do. (621)

The idea that language use is essentially social also underlies much current work in literary theory and sociolinguistics. David Bleich proposes a literature classroom in which students transform their initial responses to a text into communally negotiated and thus valid interpretations: "although the resymbolization of a text is usually a fully private affair, it is always done in reference to some communal effort" (137). Fredric Jameson, perhaps the foremost of the neo-Marxist theorists, argues that interpretation "must take place within three concentric frameworks, which mark a widening out of the sense of the social ground of a text" (75). Among linguists, William Labov is renowned for his demonstrations that the so-called verbal deprivation of children in ghetto schools is an artifact of the means of data collection, face-to-face interviews of black children by white adult investigators, and that "the consistency of certain grammatical rules [of black English vernacular] is a fine-grained index of membership in the street culture" (255). And in *Ways with Words,* a book already nearly as influential as Labov's *Language in the Inner City,* Shirley Brice Heath delineates the complex relationship between children's differential acquisition of reading and the uses of and attitudes toward texts in their home communities.

Just as such research calls for new models of the interpretation of literature and of language use, so too do the intuitively developed methods we are now beginning to use in writing classes and in literacy programs call for a new model of writing. Describing such a model explicitly will lend coherence to these intuitions by bringing out the assumptions on which they are based, illuminating aspects of writing that we have perceived but dimly heretofore through the gaps in the cognitive process model.

What I would like to propose is an ecological model of writing, whose fundamental tenet is that writing is an activity through which a person is continually engaged with a variety of socially constituted systems. Ecology, the science of natural environments, has been recently mentioned by writing researchers such as Greg Myers, who, in his analysis of the social construction of two biologists' proposals, concludes: "Like ethologists, we should not only observe and categorize the behavior of individuals, we should also consider the evolution of this behavior in its ecological context" (240). The term *ecological* is not, however, simply the newest way to say "contextual"; it points up important differences between the model I am proposing and other contextual models such as Kenneth Burke's dramatistic pentad.

Such models, oddly, abstract writing from the social context in much the way that the cognitive process model does; they perceive the context in which a piece of writing is done as unique, unconnected with other situations. Kenneth Burke's is perhaps the best contextual model that is applied to writing; Burke develops a heuristic for interrogating the immediate situation in order to impute motives for individual language acts. The terms of his pentad are conceived of as formal or transcendent, and Burke tellingly labels his description of them a "grammar," a model of "the purely internal relationships which the five terms bear to one another" (xvi). Actual statements about motives utilize these "grammatical resources," but the grammar determines the statements only in a formal sense, much as syntactic rules predict the occurrence of certain structures in sentences. One's perspective, or "philosophy," crucially guides how the terms will be applied, and, since Burke proposes no link between the grammar and the perspective, what perspective is chosen appears to be arbitrary, and, perhaps, trivial: "War may be treated as an Agency, insofar as it is a means to an end; as a collective Act, subdivisible into many individual acts; as a Purpose, in schemes proclaiming a cult of war" (xx). Thus, though the grammar allows one to assign labels to important aspects of a situation, it does not enable one to explain how the situation is causally related to other situations. Burke is perhaps more aware of the limitations of his model than are some of his disciples. The description of linguistic forms the pentad enables is, in his opinion, "preparatory": "the study of linguistic action is but beginning" (319).

In contrast, an ecology of writing encompasses much more than the individual writer and her immediate context. An ecologist explores how writers interact to form systems: all the characteristics of any individual writer or piece of writing both determine and are determined by the characteristics of all the other writers and writings in the systems. An important characteristic of ecological systems is that they are inherently dynamic; though their structures and contents can be specified at a given moment, in real time they are constantly changing, limited only by parameters that are themselves subject to change over longer spans of time. In their critique of sociobiology, R. C. Lewontin *et al.* describe how such systems operate:

> all organisms—but especially human beings—are not simply the results but are also the causes of their own environments . . . . While it may be true that at some instant the environment poses a problem or challenge to the organism, in the process of response to that challenge the organism alters the terms of its relation to the outer world and recreates the relevant aspects of that world. The relation between organism and environment is not simply one of interaction of internal and external factors, but of a dialectical development of organism and milieu in response to each other. (275)

In place of the static and limited categories of contextual models, the ecological model postulates dynamic interlocking systems which structure the social activity of writing.

The systems are not given, not limitations on writers; instead they are made and remade by writers in the act of writing. It is in this sense that writing changes social reality and not only, as Lloyd Bitzer argues, in response to exigence. A historian writes a letter of appreciation to an anthropologist whose article she has read and connects with a new writer with whom she can exchange ideas and articles. A college president who decides to write a Christmas letter to his faculty creates a new textual form that will affect his other communications and at the same time alters, slightly, the administrative structure of his institution.

Furthermore, the systems are concrete. They are structures that can be investigated, described, altered; they are not postulated mental entities, not generalizations. Every individual writer is necessarily involved in these systems: for each writer and each instance of writing one can specify the domain of ideas activated and supplemented, the purposes that stimulated the writing and that resulted from it, the interactions that took place as part of the writing, the cultural norms and textual forms that enabled and resulted from the writing.

One can abstractly distinguish different systems that operate in writing, just as one can distinguish investment patterns from consumer spending patterns from hiring patterns in a nation's economy. But in the actual activity of writing—as in the economy—the systems are entirely interwoven in their effects and manner of operation. The systems reflect the various ways writers connect with one another through writing: through systems of ideas, of purposes, of interpersonal interactions, of cultural norms, of textual forms.

The system of ideas is the means by which writers comprehend their world, to turn individual experiences and observations into knowledge. From this perspective ideas result from contact, whether face-to-face or mediated through texts. Ideas are also always continuations, as they arise within and modify particular fields of discourse. One does not begin to write about bird behavior, say, without observing birds, talking with other observers, and reading widely in the literature of animal behavior in general. One does not even begin to have ideas about a topic, even a relatively simple one, until a considerable body of already structured observations and experiences has been mastered. Even in writing where the focus is not on the development of knowledge, a writer must connect with the relevant idea system: if one is recommending ways to increase the efficiency of a particular department of a publishing firm, one must understand what the department does and how it fits into the firm as a whole.

The system of purposes is the means by which writers coordinate their actions. Arguments attempt to set agendas; promises attempt to set schedules and relationships. Purposes, like ideas, arise out of interaction, and individual purposes are modified by the larger purposes of groups; in fact, an individual impulse or need only becomes a purpose when it is recognized as such by others. A contributor to a company newspaper writes about his interest in paleontology; his individual purpose is to express himself, to gain attention, purposes we all recognize; but within the context of the company newspaper, his purpose is also to deepen his relationship with other employees.

The system of interpersonal interactions is the means by which writers regulate their access to one another. Two determinants of the nature of a writer's interactions with others are intimacy, a measure of closeness based on any similarity seen to be relevant—kinship, religion, occupation; and power, a measure of the degree to which a writer can control the action of others (for a particularly detailed discussion of these factors, see Brown and Levinson). Writers may play a number of different roles in relation to one another: editor, co-writer, or addressee, for instance. Writers signal how they view their relationship with other writers through conventional forms and strategies, but they can also change their relationship—or even initiate or terminate relationships—through the use of these conventions if others accept the new relationship that is implied.

The system of cultural norms is the means by which writers structure the larger groups of which they are members. One always writes out of a group; the notion of what role a writer takes on in a particular piece of writing derives from this fact. I write here as a member of the writing theory group, and as I write I express the attitudes and institutional arrangements of this group—and I attempt to alter some of them.

The system of textual forms is, obviously, the means by which writers communicate. Textual forms, like language forms in general, are at the same time conservative, repositories of tradition, and revolutionary, instruments of new forms of action. A textual form is a balancing act: conventional enough to be comprehensible and flexible enough to serve the changing purposes of writing. Thus, new forms usually arise by a kind of cross-breeding, or by analogy, as older forms are taken apart and recombined or modified in a wholesale fashion.

The metaphor for writing suggested by the ecological model is that of a web, in which anything that affects one strand of the web vibrates throughout the whole. To reiterate, models are ways of thinking about, or ways of seeing, complex situations. If we look at, for example, a particularly vexed problem in current writing theory, the question of audience, from the perspective of this model, we may be able to reformulate the question in a way that helps us to find new answers. Though I cannot attempt a complete analysis of the concept of audience here, I would like to outline briefly how such an analysis might proceed.

The discussion of how authors should deal with their audience has in recent years focused on the opposition between those who argue that authors must analyze the characteristics of a real audience and those who argue that authors always imagine, or create, their audience in their writing. The opposition, of course, has classical roots: in the *Phaedrus* Plato suggests that the rhetorician classify types of audiences and consider which type of speech best suits each; while, at the other extreme, epideictic rhetoric sometimes took the form of a contest in which speakers imagined an audience. Lisa Ede and Andrea Lunsford characterize "the two central perspectives on audience in composition" as "audience addressed and audience invoked" (156). Douglas Park identifies the conception of audience "as something readily identifiable and external" with Lloyd Bitzer, and the opposite conception of audience as represented to consciousness, or invented, with Walter Ong (248).

I would like to draw attention, however, to what unites both these perspectives: whether the writer is urged to analyze or invent the audience, the audience is always considered to be a construct in the writer's mind. Park specifies four meanings of audience, then argues that "the last two meanings are obviously the most important for teachers or for anyone interested in forms of discourse": "the set of conceptions or awareness in the writer's consciousness," and "an ideal conception shadowed forth in the way the discourse defines and creates contexts" (250). Park concludes, "Any systematic answers to these important questions will depend upon keeping in constant view the essential abstractness of the concept of audience" (250).

The internalization of the audience, making it into a mental construct often labeled the "general audience," is inescapable within the perspective of the cognitive process model. By focusing our attention on what goes on in an author's mind, it forces us to conceive all significant aspects of writing in terms of mental entities. Even Fred Pfister and Joanne Petrick, often cited as proponents of the idea of real audiences, begin by conceding that for writers the "audience is unseen, a phantom. . . . Students, like all writers, must fictionalize their audience. But they must construct in the imagination an audience that is as nearly a replica as is possible of those many readers who actually exist in the world of reality and who are reading the writer's words" (213–14). Less surprisingly, in her textbook Linda Flower labels one of her "problem-solving strategies for writing" "talk to your reader," but she actually recommends that the writer play both roles in the conversation (73).

Barry Kroll, who breaks down approaches to audience into three perspectives—the rhetorical, the informational, and the social—demonstrates, in his definition of the third perspective, how pervasive the tendency to internalize all aspects of writing is: "writing for readers is, like all human communication, a fundamentally social activity, entailing processes of inferring the thoughts and feelings of the other persons involved in an act of communication" ("Writing for Readers" 179). The redefinition of social activity as a cognitive process is even more striking here in that it is unmarked, mentioned as an afterthought in the gerundive phrase. Kroll goes on to conclude, "From [the social] view, the process of writing for readers inevitably involves social thinking—or 'social cognition'" (182–83). In a more recent discussion of studies of the relation between social-cognitive abilities and writing performance, Kroll more clearly advocates the social-cognitive approach to audience: "It seems reasonable that individuals who can think in more complex ways about how other people think ought to be better writers" ("Social-Cognitive Ability" 304). But, as he also admits, "successful performance (in terms of creating texts that are adapted to readers' needs) may not always reflect social-cognitive competence, because writers probably learn to employ many of the linguistic and rhetorical devices of audience-adapted writing without needing to consider their readers' characteristics, perspectives, or responses" (304).

As should be obvious, the perspective of the ecological model offers a salutary correction of vision on the question of audience. By focusing our attention on the real social context of writing, it enables us to see that writers not only analyze or invent audiences, they, more significantly, communicate with and know their audiences. They learn to employ the devices of audience-adapted writing by handing their texts to colleagues to read and respond to, by revising articles or memos or reports guided by comments from editors or superiors, by reading others' summaries or critiques of their own writing. Just as the ecological model transforms authors (people who have produced texts) into writers (people engaged in writing), it transforms the abstract "general audience" into real readers (for an insightful discussion of the use of "audience" *vs.* "reader," see Park 249–50).

These real readers do appear in discussions of audience dominated by the cognitive process model, if only in glimpses. Ruth Mitchell and Mary Taylor point out that "the audience not only judges writing, it also motivates it. A writer answers a challenge, consciously or unconsciously. The conscious challenges are assignments, demands for reports, memos, proposals, letters" (250–51). Ede and Lunsford criticize Mitchell and Taylor's model from the familiar cognitive process perspective: "no matter how much feedback writers may receive after they have written something (or in breaks while they write), as they compose writers must rely in large part upon their own vision of the reader, which they create . . . according to their own experiences and expectations" (158). But in their account of the readers of their own article, it is the real readers who are obviously most important: "a small, close-knit seminar group"; each other; Richard Larson, who "responded in writing with questions, criticisms, and suggestions, some of which we had, of course, failed to anticipate"; and readers of *College Composition and Communication,* pictured as "members of our own departments, a diverse group of individuals with widely varying degrees of interest in and knowledge of composition" (167–68). Ede and Lunsford know their readers through real social encounters; the cognitive act of analyzing them or creating them is superfluous. As Park suggests, "as a general rule it is only in highly structured situations or at particular times that writers consciously focus on audience as a discrete entity" (254).

The focus on readers as real social beings opens up new vistas for research on audience and for classroom methods. Questions we might seek answers to include: What kind of interactions do writers and readers engage in? What is the nature of the various roles readers play in the activity of writing? What institutional arrangements encourage writer-reader interaction? How do writers find readers to work with? How do writers and readers develop ideas together? How do writers and readers alter textual forms together?

In the classroom, we can enable our students to see each other as real readers, not as stand-ins for a general audience. Students learn about how to deal with their readers not "by internalizing and generalizing the reactions of a number of specific readers" and thereby developing a "sense of audience" (Kroll, "Writing for Readers" 181), but by developing the habits and skills involved in finding readers and making use of their responses. Students, like all writers, need to find out what kind of readers best help them in the role of editor, how to work with co-writers, how to interpret criticisms, how to enter into dialogue with their addressees.

In contrast, then, to the solitary author projected by the cognitive process model, the ideal image the ecological model projects is of an infinitely extended group of people who interact through writing, who are connected by the various systems that constitute the activity of writing. For these "engaged writers" ideas are not so much fixed constructs to be transferred from one mind to the page and thence to another mind; instead, ideas are out there in the world, a landscape that is always being modified by ongoing human discourse. They "find ideas" in writing because they thus enter the field of discourse, finding in the exchange of language certain structures that they modify to suit their purposes. Nor for them do purposes arise solely out of individual desires, but rather arise out of the interaction between their needs and the needs of the various groups that structure their society. As Dell Hymes says about purposes in speaking, "Ultimately, the functions served . . . must be derived directly from the purposes and needs of human persons engaged in social action, and are what they are: talking [or writing] to seduce, to stay awake, to avoid a war" (70). The various roles people take on in writing also arise out of this social structure: through interacting with others, in writing and speaking, they learn the functions and textual forms of impersonal reporting, effective instruction, irony, story-telling. In the same way they learn the attitudes toward these roles and toward purposes and ideas held by the various groups they interact with, and they come to understand how these interactions are themselves partly structured by institutional procedures and arrangements. These attitudes, procedures, and arrangements make up a system of cultural norms which are, however, neither stable nor uniform throughout a culture. People move from group to group, bringing along with them different complexes of ideas, purposes, and norms, different ways of interacting, different interpersonal roles and textual forms. Writing, thus, is seen to be both constituted by and constitutive of these ever-changing systems, systems through which people relate as complete, social beings, rather than imagining each other as remote images: an author, an audience.

It is important to remember that the image the ecological model projects is again an ideal one. In reality, these systems are often resistent to change and not easily accessible. Whenever ideas are seen as commodities they are not shared; whenever individual and group purposes cannot be negotiated someone is shut out; differences in status, or power, or intimacy curtail interpersonal interactions; cultural institutions and attitudes discourage writing as often as they encourage it; textual forms are just as easily used as barriers to discourse as they are used as means of discourse. A further value of the ecological model is that it can be used to diagnose and analyze such situations, and it encourages us to direct our corrective energies away from the characteristics of the individual writer and toward imbalances in social systems that prevent good writing; one such analysis by my colleague Michael Holzman appeared recently in *CE*.

Writing is one of the activities by which we locate ourselves in the enmeshed stems that make up the social world. It is not simply a way of thinking but more fundamentally a way of acting. As Wilhelm von Humboldt says of language, it "is not work *(ergon)* but activity *(energia)*" (27), an activity through which we become most truly human. By looking at writing ecologically we understand better how important writing is—and just how hard it is to teach.

Works Cited

Barthes, Roland. *S/Z*. 1970. Trans. Richard Miller. New York: Hill, 1974.
Berlin, James. "Contemporary Composition: The Major Pedagogical Theories."
    College English 44 (1982): 765–77.

Bitzer, Lloyd F. "The Rhetorical Situation." *Philosophy and Rhetoric* 1 (1968): 1–14.

Bleich, David. *Subjective Criticism.* Baltimore: Johns Hopkins UP, 1978.

Brown, Penelope, and Stephen Levinson. "Universals in Language Usage: Politeness Phenomena." *Questions and Politeness: Strategies in Social Interaction.* Ed. Esther N. Goody. Cambridge: Cambridge UP, 1978. 56–289.

Bruffee, Kenneth. "Collaborative Learning." *College English* 43 (1981): 745–46.

Burke, Kenneth. *A Grammar of Motives.* Berkeley: U of California P, 1969.

Culler, Jonathan. *Structuralist Poetics: Structuralism, Linguistics, and the Study of Literature.* Ithaca, NY: Cornell UP, 1975.

Dillon, George. *Constructing Texts: Elements of a Theory of Composition and Style.* Bloomington: Indiana UP, 1981.

Ede, Lisa, and Andrea Lunsford. "Audience Addressed/Audience Invoked: The Role of Audience in Composition Theory and Pedagogy." *College Composition and Communication* 35 (1984): 155–71.

Fish, Stanley. *Is There a Text in This Class? The Authority of Interpretive Communities.* Cambridge: Harvard UP, 1980.

Flower, Linda. *Problem-Solving Strategies for Writing.* New York: Harcourt, 1981.

Goffman, Erving. *Forms of Talk.* Oxford: Blackwell, 1981.

Hairston, Maxine. "The Winds of Change: Thomas Kuhn and the Revolution in the Teaching of Writing." *College Composition and Communication* 33 (1982): 76–88.

Halliday, M. A. K. *Language as Social Semiotic.* Baltimore: University Park, 1978.

Heath, Shirley Brice. *Ways with Words: Language, Life, and Work in Communities and Classrooms.* Cambridge: Cambridge UP, 1983.

Holzman, Michael. "The Social Context of Literacy Education." *College English* 48 (1986): 27–33.

Humboldt, Wilhelm von. *Linguistic Variability and Intellectual Development.* 1836. Trans. George C. Buck and Frithjof A. Raven. Philadelphia: U of Pennsylvania P, 1971.

Hymes, Dell. "Models of the Interaction of Language and Social Life." *Directions in Sociolinguistics.* Ed. John J. Gumperz and Dell Hymes. New York: Holt, 1972. 35–71.

Jameson, Fredric. *The Political Unconscious: Narrative as a Socially Symbolic Act.* Ithaca, NY: Cornell UP, 1981.

Kinneavy, James. *A Theory of Discourse.* Englewood Cliffs, NJ: Prentice, 1971.

Kroll, Barry M. "Writing for Readers: Three Perspectives on Audience." *College Composition and Communication* 35 (1984): 172–85.

———. "Social-Cognitive Ability and Writing Performance: How Are They Related?" *Written Communication* 2 (1985): 293–305.

Labov, William. *Language in the Inner City: Studies in the Black English Vernacular.* Philadelphia: U of Pennsylvania P, 1972.

Lewontin, R. C., Steven Rose, and Leon J. Kamin. *Not in Our Genes: Biology, Ideology, and Human Nature.* New York: Pantheon Books, 1984.

Mitchell, Ruth, and Mary Taylor. "The Integrating Perspective: An Audience-Response Model for Writing." *College English* 41 (1979): 247–71.

Myers, Greg. "The Social Construction of Two Biologists' Proposals." *Written Communication* 2 (1985): 219–45.

Park, Douglas B. "The Meanings of 'Audience.'" *College English* 44 (1982): 247–57.

Pfister, Fred R., and Joanne F. Petrick. "A Heuristic Model for Creating a Writer's Audience." *College Composition and Communication* 31 (1980): 213–20.

Reddy, Michael J. "The Conduit Metaphor—A Case of Frame Conflict in Our Language About Language." *Metaphor and Thought.* Ed. Andrew Ortony. Cambridge: Cambridge UP, 1979. 284–324.

Reither, James A. "Writing and Knowing: Toward Redefining the Writing Process." *College English* 47 (1985): 620–28.

Williams, Joseph. *Style: Ten Lessons in Clarity and Grace.* Glenview, IL: Scott, 1981.

Additional Sources

Barton, Ellen L. "Evidentials, Argumentation, and Epistemological Stance." *College English* 55 (November 1993): 745–69.

Studies the difference in uses of evidentials in student and scholarly writing.

Flower, Linda. "Negotiating the Meaning of Difference." *Written Communication* Vol. 13, 1 (January 1996): 44–92.

Describes the experiences of people working in a Community Literacy Collaboration project, with special emphasis on the cultural conflicts.

Young, Art, and Toby Fulwiler, Eds. *Writing across the Disciplines; Research into Practice.* Portsmouth, NH: Boynton/Cook Publishers, Inc., 1986.

Discusses one university writing-across-the-curriculum program at a campus, programmatic, and individual course level, with recommendations for program creation and assessment.

Chapter 6
Grammar and Usage

Although Patrick Hartwell begins his essay "Grammar, Grammars, and the Teaching of Grammar" with a statement about how and when the grammar issue was settled for him, the recent debacle over Ebonics demonstrates just how unsettling most people find the topic. Unfortunately, the misunderstandings and misrepresentations of the Ebonics debate typify what happens even when teachers of English discuss the role of grammar and usage in the teaching of writing. For instance, far too often when someone criticizes a particular *method* of teaching grammar, the person is perceived as attacking the goal of enabling students to use standard edited English. Yet, for the most part, few people dispute the importance of paying attention to standard edited English; where people (especially linguists) take issue is with *how* that attention is paid.

Linguists generally have two main objections to many current methods of grammar and usage instruction: what English teachers say about "correct" grammar and how "rules" are explained. Educational researchers typically have a third objection: Instructors are too often wed to methods which have never been shown to have any effect on writing practice.

Dennis Baron ends his *Grammar and Good Taste,* a book that traces the history of grammar reform in America, with an impassioned statement about what happens when the people teaching grammar are not philologists. The point Baron makes is that grammar reformers invariably appeal to mutually contradictory principles about what constitutes "correct" usage: At one moment reformers are appealing to the history of usage and the next are rejecting the history in favor of current usage, defending one usage on the grounds of perspicacity and rejecting another as pedantic. A linguist friend once pointed out his personal "pet peeve" about the whole argument: Defenders of correctness often themselves violate the rules they claim to hold so dear, such as when they say that a writer "can't" use a word a particular way when they mean that they think people "shouldn't."

The distinction between "can" and "should" is not pedantic, as it is at the center of linguists' two objections. People often discuss rules of grammar and usage as though they were discussing rules of physics, but the rules of grammar and usage are much closer to rules of etiquette. As Noam Chomsky has shown, there are some rules of grammar which cannot be violated (even people with neurological disorders that cause them to transpose words in a sentence will rarely transpose a noun for a verb, for instance). Those "rules"—because they cannot be violated—do not need to be taught, so they are of little concern to

teachers of writing. Instead, most of the rules with which we need to be concerned are the ones that students *can* violate (just as a person can make
breaches of etiquette), but we too often discuss these rules as though they were
at the same level of importance and inviolability as the rules which do serve as
the foundations of language. For instance, sentence fragments and comma
splices are often described as fundamental violations of sentence boundaries—in
fact, they are fairly trivial to communication: British English does not forbid
comma splices, and neither sentence fragments nor comma splices exist as errors
in spoken language. In other words, a person who uses a comma splice will get
her point across in ways that a person who transposes the subject and object of
an English sentence may not.

People tend to explain the rules of standard edited English as though they
were a stable entity, and this tendency necessarily traps teachers of writing into
unproductive falsehoods. That is, if we try to explain to students that correct
usage is important because incorrect usage will keep them from being understood, we have told them something that they know to be a lie. They have been
told by many teachers and readers that their "grammar" is filled with errors, but
they also know that they go through large parts of their days making themselves
understood.

Many of the "rules" that our students have been taught are themselves
errors (such as the "rule" that a semicolon is always required before *however*);
extremely recent impositions (the distinction between *that* and *which*); conventions about which there is considerable disagreement (whether *none* takes a
singular or plural verb); or regional variations (in British English, what Americans call a comma splice is perfectly acceptable). There is an extraordinary range
of linguistic infelicity about which an instructor might want to comment: things
that are minor violations of the teacher's own stylistic preferences (using the first
person); things that are violations of genre conventions (using the second person
in a college paper); violations of standard edited English that do not confuse the
meaning (noun-verb agreement); violations that will mislead a reader (reference
error). Too often we describe those very different practices as though they were
the same or as though they had the same consequences for communication.
Because some of those rules are trivial, some students will conclude that all consideration of grammar and usage is trivial (as when one student objected to her
grade having been affected by what she called "technical" issues in regard to a
paper with long sections that were actually unintelligible). Because some of those
rules are important, some students conclude that they can never write without
mastering all the rules (as when one student said that she was a good writer until
she tried to memorize the twenty-eight comma rules her teacher had listed).
Most importantly, because some of those rules are shared by other teachers and
some are not, many students conclude that grammar and usage is something
they cannot know, like the rules of a game that change at will.

Yet, as Hartwell and others have argued, students do know grammar. They
may not be able to articulate the rules of their grammar, but, then again, neither
can many teachers. This is the second objection which linguists make about pre-

scriptive grammarians—we inaccurately describe the rules themselves. In addition to the above list of problems (instances of hypercorrectness, confusing style and grammar, conflating errors which have very different consequences), we often describe as rules of nature things that are rules of thumb. Chomsky has numerous examples of this problem, one of which regards the "rule" that the pronoun *everyone* always takes a singular verb. If this really were a rule of nature, the "correct" usage would be: "If everyone comes to the party, he will have no place to sit."

The analogy of grammar and usage as rules of etiquette, mentioned earlier, is the one that I find most useful. Students know that there are some rules that are necessary in order for people to get along because interaction will stop once they are broken (such as avoiding yelling). And students recognize that there are other rules that facilitate communication, for they prevent certain kinds of distractions (such as avoiding chewing with one's mouth open). Some breaches of etiquette are simply irritating, and one can overlook them in small amounts (such as failing to say "please" or "thank you"). Some points of etiquette are insisted upon with great dogmatism, despite there being substantial variation (such as when one serves the salad) and some are pure class markers (such as how one uses the spoon when drinking soup). And, of course, there are regional variations (such as the distinction between American and Continental ways of holding the knife and fork).

Working with this sort of analogy helps with some of the problems of teaching grammar and usage, but only a few. One problem which remains is that it is difficult to find a method that effects change in student practice. As Knoblach and Brannon first asserted, and Hillocks later confirmed, research has yet to find any methods of formal instruction that cause students to write fewer errors in their papers (with the possible exception of sentence embedding). Despite the fact that this has been demonstrated time after time, many instructors still cling to taking class time for formal instruction in grammar and usage, and it is worth considering their reasons.

First, many instructors remember such instruction having worked with them—they remember when someone explained modification in such a way that they stopped writing dangling modifiers. When we replicate practices that worked with us, however, we forget that we are hardly typical of our students— how many of them are interested enough in language that they are likely to become English teachers? So, does it make sense to stand in front of a class lecturing about grammar and usage because one student might have something click? If it is likely to reach only one student, why not explain it to one student outside of class, and use class time for instruction that is likely to benefit the majority? These rhetorical questions call forth the second reason that instructors are likely to cling to lecturing, handing out worksheets, or engaging in highly punitive marking systems: They are not sure what else to do.

The research that shows such a dismal view of grammar instruction regards *formal* instruction in grammar. As Martha Kolln has argued, the research has little to say about working with students individually, asking that students resubmit papers with errors corrected, or referring students to writing centers. A friend who has the greatest success that I have ever seen at getting students to write more felicitous prose uses handbook notations—simply noting in the margin the handbook section that deals with the error(s) in that area of the paper. It is then the student's responsibility to read and interpret that section of the handbook in order to correct the error before the next submission. The instructor is, of course, happy to answer any questions that students may have about the handbook explanation or his notations, but he rarely uses class time to do so. Furthermore, he does not correct the errors; doing so simply leads to what Elaine Lees has called "created blueprints" for papers addressing that particular assignment.

Grammar, Grammars, and the Teaching of Grammar
Patrick Hartwell

For me the grammar issue was settled at least twenty years ago with the conclusion offered by Richard Braddock, Richard Lloyd-Jones, and Lowell Schoer in 1963.

> In view of the widespread agreement of research studies based upon many types of students and teachers, the conclusion can be stated in strong and unqualified terms: the teaching of formal grammar has a negligible or, because it usually displaces some instruction and practice in composition, even a harmful effect on improvement in writing.[1]

Indeed, I would agree with Janet Emig that the grammar issue is a prime example of "magical thinking": the assumption that students will learn only what we teach and only because we teach.[2]

But the grammar issue, as we will see, is a complicated one. And, perhaps surprisingly, it remains controversial, with the regular appearance of papers defending the teaching of formal grammar or attacking it.[3] Thus Janice Neuleib,

---

[1] *Research in Written Composition* (Urbana, Ill.: National Council of Teachers of English, 1963), pp. 37–38.

[2] "Non-magical Thinking: Presenting Writing Developmentally in Schools," in *Writing Process, Development and Communication,* Vol. II of *Writing: The Nature, Development and Teaching of Written Communication,* ed. Charles H. Frederiksen and Joseph F. Dominic (Hillsdale, N.J.: Lawrence Erlbaum, 1980), pp. 21–30.

[3] For arguments in favor of formal grammar teaching, see Patrick F. Basset, "Grammar—Can We Afford Not to Teach It?" *NASSP Bulletin,* 64, No. 10 (1980), 55–63; Mary Epes, et al., "The COMP-LAB Project: Assessing the Effectiveness of a Laboratory-Centered Basic Writing Course on the College Level" (Jamaica, N. Y.: York College, CUNY, 1979) ERIC 194 908; June B. Evans, "The Analogous Ounce: The Analgesic for Relief," *English Journal,* 70, No. 2 (1981), 38–39: Sydney Greenbaum, "What Is Grammar and Why Teach It?" (a paper presented at the meeting of the National Council of Teachers of English, Boston, Nov. 1982) ERIC 222 917; Marjorie Smelstor, *A Guide to the Role of Grammar in Teaching Writing* (Madison: University of Wisconsin School of Education, 1978) ERIC 176 323; and A. M. Tibbetts, *Working Papers: A Teacher's Observations on Composition* (Glenview, Ill.: Scott, Foresman, 1982).

For attacks on formal grammar teaching, see Harvey A. Daniels, *Famous Last Words: The American Language Crisis Reconsidered* (Carbondale: Southern Illinois University Press, 1983); Suzette Haden Elgin, *Never Mind the Trees: What the English Teacher Really Needs to Know about Linguistics* (Berkeley: University of California College of Education, Bay Area Writing Project Occasional Paper No. 2. 1980) ERIC 198 536; Mike Rose, "Remedial Writing Courses: A Critique and a Proposal." *College English,* 45 (1983), 109–128; and Ron Shook, "Response to Martha Kolln," *College Composition and Communication,* 34 (1983), 491–495.

writing on "The Relation of Formal Grammar to Composition" in *College Composition and Communication* (23 [1977], 247–50), is tempted "to sputter on paper" at reading the quotation above (p. 248), and Martha Kolln, writing in the same journal three years later ("Closing the Books on Alchemy," *CCC*, 32 [1981], 139–51), labels people like me "alchemists" for our perverse beliefs. Neuleib reviews five experimental studies, most of them concluding that formal grammar instruction has no effect on the quality of students' writing nor on their ability to avoid error. Yet she renders in effect a Scots verdict of "Not proven" and calls for more research on the issue. Similarly, Kolln reviews six experimental studies that arrive at similar conclusions, only one of them overlapping with the studies cited by Neuleib. She calls for more careful definition of the word *grammar*—her definition being "the internalized system that native speakers of a language share" (p. 140)—and she concludes with a stirring call to place grammar instruction at the center of the composition curriculum: "our goal should be to help students understand the system they know unconsciously as native speakers, to teach them the necessary categories and labels that will enable them to think about and talk about their language" (p. 150). Certainly our textbooks and our pedagogies—though they vary widely in what they see as "necessary categories and labels"—continue to emphasize mastery of formal grammar, and popular discussions of a presumed literacy crisis are almost unanimous in their call for a renewed emphasis on the teaching of formal grammar, seen as basic for success in writing.[4]

An Instructive Example

It is worth noting at the outset that both sides in this dispute—the grammarians and the anti-grammarians—articulate the issue in the same positivistic terms: what does experimental research tell us about the value of teaching formal grammar? But seventy-five years of experimental research has for all practical purposes told us nothing. The two sides are unable to agree on how to interpret such research. Studies are interpreted in terms of one's prior assumptions about the value of teaching grammar: their results seem not to change those assumptions. Thus the basis of the discussion, a basis shared by Kolln and Neuleib and by Braddock and his colleagues—"what does educational research tell us?"— seems designed to perpetuate, not to resolve, the issue. A single example will be instructive. In 1976 and then at greater length in 1979, W. B. Elley, I. H.

---

[4]See, for example, Clifton Fadiman and James Howard, *Empty Pages: A Search for Writing Competence in School and Society* (Belmont, Cal.: Fearon Pitman, 1979); Edwin Newman, *A Civil Tongue* (Indianapolis, Ind.: Bobbs-Merrill, 1976); and *Strictly Speaking* (New York: Warner Books, 1974); John Simons, *Paradigms Lost* (New York: Clarkson N. Potter, 1980); A. M. Tibbets and Charlene Tibbets, *What's Happening to American English?* (New York: Scribner's, 1978); and "Why Johnny Can't Write," *Newsweek*, 8 Dec. 1975, pp. 58–63.

Barham, H. Lamb, and M. Wyllie reported on a three-year experiment in New Zealand, comparing the relative effectiveness at the high school level of instruction in transformational grammar, instruction in traditional grammar, and no grammar instruction.[5] They concluded that the formal study of grammar, whether transformational or traditional, improved neither writing quality nor control over surface correctness.

> After two years, no differences were detected in writing performance or language competence; after three years small differences appeared in some minor conventions favoring the TG [transformational grammar] group, but these were more than offset by the less positive attitudes they showed towards their English studies. (p. 18)

Anthony Petroskey, in a review of research ("Grammar Instruction: What We Know," *English Journal,* 66, No. 9 [1977], 86–88), agreed with this conclusion, finding the study to be carefully designed, "representative of the best kind of educational research" (p. 86), its validity "unquestionable" (p. 88). Yet Janice Neuleib in her essay found the same conclusions to be "startling" and questioned whether the findings could be generalized beyond the target population, New Zealand high school students. Martha Kolln, when her attention is drawn to the study ("Reply to Ron Shook," *CCC,* 32 [1981], 139–151), thinks the whole experiment "suspicious." And John Mellon has been willing to use the study to defend the teaching of grammar; the study of Elley and his colleagues, he has argued, shows that teaching grammar does no harm.[6]

It would seem unlikely, therefore, that further experimental research, in and of itself, will resolve the grammar issue. Any experimental design can be nit-picked, any experimental population can be criticized, and any experimental conclusion can be questioned or, more often, ignored. In fact, it may well be that the grammar question is not open to resolution by experimental research, that, as Noam Chomsky has argued in *Reflections on Language* (New York: Pantheon, 1975), criticizing the trivialization of human learning by behavioral psychologists, the issue is simply misdefined.

> There will be "good experiments" only in domains that lie outside the organism's cognitive capacity. For example, there will be no "good experiments" in the study of human learning.
> This discipline . . . will, of necessity, avoid those domains in which an organism is specially designed to acquire rich cognitive structures that enter into its life in an intimate fashion. The discipline will be of vir-

[5]"The Role of Grammar in a Secondary School English Curriculum." *Research in the Teaching English,* 10 (1976), 5–21; *The Role of Grammar in a Secondary School Curriculum* (Wellington: New Zealand Council of Teachers of English, 1979).

[6]"A Taxonomy of Compositional Competencies," in *Perspectives on Literacy,* ed. Richard Beach and P. David Pearson (Minneapolis: University of Minnesota College of Education, 1979), pp. 247–272.

tually no intellectual interest, it seems to me, since it is restricting itself in principle to those questions that are guaranteed to tell us little about the nature of organisms. (p. 36)

Asking the Right Questions

As a result, though I will look briefly at the tradition of experimental research, my primary goal in this essay is to articulate the grammar issue in different and, I would hope, more productive terms. Specifically, I want to ask four questions:

1. Why is the grammar issue so important? Why has it been the dominant focus of composition research for the last seventy-five years?
2. What definitions of the word *grammar* are needed to articulate the grammar issue intelligibly?
3. What do findings in cognate disciplines suggest about the value of formal grammar instruction?
4. What is our theory of language, and what does it predict about the value of formal grammar instruction? (This question—"what does our theory of language predict?"—seems a much more powerful question than "what does educational research tell us?")

In exploring these questions I will attempt to be fully explicit about issues, terms, and assumptions. I hope that both proponents and opponents of formal grammar instruction would agree that these are useful as shared points of reference: care in definition, full examination of the evidence, reference to relevant work in cognate disciplines, and explicit analysis of the theoretical bases of the issue.

But even with that gesture of harmony it will be difficult to articulate the issue in a balanced way, one that will be acceptable to both sides. After all, we are dealing with a professional dispute in which one side accuses the other of "magical thinking," and in turn that side responds by charging the other as "alchemists." Thus we might suspect that the grammar issue is itself embedded in larger models of the transmission of literacy, part of quite different assumptions about the teaching of composition.

Those of us who dismiss the teaching of formal grammar have a model of composition instruction that makes the grammar issue "uninteresting" in a scientific sense. Our model predicts a rich and complex interaction of learner and environment in mastering literacy, an interaction that has little to do with sequences of skills instruction as such. Those who defend the teaching of grammar tend to have a model of composition instruction that is rigidly skills-centered and rigidly sequential: the formal teaching of grammar, as the first step in that sequence, is the cornerstone or linchpin. Grammar teaching is thus supremely interesting, naturally a dominant focus for educational research. The controversy over the value of grammar instruction, then, is inseparable from two other issues: the issues of sequence in the teaching of composition and of the role of the composition teacher. Consider, for example, the force of these two issues in Janice Neuleib's conclusion: after calling for yet more experimental research on the value of teaching grammar, she ends with an absolute (and unsupported) claim about sequences and teacher roles in composition.

> We do know, however, that some things must be taught at different levels. Insistence on adherence to usage norms by composition teachers does improve usage. Students can learn to organize their papers if teachers do not accept papers that are disorganized. Perhaps composition teachers can teach those two abilities before they begin the more difficult tasks of developing syntactic sophistication and a winning style. ("The Relation of Formal Grammar to Composition," p. 250)

(One might want to ask, in passing, whether "usage norms" exist in the monolithic fashion the phrase suggests and whether refusing to accept disorganized papers is our best available pedagogy for teaching arrangement.)[7]

But I want to focus on the notion of sequence that makes the grammar issue important: first grammar, then usage, then some absolute model of organization, all controlled by the teacher at the center of the learning process, with other matters, those of rhetorical weight—"syntactic sophistication and a winning style"—pushed off to the future. It is not surprising that we call each other names: those of us who question the value of teaching grammar are in fact shaking the whole elaborate edifice of traditional composition instruction.

The Five Meanings of "Grammar"

Given its centrality to a well-established way of teaching composition, I need to go about the business of defining grammar rather carefully, particularly in view Kolln's criticism of the lack of care in earlier discussions. Therefore I will build upon a seminal discussion of the word *grammar* offered a generation ago, in 1954, by W. Nelson Francis, often excerpted as "The Three Meanings of Grammar."[8] It is worth reprinting at length, if only to re-establish it as a reference point for future discussions.

> The first thing we mean by "grammar" is "the set of formal patterns in which the words of a language are arranged in order to convey larger meanings." It is not necessary that we be able to discuss these patterns self-consciously in order to be able to use them. In fact, all speakers of a language above the age of five or six know how to use its complex

---

[7]On usage norms, see Edward Finegan, *Attitudes toward English Usage: The History of a War of Words* (New York: Teachers College Press, 1980), and Jim Quinn, *American Tongue in Cheek: A Populist Guide to Language* (New York: Pantheon, 1980); on arrangement, see Patrick Hartwell, Teaching Arrangement: A Pedagogy," *CE,* 40 (1979), 548–554.

[8]"Revolution in Grammar," *Quarterly Journal of Speech,* 40 (1954), 299–312.

forms of organization with considerable skill; in this sense of the word—call it "Grammar 1"—they are thoroughly familiar with its grammar.

The second meaning of "grammar"—call it "Grammar 2"—is "the branch of linguistic science which is concerned with the description, analysis, and formulization of formal language patterns." Just as gravity was in full operation before Newton's apple fell, so grammar in the first sense was in full operation before anyone formulated the first rule that began the history of grammar as a study.

The third sense in which people use the word "grammar" is "linguistic etiquette." This we may call "Grammar 3." The word in this sense is often coupled with a derogatory adjective: we say that the expression "he ain't here" is "bad grammar.". . .

As has already been suggested, much confusion arises from mixing these meanings. One hears a good deal of criticism of teachers of English couched in such terms as "they don't teach grammar any more." Criticism of this sort is based on the wholly unproven assumption that teaching Grammar 2 will improve the student's proficiency in Grammar 1 or improve his manners in Grammar 3. Actually, the form of Grammar 2 which is usually taught is a very inaccurate and misleading analysis of the facts of Grammar 1; and it therefore is of highly questionable value in improving a person's ability to handle the structural patterns of his language. (pp. 300–301)

Francis' Grammar 3 is, of course, not grammar at all, but usage. One would like to assume that Joseph Williams' recent discussion of usage ("The Phenomenology of Error," *CCC*, 32 (1981), 152–168), along with his references, has placed those shibboleths in a proper perspective. But I doubt it, and I suspect that popular discussions of the grammar issue will be as flawed by the intrusion of usage issues as past discussions have been. At any rate I will make only passing reference to Grammar 3—usage—naively assuming that this issue has been discussed elsewhere and that my readers are familiar with those discussions.

We need also to make further discriminations about Francis' Grammar 2, given that the purpose of his 1954 article was to substitute for one form of Grammar 2, that "inaccurate and misleading" form "which is usually taught," another form, that of American structuralist grammar. Here we can make use of a still earlier discussion, one going back to the days when *PMLA* was willing to publish articles on rhetoric and linguistics, to a 1927 article by Charles Carpenter Fries, "The Rules of the Common School Grammars" (42 [1927], 221–237). Fries there distinguished between the scientific tradition of language study (to which we will now delimit Francis' Grammar 2, scientific grammar) and the separate tradition of "the common school grammars," developed unscientifically, largely based on two inadequate principles—appeals to "logical principles," like "two negatives make a positive," and analogy to Latin grammar; thus, Charlton Laird's characterization, "the grammar of Latin, ingeniously warped to suggest English" (*Language in America* [New York: World, 1970], p. 294). There is, of course, a direct link between the "common school grammars" that Fries criticized in 1927 and the grammar-based texts of today, and thus it seems wise, as Karl W. Dykema suggests ("Where Our Grammar Came From," *CE,* 22 (1961), 455–465), to separate Grammar 2, "scientific grammar," from Grammar 4, "school grammar," the latter meaning, quite literally, "the grammars used in the schools."

Further, since Martha Kolln points to the adaptation of Christensen's sentence rhetoric in a recent sentence-combining text as an example of the proper emphasis on "grammar" ("Closing the Books on Alchemy," p. 140), it is worth separating out, as still another meaning of *grammar,* Grammar 5, "stylistic grammar," defined as "grammatical terms used in the interest of teaching prose style." And, since stylistic grammars abound, with widely variant terms and emphases, we might appropriately speak parenthetically of specific forms of Grammar 5—Grammar 5 (Lanham); Grammar 5 (Strunk and White); Grammar 5 (Williams, *Style*); even Grammar 5 (Christensen, as adapted by Daiker, Kerek, and Morenberg).[9]

The Grammar in Our Heads

With these definitions in mind, let us return to Francis' Grammar 1, admirably defined by Kolln as "the internalized system of rules that speakers of a language share" ("Closing the Books on Alchemy," p. 140), or, to put it more simply, the grammar in our heads. Three features of Grammar 1 need to be stressed: first, its special status as an "internalized system of rules," as tacit and unconscious knowledge; second, the abstract, even counterintuitive, nature of these rules, insofar as we are able to approximate them indirectly as Grammar 2 statements; and third, the way in which the form of one's Grammar 1 seems profoundly affected by the acquisition of literacy. This sort of review is designed to firm up our theory of language, so that we can ask what it predicts about the value of teaching formal grammar.

A simple thought experiment will isolate the special status of Grammar 1 knowledge. I have asked members of a number of different groups—from sixth graders to college freshmen to high-school teachers—to give me the rule for ordering adjectives of nationality, age, and number in English. The response is alwaays the same: "We don't know the rule." Yet when I ask these groups to perform an active language task, they show productive control over the rule they have denied knowing. I ask them to arrange the following words in a natural order:

French   the   young   girls   four

I have never seen a native speaker of English who did not immediately produce the natural order, "the four young French girls." The rule is that in English the

---

[9]Richard A. Lanham, *Revising Prose* (New York: Scribner's, 1979): William Strunk and E. B. White, *The Elements of Style,* 3rd ed. (New York: Macmillan, 1979); Joseph Williams. *Style: Ten Lessons in Clarity and Grace* (Glenview, Ill.: Scott, Foresman, 1981); Christensen, "A Generative Rhetoric of the Sentence," *CCC,* 14 (1963), 155–161; Donald A. Daiker, Andrew Kerek, and Max Morenberg, *The Writer's Options: Combining to Composing,* 2nd ed. (New York: Harper & Row, 1982).

order of adjectives is first, number, second, age, and third, nationality. Native speakers can create analogous phrases using the rule—"the seventy-three aged Scandinavian lechers"; and the drive for meaning is so great that they will create contexts to make sense out of violations of the rule, as in foregrounding' for emphasis: "I want to talk to the French four young girls." (I immediately envision a large room, perhaps a banquet hall, filled with tables at which are seated groups of four young girls, each group of a different nationality.) So Grammar 1 is eminently usable knowledge—the way we make our life through language—but it is not accessible knowledge; in a profound sense, we do not know that we have it. Thus neurolinguist Z. N. Pylyshyn speaks of Grammar 1 as "autonomous," separate from common-sense reasoning, and as "cognitively impenetrable," not available for direct examination.[10] In philosophy and linguistics, the distinction is made between formal, conscious, "knowing about" knowledge (like Grammar 2 knowledge) and tacit, unconscious, "knowing how" knowledge (like Grammar 1 knowledge). The importance of this distinction for the teaching of composition—it provides a powerful theoretical justification for mistrusting the ability of Grammar 2 (or Grammar 4) knowledge to affect Grammar 1 performance—was pointed out in this journal by Martin Steinmann, Jr., in 1966 ("Rhetorical Research," *CE,* 27 [1966], 278–285).

Further, the more we learn about Grammar 1—and most linguists would agree that we know surprisingly little about it—the more abstract and implicit it seems. This abstractness can be illustrated with an experiment, devised by Lise Menn and reported by Morris Halle,[11] about our rule for forming plurals in speech. It is obvious that we do indeed have a "rule" for forming plurals, for we do not memorize the plural of each noun separately. You will demonstrate productive control over that rule by forming the spoken plurals of the nonsense words below:

thole   flitch   plast

Halle offers two ways of formalizing a Grammar 2 equivalent of this Grammar 1 ability. One form of the rule is the following, stated in terms of speech sounds:

a. If the noun ends in /s z š ž č ǰ/, add /ɨz/;
b. otherwise, if the noun ends in /p t k f Ø/, add /s/;
c. otherwise, add /z/.[11]

[10]"A Psychological Approach," in *Psychobiology of Language,* ed. M. Studdert-Kennedy (Cambridge, Mass.: MIT Press, 1983), pp. 16–19. See also Noam Chomsky, "Language and Unconscious Knowledge," in *Psychoanalysis and Language: Psychiatry and the Humanities.* Vol. III, ed. Joseph H. Smith (New Haven, Conn.: Yale University Press, 1978), pp. 3–44.

[11]Morris Halle, "Knowledge Unlearned and Untaught: What Speakers Know about the Sounds of Their Language," in *Linguistic Theory and Psychological Reality.* ed. Halle, Joan Bresnan, and George A. Miller (Cambridge, Mass.: MIT Press, 1978), pp. 135–140.

This rule comes close to what we literate adults consider to be an adequate rule for plurals in writing, like the rules, for example, taken from a recent "common school grammar," Eric Gould's *Reading into Writing: A Rhetoric, Reader, and Handbook* (Boston: Houghton Mifflin, 1983):

> *Plurals* can be tricky. If you are unsure of a plural, then check it in the dictionary.
> The general rules are
> Add *s* to the singular: *girls, tables*
> Add *es* to nouns ending in *ch, sh, x* or *s: churches, boxes, wishes*
> Add *es* to nouns ending in *y* and preceded by a vowel once you have changed *y* to *i: monies, companies.* (p. 666)

(But note the persistent inadequacy of such Grammar 4 rules: here, as I read it, the rule is inadequate to explain the plurals of *ray* and *tray,* even to explain the collective noun *monies,* not a plural at all, formed from the mass noun *money* and offered as an example.) A second form of the rule would make use of much more abstract entities, sound features:

> a. If the noun ends with a sound that is [coronal, strident], add /ɪz/;
> b. otherwise, if the noun ends with a sound that is [non-voiced], add /s/;
> c. otherwise, add /z/.

(The notion of "sound features" is itself rather abstract, perhaps new to readers not trained in linguistics. But such readers should be able to recognize that the spoken plurals of *lip* and *duck,* the sound [s], differ from the spoken plurals of *sea* and *gnu,* the sound [z], only in that the sounds of the latter are "voiced"—one's vocal cords vibrate—while the sounds of the former are "non-voiced.")

To test the psychologically operative rule, the Grammar 1 rule, native speakers of English were asked to form the plural of the last name of the composer Johann Sebastian *Bach,* a sound [x], unique in American (though not in Scottish) English. If speakers follow the first rule above, using word endings, they would reject a) and b), then apply c), producing the plural as /baxz/, with word-final /z/. (If writers were to follow the rule of the common school grammar, they would produce the written plural *Baches,* apparently, given the form of the rule, on analogy with *churches.*) If speakers follow the second rule, they would have to analyze the sound [x] as [non-labial, non-coronal, dorsal, non-voiced, and non-strident], producing the plural as /baxs/, with word-final /s/. Native speakers of American English overwhelmingly produce the plural as /baxs/. They use knowledge that Halle characterizes as "unlearned and untaught" (p. 140).

Now such a conclusion is counterintuitive—certainly it departs maximally from Grammar 4 rules for forming plurals. It seems that native speakers of English behave as if they have productive control, as Grammar 1 knowledge, of abstract sound features (± coronal, ± strident, and so on) which are available as conscious, Grammar 2 knowledge only to trained linguists—and, indeed, formally available only within the last hundred years or so. ("Behave as if," in that last sentence, is a necessary hedge, to underscore the difficulty of "knowing about" Grammar 1.)

Moreover, as the example of plural rules suggests, the form of the Grammar 1 in the heads of literate adults seems profoundly affected by the acquisition of literacy. Obviously, literate adults have access to different morphological codes: the abstract print -*s* underlying the predictable /s/ and /z/ plurals, the abstract print -*ed* underlying the spoken past tense markers /t/, as in "walked," /əd/, as "surrounded," /d/, as in "scored," and the symbol /∅/ for no surface realization, as in the relaxed standard pronunciation of "I walked to the store." Literate adults also have access to distinctions preserved only in the code of print (for example, the distinction between "a good sailer" and "a good sailor" that Mark Aranoff points out in "An English Spelling Convention," *Linguistic Inquiry,* 9 [1978], 299–303). More significantly, Irene Moscowitz speculates that the ability of third graders to form abstract nouns on analogy with pairs like *divine::divinity* and *serene::serenity,* where the spoken vowel changes but the spelling preserves meaning, is a factor of knowing how to read. Carol Chomsky finds a three-stage developmental sequence in the grammatical performance of seven-year-olds, related to measures of kind and variety of reading; and Rita S. Brause finds a nine-stage developmental sequence in the ability to understand semantic ambiguity, extending from fourth graders to graduate students.[12] John Mills and Gordon Hemsley find that level of education, and presumably level of literacy, influence judgments of grammaticality, concluding that literacy changes the deep structure of one's internal grammar; Jean Whyte finds that oral language functions develop differently in readers and non-readers; José Morais, Jésus Alegria, and Paul Bertelson find that illiterate adults are unable to add or delete sounds at the beginning of nonsense words, suggesting that awareness of speech as a series of phones is provided by learning to read an alphabetic code. Two experiments—one conducted by Charles A. Ferguson, the other by Mary E. Hamilton and David Barton—find that adults' ability to recognize segmentation in speech is related to degree of literacy, not to amount of schooling or general ability.[13]

[12]Moscowitz, "On the Status of Vowel Shift in English," in *Cognitive Development and the acquisition of Language,* ed. T. E. Moore (New York: Academic Press, 1973), pp. 223–60: Chomsky, "Stages in Language Development and Reading Exposure," *Harvard Educational Review,* 42 (1972), 1–33; and Brause, "Developmental Aspects of the Ability to Understand Semantic Ambiguity, with Implications for Teachers," *RTE,* 11 (1977), 39–48.

[13]Mills and Hemsley, "The Effect of Levels of Education on Judgments of Grammatical Acceptability," *Language and Speech,* 19 (1976), 324–342; Whyte, "Levels of Language Competence and Reading Ability: An Exploratory Investigation," *Journal of Research in Reading,* 5 (1982), 123–132; Morais, et al., "Does Awareness of Speech as a Series of Phones Arise Spontaneously?" *Cognition,* 7 (1979), 323–331; Ferguson, *Cognitive Effects of Literacy: Linguistic Awareness in Adult Non-readers* (Washington, D.C.: National Institute of Education Final Report, 1981) ERIC 222 857; Hamilton and Barton. "A Word is a Word: Metalinguistic Skills in Adults of Varying Literacy Levels" (Stanford, Cal.: Stanford University Department of Linguistics, 1980) ERIC 222 859.

It is worth noting that none of these investigators would suggest that the developmental sequences they have uncovered be isolated and taught as discrete skills. They are natural concomitants of literacy, and they seem best characterized not as isolated rules but as developing schemata, broad strategies for approaching written language.

Grammar 2

We can, of course, attempt to approximate the rules or schemata of Grammar 1 by writing fully explicit descriptions that model the competence of a native speaker. Such rules, like the rules for pluralizing nouns or ordering adjectives discussed above, are the goal of the science of linguistics, that is, Grammar 2. There are a number of scientific grammars—an older structuralist model and several versions within a generative-transformational paradigm, not to mention isolated schools like tagmemic grammar, Montague grammar, and the like. In fact, we cannot think of Grammar 2 as a stable entity, for its form changes with each new issue of each linguistics journal, as new "rules of grammar" are proposed and debated. Thus Grammar 2, though of great theoretical interest to the composition teacher, is of little practical use in the classroom, as Constance Weaver has pointed out (*Grammar for Teachers* [Urbana, Ill.: NCTE, 1979], pp. 3–6). Indeed Grammar 2 is a scientific model of Grammar 1, not a description of it, so that questions of psychological reality, while important, are less important than other, more theoretical factors, such as the elegance of formulation or the global power of rules. We might, for example, wish to replace the rule for ordering adjectives of age, number, and nationality cited above with a more general rule—what linguists call a "fuzzy" rule—that adjectives in English are ordered by their abstract quality of "nouniness": adjectives that are very much like nouns, like *French* or *Scandinavian,* come physically closer to nouns than do adjectives that are less "nouny," like *four* or *aged.* But our motivation for accepting the broader rule would be its global power, not its psychological reality.[14]

I try to consider a hostile reader, one committed to the teaching of grammar, and I try to think of ways to hammer in the central point of this distinction, that the rules of Grammar 2 are simply unconnected to productive control over Gammar 1. I can argue from authority: Noam Chomsky has touched on this point whenever he has concerned himself with the implications of linguistics for language teaching, and years ago transformationalist Mark Lester stated

---

[14]On the question of the psychological reality of Grammar 2 descriptions, see Maria Black and Shulamith Chiat, "Psycholinguistics without "Psychological Reality'," *Linguistics,* 19 (1981), 37–61; Joan Bresnan, ed., *The Mental Representation of Grammatical Relations* (Cambridge, Mass.: MIT Press, 1982); and Michael H. Long, "Inside the 'Black Box': Methodological Issues in Classroom Research on Language Learning," *Language Learning,* 30 (1980), 1–42.

unequivocally, "there simply appears to be no correlation between a writer's study of language and his ability to write."[15] I can cite analogies offered by others: Francis Christensen's analogy in an essay originally published in 1962 that formal grammar study would be "to invite a centipede to attend to the sequence of his legs in motion,"[16] or James Britton's analogy, offered informally after a conference presentation, that grammar study would be like forcing starving people to master the use of a knife and fork before allowing them to eat. I can offer analogies of my own, contemplating the wisdom of asking a pool player to master the physics of momentum before taking up a cue or of making a prospective driver get a degree in automotive engineering before engaging the clutch. I consider a hypothetical argument, that if Grammar 2 knowledge affected Grammar 1 performance, then linguists would be our best writers. (I can certify that they are, on the whole, not.) Such a position, after all, is only in accord with other domains of science: the formula for catching a fly ball in baseball ("Playing It by Ear," *Scientific American,* 248, No. 4 [1983], 76) is of such complexity that it is beyond my understanding—and, I would suspect, that of many workaday centerfielders. But perhaps I can best hammer in this claim—that Grammar 2 knowledge has no effect on Grammar 1 performance—by offering a demonstration.

The diagram on the next page is an attempt by Thomas N. Huckin and Leslie A. Olsen (*English for Science and Technology* [New York: McGraw-Hill, 1983]) to offer, for students of English as a second language, a fully explicit formulation of what is, for native speakers, a trivial rule of the language—the choice of definite article, indefinite article, or no definite article. There are obvious limits to such a formulation, for article choice in English is less a matter of rule than of idiom ("I went to college" versus "I went to a university" versus British "I went to university"), real-world knowledge (using indefinite "I went into a house" instantiates definite "I looked at the ceiling," and indefinite "I visited a university" instantiates definite "I talked with the professors"), and stylistic choice (the last sentence above might alternatively end with "the choice of the definite article, the indefinite article, or no article"). Huckin and Olsen invite non-native speakers to use the rule consciously to justify article choice in technical prose, such as the passage below from P. F. Brandwein (*Matter: An Earth Science* [New York: Harcourt Brace Jovanovich, 1975]). I invite you to spend a couple of minutes doing the same thing, with the understanding that this exercise is a test case: you are using a very explicit rule to justify a fairly straightforward issue of grammatical choice.

[15]Chomsky, "The Current Scene in Linguistics," *College English,* 27 (1966), 587–595; and "Linguistic Theory," in *Language Teaching: Broader Contexts,* ed. Robert C. Meade, Jr. (New York: Modern Language Association, 1966), pp. 43–49; Mark Lester, "The Value of Transformational Grammar in Teaching Composition," *CCC,* 16 (1967), 228.

[16]Christensen, "Between Two Worlds," in *Notes toward a New Rhetoric: Nine Essays for Teachers,* rev. ed., ed. Bonniejean Christensen (New York: Harper & Row, 1978), pp. 1–22.

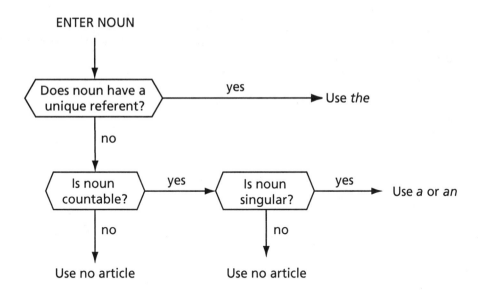

ENTER NOUN

Does noun have a unique referent? — yes → Use *the*

no

Is noun countable? — yes → Is noun singular? — yes → Use *a* or *an*

no → Use no article   no → Use no article

Imagine a cannon on top of _____ highest mountain on earth. It is firing _____ cannonballs horizontally. _____ first cannonball fired follows its path. As _____ cannonball moves, _____ gravity pulls it down, and it soon hits _____ ground. Now _____ velocity with which each succeeding cannonball is fired is increased. Thus, _____ cannonball goes farther each time. Cannonball 2 goes farther than _____ cannonball 1 although each is being pulled by _____ gravity toward the earth all _____ time. _____ last cannonball is fired with such tremendous velocity that it goes completely around _____ earth. It returns to _____ mountaintop and continues around the earth again and again. _____ cannonball's inertia causes it to continue in motion indefinitely in _____ orbit around earth. In such a situation, we could consider _____ cannonball to be _____ artificial satellite, just like _____ weather satellites launched by _____ U.S. Weather Service. (p. 209)

Most native speakers of English who have attempted this exercise report a great deal of frustration, a curious sense of working against, rather than with, the rule. The rule, however valuable it may be for non-native speakers, is, for the most part, simply unusable for native speakers of the language.

Cognate Areas of Research

We can corroborate this demonstration by turning to research in two cognate areas, studies of the induction of rules of artificial languages and studies of the role of formal rules in second language acquisition. Psychologists have studied the ability of subjects to learn artificial languages, usually constructed of nonsense syllables or letter strings. Such languages can be described by phrase structure rules:

$$S \Rightarrow VX$$
$$X \Rightarrow MX$$

More clearly, they can be presented as flow diagrams, as below:

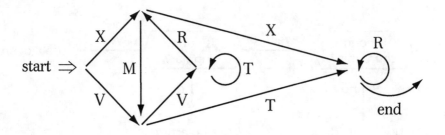

This diagram produces "sentences" like the following:

VVTRXRR.	XMVTTRX.	XXRR.
XMVRMT.	VVTTRMT.	XMTRRR.

The following "sentences" would be "ungrammatical" in this language:

*VMXTT.	*RTXVVT.	*TRVXXVVM.

Arthur S. Reber, in a classic 1967 experiment, demonstrated that mere exposure to grammatical sentences produced tacit learning: subjects who copied several grammatical sentences performed far above chance in judging the grammaticality of other letter strings. Further experiments have shown that providing subjects with formal rules—giving them the flow diagram above, for example—remarkably degrades performance: subjects given the "rules of the language" do much less well in acquiring the rules than do subjects not given the rules. Indeed, even telling subjects that they are to induce the rules of an artificial language degrades performance. Such laboratory experiments are admittedly contrived, but they confirm predictions that our theory of language would make about the value of formal rules in language learning.[17]

The thrust of recent research in second language learning similarly works to constrain the value of formal grammar rules. The most explicit statement of the

[17]Reber, "Implicit Learning of Artificial Grammars," *Journal of Verbal Learning and Verbal Behavior,* 6 (1967), 855–863; "Implicit Learning of Synthetic Languages: The Role of Instructional Set," *Journal of Experimental Psychology: Human Learning and Memory,* 2 (1976), 889–94; and Reber, Saul M. Kassin, Selma Lewis, and Gary Cantor, "On the Relationship Between Implicit and Explicit Modes in the Learning of a Complex Rule Structure," *Journal of Experimental Psychology: Human Learning and Memory,* 6 (1980), 492–502.

value of formal rules is that of Stephen D. Krashen's monitor model.[18] Krashen divides second language mastery into *acquisition*—tacit, informal mastery, akin to first language acquisition—and formal learning—conscious application of Grammar 2 rules, which he calls "monitoring" output. In another essay Krashen uses his model to predict a highly individual use of the monitor and a highly constrained role for formal rules:

> Some adults (and very few children) are able to use conscious rules to increase the grammatical accuracy of their output, and even for these people, very strict conditions need to be met before the conscious grammar can be applied.[19]

In *Principles and Practice in Second Language Acquisition* (New York: Pergamon, 1982) Krashen outlines these conditions by means of a series of concentric circles, beginning with a large circle denoting the rules of English and a smaller circle denoting the subset of those rules described by formal linguists (adding that most linguists would protest that the size of this circle is much too large):

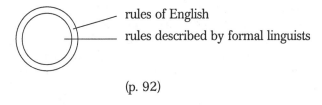

rules of English
rules described by formal linguists

(p. 92)

Krashen then adds smaller circles, as shown below—a subset of the rules described by formal linguists that would be known to applied linguists, a subset of those rules that would be available to the best teachers, and then a subset of those rules that teachers might choose to present to second language learners:

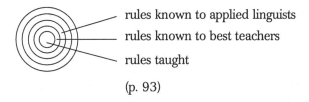

rules known to applied linguists
rules known to best teachers
rules taught

(p. 93)

---

[18]"Individual Variation in the Use of the Monitor," in *Principles of Second Language Learning,* ed. W. Richie (New York: Academic Press, 1978), pp. 175–185.

[19]"Applications of Psycholinguistic Research to the Classroom," in *Practical Applications of Research in Foreign Language Teaching,* ed. D. J. James (Lincolnwood, Ill.: National Textbook, 1983), p. 61.

Of course, as Krashen notes, not all the rules taught will be learned, and not all those learned will be available, as what he calls "mental baggage" (p. 94), for conscious use.

An experiment by Ellen Bialystock, asking English speakers learning French to judge the grammaticality of taped sentences, complicates this issue, for reaction time data suggest that learners first make an intuitive judgment of grammaticality, using implicit or Grammar 1 knowledge, and only then search for formal explanations, using explicit or Grammar 2 knowledge.[20] This distinction would suggest that Grammar 2 knowledge is of use to second language learners only after the principle has already been mastered as tacit Grammar 1 knowledge. In the terms of Krashen's model, learning never becomes acquisition *Principles,* p. 86).

An ingenious experiment by Herbert W. Seliger complicates the issue yet further ("On the Nature and Function of Language Rules in Language Learning," *TESOL Quarterly,* 13 [1979], 359–369). Seliger asked native and non-native speakers of English to orally identify pictures of objects (e.g., "an apple," "a pear," "a book," "an umbrella"), noting whether they used the correct form of the indefinite articles *a* and *an*. He then asked each speaker to state the rule for choosing between *a* and *an*. He found no correlation between the ability to state the rule and the ability to apply it correctly, either with native or non-native speakers. Indeed, three of four adult non-native speakers in his sample produced a correct form of the rule, but they did not apply it in speaking. A strong conclusion from this experiment would be that formal rules of grammar seem to have no value whatsoever. Seliger, however, suggests a more paradoxical interpretation. Rules are of no use, he agrees, but some people think they are, and for these people, assuming that they have internalized the rules, even inadequate rules are of heuristic value, for they allow them to access the internal rules they actually use.

The Incantations of the "Common School Grammars"

Such a paradox may explain the fascination we have as teachers with "rules of grammar" of the Grammar 4 variety, the "rules" of the "common school grammars." Again and again such rules are inadequate to the facts of written language; you will recall that we have known this since Francis' 1927 study. R. Scott Baldwin and James M. Coady, studying how readers respond to punctuation signals ("Psycholinguistic Approaches to a Theory of Punctuation," *Journal of Reading Behavior,* 10 [1978], 363–83), conclude that conventional rules of punctuation are "a complete sham" (p. 375). My own favorite is the Grammar 4 rule for showing possession, always expressed in terms of adding -'s or -s' to nouns, while our internal grammar, if you think about it, adds possession to noun phrases, albeit under severe stylistic constraints: "the horses of the Queen

---

[20]"Some Evidence for the Integrity and Interaction of Two Knowledge Sources," In *New Dimensions in Second Language Acquisition Research,* ed. Roger W. Andersen (Rowley, Mass.: Newbury House, 1981), pp. 62–74.

of England" are "the Queen of England's horses" and "the feathers of the duck over there" are "the duck over there's feathers." Suzette Haden Elgin refers to the "rules" of Grammar 4 as "incantations" (*Never Mind the Trees,* p. 9: see footnote 3).

It may simply be that as hyperliterate adults we are conscious of "using rules" when we are in fact doing something else, something far more complex, accessing tacit heuristics honed by print literacy itself. We can clarify this notion by reaching for an acronym coined by technical writers to explain the readability of complex prose—COIK: "clear only if known." The rules of Grammar 4—no, we can at this point be more honest—the incantations of Grammar 4 are COIK. If you know how to signal possession in the code of print, then the advice to add -'s to nouns makes perfect sense, just as the collective noun *monies* is a fine example of changing -*y* to -*i* and adding -es to form the plural. But if you have not grasped, tacitly, the abstract representation of possession in print, such incantations can only be opaque.

Worse yet, the advice given in "the common school grammars" is unconnected with anything remotely resembling literate adult behavior. Consider, as an example, the rule for not writing a sentence fragment as the rule is described in the best-selling college grammar text, John C. Hodges and Mary S. Whitten's *Harbrace College Handbook,* 9th ed. (New York: Harcourt Brace Jovanovich, 1982). In order to get to the advice, "as a rule, do not write a sentence fragment" (p. 25), the student must master the following learning tasks:

Recognizing verbs.
Recognizing subjects and verbs.
Recognizing all parts of speech. (*Harbrace* lists eight.)
Recognizing phrases and subordinate clauses. (*Harbrace* lists six types of
     phrases, and it offers incomplete lists of eight relative pronouns and
     eighteen subordinating conjunctions.)
Recognizing main clauses and types of sentences.

These learning tasks completed, the student is given the rule above, offered a page of exceptions, and then given the following advice (or is it an incantation?):

> Before handing in a composition, . . . proofread each word group
> written as a sentence. Test each one for completeness. First, be sure that
> it has at least one subject and one predicate. Next, be sure that the word
> group is not a dependent clause beginning with a subordinating con-
> junction or a relative clause. (p. 27)

The school grammar approach defines a sentence fragment as a conceptual error—as not having conscious knowledge of the school grammar definition of *sentence.* It demands heavy emphasis on rote memory, and it asks students to behave in ways patently removed from the behaviors of mature writers. (I have never in my life tested a sentence for completeness, and I am a better writer—and probably a better person—as a consequence.) It may be, of course, that some developing writers, at some points in their development, may benefit from such advice—or, more to the point, may think that they benefit—but, as Thomas

Friedman points out in "Teaching Error, Nurturing Confusion" (*CE,* 45 [1983], 390–399), our theory of language tells us that such advice is, at the best, COIK. As the Maine joke has it, about a tourist asking directions from a farmer, "you can't get there from here."

Redefining Error

In the specific case of sentence fragments, Mina P. Shaughnessy (*Errors and Expectations* [New York: Oxford University Press, 1977]) argues that such errors are not conceptual failures at all, but performance errors—mistakes in punctuation. Muriel Harris' error counts support this view ("Mending the Fragmented Free Modifier," *CCC,* 32 [1981], 175–182). Case studies show example after example of errors that occur *because of* instruction—one thinks, for example, of David Bartholmae's student explaining that he added an -*s* to *children* "because it's a plural" ("The Study of Error," *CCC,* 31 [1980], 262). Surveys, such as that by Muriel Harris ("Contradictory Perceptions of the Rules of Writing," *CCC,* 30 [1979], 218–220), and our own observations suggest that students consistently misunderstand such Grammar 4 explanations (COIK, you will recall). For example, from Patrick Hartwell and Robert H. Bentley and from Mike Rose, we have two separate anecdotal accounts of students, cited for punctuating a *because*-clause as a sentence, who have decided to avoid using *because.* More generally, Collette A. Daiute's analysis of errors made by college students shows that errors tend to appear at clause boundaries, suggesting short-term memory load and not conceptual deficiency as a cause of error.[21]

Thus, if we think seriously about error and its relationship to the worship of formal grammar study, we need to attempt some massive dislocation of our traditional thinking, to shuck off our hyperliterate perception of the value of formal rules, and to regain the confidence in the tacit power of unconscious knowledge that our theory of language gives us. Most students, reading their writing aloud, will correct in essence all errors of spelling, grammar, and, by intonation, punctuation, but usually without noticing that what they read departs from what they wrote.[22] And Richard H. Haswell ("Minimal Marking," *CE,* 45 [1983], 600–604) notes that his students correct 61.1% of their errors when they are identified with a simple mark in the margin rather than by error type. Such findings suggest that we need to redefine error, to see it not as a cognitive or linguistic problem, a problem of not knowing a "rule of grammar" (whatever that may mean), but

[21]Hartwell and Bentley, *Some Suggestions for Using Open to Language* (New York: Oxford University Press, 1982), p. 73; Rose, *Writer's Block: The Cognitive Dimension* (Carbondale: Southern Illinois University Press, 1983), p. 99; Daiute, "Psycholinguistic Foundations of the Writing Process," *RTE,* 15 (1981), 5–22.

[22]See Bartholmae, "The Study of Error"; Patrick Hartwell, "The Writing Center and the Paradoxes of Written-Down Speech," in *Writing Centers: Theory and Administration,* ed. Gary Olson (Urbana, Ill.: NCTE, 1984), pp. 48–61; and Sondra Perl, "A Look at Basic Writers in the Process of Composing," in *Basic Writing: A Collection of Essays for Teachers, Researchers, and Administrators* (Urbana, Ill.: NCTE, 1980), pp. 13–32.

rather, following the insight of Robert J. Bracewell ("Writing as a Cognitive Activity," *Visible Language,* 14 [1980], 400–422), as a problem of metacognition and metalinguistic awareness, a matter of accessing knowledges that, to be of any use, learners must have already internalized by means of exposure to the code. (Usage issues—Grammar 3—probably represent a different order of problem. Both Joseph Emonds and Jeffrey Jochnowitz establish that the usage issues we worry most about are linguistically unnatural, departures from the grammar in our heads.)[23]

The notion of metalinguistic awareness seems crucial. The sentence below, created by Douglas R. Hofstadter ("Metamagical Themas," *Scientific American,* 235, No. 1 [1981], 22–32), is offered to clarify that notion; you are invited to examine it for a moment or two before continuing.

Their is four errors in this sentence. Can you find them?

Three errors announce themselves plainly enough, the misspellings of *there* and *sentence* and the use of *is* instead of *are.* (And, just to illustrate the perils of hyperliteracy, let it be noted that, through three years of drafts, I referred to the choice of *is* and *are* as a matter of "subject-verb agreement.") The fourth error resists detection, until one assesses the truth value of the sentence itself—the fourth error is that there are not four errors, only three. Such a sentence (Hofstadter calls it a "self-referencing sentence") asks you to look at it in two ways, simultaneously as statement and as linguistic artifact—in other words, to exercise metalinguistic awareness.

A broad range of cross-cultural studies suggest that metalinguistic awareness is a defining feature of print literacy. Thus Sylvia Scribner and Michael Cole, working with the triliterate Vai of Liberia (variously literate in English, through schooling; in Arabic, for religious purposes; and in an indigenous Vai script, used for personal affairs), find that metalinguistic awareness, broadly conceived, is the only cognitive skill underlying each of the three literacies. The one statistically significant skill shared by literate Vai was the recognition of word boundaries. Moreover, literate Vai tended to answer "yes" when asked (in Vai), "Can you call the sun the moon and the moon the sun?" while illiterate Vai tended to have grave doubts about such metalinguistic play. And in the United States Henry and Lila R. Gleitman report quite different responses by clerical workers and PhD candidates asked to interpret nonsense compounds like "house-bird glass": clerical workers focused on meaning and plausibility (for example, "a house-bird made of glass"), while PhD candidates focused on syntax (for example, "a very small drinking cup for canaries" or "a glass that protects house-birds").[24] More

---

[23]Emonds, *Adjacency in Grammar: The Theory of Language-Particular Rules* (New York: Academic, 1983); and Jochnowitz, "Everybody Likes Pizza, Doesn't He or She?" *American Speech,* 57 (1982), 198–203.

[24]Scribner and Cole, *Psychology of Literacy* (Cambridge, Mass.: Harvard University Press, 1981); Gleitman and Gleitman, "Language Use and Language Judgment," in *Individual Differences in Language Ability and Language Behavior,* ed. Charles J. Fillmore, Daniel Kemper, and William S.-Y. Wang (New York: Academic Press, 1979), pp. 103–126.

general research findings suggest a clear relationship between measures of metalinguistic awareness and measures of literacy level.[25] William Labov, speculating on literacy acquisition in inner-city ghettoes, contrasts "stimulus-bound" and "language-bound" individuals, suggesting that the latter seem to master literacy more easily.[26] The analysis here suggests that the causal relationship works the other way, that it is the mastery of written language that increases one's awareness of language as language.

This analysis has two implications. First, it makes the question of socially nonstandard dialects, always implicit in discussions of teaching formal grammar, into a non-issue.[27] Native speakers of English, regardless of dialect, show tacit mastery of the conventions of Standard English, and that mastery seems to transfer into abstract orthographic knowledge through interaction with print.[28] Developing writers show the same patterning of errors, regardless of dialect.[29]

[25]There are several recent reviews of this developing body of research in psychology and child development: Irene Athey. "Language Development Factors Related to Reading Development," *Journal of Educational Research,* 76 (1983), 197–203; James Flood and Paula Menyuk, "Metalinguistic Development and Reading/Writing Achievement," *Claremont Reading Conference Yearbook,* 46 (1982). 122–132; and the following four essays: David T. Hakes, "The Development of Metalinguistic Abilities: What Develops?." pp. 162–210; Stan A. Kuczaj, II, and Brooke Harbaugh, "What Children Think about the Speaking Capabilities of Other Persons and Things," pp. 211–227; Karen Saywitz and Louise Cherry Wilkinson, "Age-Related Differences in Metalinguistic Awareness," pp. 229–250; and Harriet Salatas Waters and Virginia S. Tinsley. "The Development of Verbal Self-Regulation: Relationships between Language, Cognition, and Behavior." pp. 251–277; all in *Language, Thought, and Culture,* Vol. II of *Language Development,* ed. Stan Kuczaj, Jr. (Hillsdale, N.J.: Lawrence Erlbaum, 1982). See also Joanne R. Nurss, "Research in Review: Linguistic Awareness and Learning to Read," *Young Children,* 35, No. 3 (1980), 57–66.

[26]"Competing Value Systems in Inner City Schools," in *Children In and Out of School: Ethnography and Education,* ed. Perry Gilmore and Allan A. Glatthorn (Washington, D.C.: Center for Applied Linguistics, 1982). pp. 148–171; and "Locating the Frontier between Social and Psychological Factors in Linguistic Structure," in *Individual Differences in Language Ability and Language Behavior,* ed. Fillmore, Kemper, and Wang, pp. 327–340.

[27]See, for example, Thomas Farrell, "IQ and Standard English," *CCC,* 34 (1983), 470–484; and responses by Karen L. Greenberg and Patrick Hartwell, *CCC,* in press.

[28]Jane W. Torrey, "Teaching Standard English to Speakers of Other Dialects," in *Applications of Linguistics: Selected Papers of the Second International Conference of Applied Linguistics,* ed. G. E. Perren and J. L. M. Trim (Cambridge, Mass.: Cambridge University Press, 1971), pp. 423–428; James W. Beers and Edmund H. Henderson, "A Study of the Developing Orthographic Concepts among First Graders," *RTE,* 11 (1977), 133–148.

[29]See the error counts of Samuel A. Kirschner and G. Howard Poteet, "Non-Standard English Usage in the Writing of Black, White, and Hispanic Remedial English Students in an Urban Community College," *RTE,* 7 (1973), 351–355; and Marilyn Sternglass, "Close Similarities in Dialect Features of Black and White College Students in Remedial Composition Classes," *TESOL Quarterly,* 8 (1974), 271–283.

Studies of reading and of writing suggest that surface features of spoken dialect are simply irrelevant to mastering print literacy.[30] Print is a complex cultural code—or better yet, a system of codes—and my bet is that, regardless of instruction, one masters those codes from the top down, from pragmatic questions of voice, tone, audience, register, and rhetorical strategy, not from the bottom up, from grammar to usage to fixed forms of organization.

Second, this analysis forces us to posit multiple literacies, used for multiple purposes, rather than a single static literacy, engraved in "rules of grammar." These multiple literacies are evident in cross-cultural studies.[31] They are equally evident when we inquire into the uses of literacy in American communities.[32] Further, given that students, at all levels, show widely variant interactions with print literacy, there would seem to be little to do with grammar—with Grammar 2 or with Grammar 4—that we could isolate as a basis for formal instruction.[33]

[30]For reading, see the massive study by Kenneth S. Goodman and Yetta M. Goodman, *Reading of American Children whose Language Is a Stable Rural Dialect of English or a Language other than English* (Washington, D.C.: National Institute of Education Final Report, 1978) ERIC 175 754; and the overview by Rudine Sims, "Dialect and Reading: Toward Redefining the Issues," in *Reader Meets Author/Bridging the Gap: A Psycholinguistic and Sociolinguistic Approach,* ed. Judith A. Langer and M. Tricia Smith-Burke (Newark, Del.: International Reading Association, 1982), pp. 222–232. For writing, see Patrick Hartwell, "Dialect Interference in Writing: A Critical View," *RTE,* 14 (1980), 101–118; and the anthology edited by Barry M. Kroll and Roberta J. Vann, *Exploring Speaking-Writing Relationships: Connections and Contrasts* (Urbana, Ill.: NCTE, 1981).

[31]See, for example, Eric A. Havelock, *The Literary Revolution in Greece and its Cultural Conquences* (Princeton, N.J.: Princeton University Press, 1982); Lesley Milroy on literacy in Dublin, *Language and Social Networks* (Oxford: Basil Blackwell, 1980); Ron Scollon and Suzanne B. K. Scollon on literacy in central Alaska, *Interethnic Communication: An Athabascan Case* (Austin, Tex.: Southwest Educational Development Laboratory Working Papers in Sociolinguistics, No. 59, 199) ERIC 175 276; and Scribner and Cole on literacy in Liberia, *Psychology of Literacy* (see footnote 24).

[32]See, for example, the anthology edited by Deborah Tannen, *Spoken and Written Language: Exploring Orality and Literacy* (Norwood, N.J.: Ablex, 1982); and Shirley Brice Heath's continuing work: "Protean Shapes in Literacy Events: Ever-Shifting Oral and Literate Traditions," in *Spoken and Written Language,* pp. 91–117; *Ways with Words: Language, Life and Work in Communities and Classrooms* (New York: Cambridge University Press, 1983); and "What No Bedtime Story Means," *Language in Society,* 11 (1982), 49–76.

[33]For studies at the elementary level, see Dell H. Hymes, et al., eds., *Ethnographic Monitoring of Children's Acquisition of Reading/Language Arts Skills In and Out of the Classroom* (Washington, D.C.: National Institute of Education Final Report. 1981) ERIC 208 096. For studies at the secondary level, see James L. Collins and Michael M. Williamson, "Spoken Language and Semantic Abbreviation in Writing," *RTE,* 15 (1981), 23–36. And for studies at the college level, see Patrick Hartwell and Gene LoPresti. "Sentence Combining as Kid-Watching," in *Sentence Combining: Toward a Rhetorical Perspective,* ed. Donald A. Daiker, Andrew Kerek, and Max Morenberg (Carbondale: Southern Illinois University Press, in press).

Grammar 5: Stylistic Grammar

Similarly, when we turn to Grammar 5, "grammatical terms used in the interest of teaching prose style," so central to Martha Kolln's argument for teaching formal grammar, we find that the grammar issue is simply beside the point. There are two fully-articulated positions about "stylistic grammar," which I will label "romantic" and "classic," following Richard Lloyd-Jones and Richard E. Young.[34] The romantic position is that stylistic grammars, though perhaps useful for teachers, have little place in the teaching of composition, for students must struggle with and through language toward meaning. This position rests on a theory of language ultimately philosophical rather than linguistic (witness, for example, the contempt for linguists in Ann Berthoff's *The Making of Meaning: Metaphors, Models, and Maxims for Writing Teachers* [Montclair, N.J.: Boynton/Cook, 1981]); it is articulated as a theory of style by Donald A. Murray and, on somewhat different grounds (that stylistic grammars encourage overuse of the monitor), by Ian Pringle. The classic position, on the other hand, is that we can find ways to offer developing writers helpful suggestions about prose style, suggestions such as Francis Christensen's emphasis on the cumulative sentence, developed by observing the practice of skilled writers, and Joseph Williams' advice about predication, developed by psycholinguistic studies of comprehension.[35] James A. Berlin's recent survey of composition theory (*CE,* 45 [1982], 765–777) probably understates the gulf between these two positions and the radically different conceptions of language that underlie them, but it does establish that they share an overriding assumption in common: that one learns to control the language of print by manipulating language in meaningful contexts, not by learning about language in isolation, as by the study of formal grammar. Thus even classic theorists, who choose to present a vocabulary of style to students, do so only as a vehicle for encouraging productive control of communicative structures.

We might put the matter in the following terms. Writers need to develop skills at two levels. One, broadly rhetorical, involves communication in meaningful contexts (the strategies, registers, and procedures of discourse across a range of modes, audiences, contexts, and purposes). The other, broadly metalinguistic rather than linguistic, involves active manipulation of language with conscious attention to surface form. This second level may be developed tacitly, as a natural

[34]Lloyd-Jones, "Romantic Revels—I Am Not You," *CCC,* 23 (1972), 251–271; and Young, "Concepts of Art and the Teaching of Writing," in *The Rhetorical Tradition and Modern Writing,* ed. James J. Murphy (New York: Modern Language Association, 1982), pp. 130–141.

[35]For the romantic position, see Ann E. Berthoff, "Tolstoy, Vygotsky, and the Making of Meaning," *CCC,* 29 (1978), 249–255; Kenneth Dowst, "The Epistemic Approach," in *Eight Approaches to Teaching Composition,* ed. Timothy Donovan and Ben G. McClellan (Urbana, Ill.: NCTE, 1980), pp. 65–85; Peter Elbow, "The Challenge for Sentence Combining"; and Donald Murray, "Following Language toward Meaning," both in *Sentence Combining: Toward a Rhetorical Perspective* (in press: see footnote 33); and Ian Pringle, "Why Teach Style? A Review-Essay," *CCC,* 34 (1983), 91–98.

adjunct to developing rhetorical competencies—I take this to be the position of romantic theorists. It may be developed formally, by manipulating language for stylistic effect, and such manipulation may involve, for pedagogical continuity, a vocabulary of style. But it is primarily developed by any kind of language activity that enhances the awareness of language as language.[36] David T. Hakes, summarizing the research on metalinguistic awareness, notes how far we are from understanding this process:

> the optimal conditions for becoming metalinguistically competent involve growing up in a literate environment with adult models who are themselves metalinguistically competent and who foster the growth of that competence in a variety of ways as yet little understood. ("The Development of Metalinguistic Abilities," p. 205: see footnote 25)

Such a model places language, at all levels, at the center of the curriculum, but not as "necessary categories and labels" (Kolln, "Closing the Books on Alchemy," p. 150), but as literal stuff, verbal clay, to be molded and probed, shaped and reshaped, and, above all, enjoyed.

The Tradition of Experimental Research

Thus, when we turn back to experimental research on the value of formal grammar instruction, we do so with firm predictions given us by our theory of language. Our theory would predict that formal grammar instruction, whether instruction in scientific grammar or instruction in "the common school grammar," would have little to do with control over surface correctness nor with quality of writing. It would predict that any form of active involvement with language would be preferable to instruction in rules or definitions (or incantations). In essence, this is what the research tells us. In 1893, the Committee of Ten (*Report of the Committee of Ten on Secondary School Studies* [Washington, D.C.: U.S. Government Printing Office, 1893]) put grammar at the center of the English curriculum, and its report established the rigidly sequential mode of instruction common for the last century. But the committee explicitly noted that grammar instruction did not aid correctness, arguing instead that it improved the ability to think logically (an argument developed from the role of the "grammarian" in the classical rhetorical tradition, essentially a teacher of literature—see, for example, the etymology of *grammar* in the *Oxford English Dictionary*).

But Franklin S. Hoyt, in a 1906 experiment, found no relationship between the study of grammar and the ability to think logically; his research led him to conclude what I am constrained to argue more than seventy-five years later, that there is no "relationship between a knowledge of technical grammar and the

---

For the classic position, see Christensen's "A Generative Rhetoric of the Sentence"; and Joseph Williams' "Defining Complexity." *CE,* 41 (1979), 595–609; and his *Style: Ten Lessons in Clarity and Grace* (see footnote 9).

ability to use English and to interpret language" ("The Place of Grammar in the Elementary Curriculum," *Teachers College Record,* 7 [1906], 483–484). Later studies, through the 1920s, focused on the relationship of knowledge of grammar and ability to recognize error; experiments reported by James Boraas in 1917 and by William Asker in 1923 are typical of those that reported no correlation. In the 1930s, with the development of the functional grammar movement, it was common to compare the study of formal grammar with one form or another of active manipulation of language; experiments by I. O. Ash in 1935 and Ellen Frogner in 1939 are typical of studies showing the superiority of active involvement with language.[37] In a 1959 article, "Grammar in Language Teaching" (*Elementary English,* 36 [1959], 412–421), John J. DeBoer noted the consistency of these findings.

> The impressive fact is . . . that in all these studies, carried out in places and at times far removed from each other, often by highly experienced and disinterested investigators, the results have been consistently negative so far as the value of grammar in the improvement of language expression is concerned. (p. 417)

In 1960 Ingrid M. Strom, reviewing more than fifty experimental studies, came to a similarly strong and unqualified conclusion:

> direct methods of instruction, focusing on writing activities and the structuring of ideas, are more efficient in teaching sentence structure, usage, punctuation, and other related factors than are such methods as nomenclature drill, diagramming, and rote memorization of grammatical rules.[38]

In 1963 two research reviews appeared, one by Braddock, Lloyd-Jones, and Schorer, cited at the beginning of this paper, and one by Henry C. Meckel, whose conclusions, though more guarded, are in essential agreement.[39] In 1969 J. Stephen Sherwin devoted one-fourth of his *Four Problems in Teaching English:*

---

[36]Courtney B. Cazden and David K. Dickinson, "Language and Education: Standardization versus Cultural Pluralism," in *Language in the USA,* ed. Charles A. Ferguson and Shirley Brice Heath (New York: Cambridge University Press, 1981), pp. 446–468; and Carol Chomsky. "Developing Facility with Language Structure," in *Discovering Language with Children,* ed. Gay Su Pinnell Urbana, Ill.: NCTE, 1980), pp. 56–59.

[37]Boraas, "Formal English Grammar and the Practical Mastery of English." Diss. University of Illinois. 1917; Asker, "Does Knowledge of Grammar Function?" *School and Society,* 17 (27 January 1923), 109–111: Ash, "An Experimental Evaluation of the Stylistic Approach in Teaching Composition in the Junior High School," *Journal of Experimental Education,* 4 (1935), 54–62; and Frogner, "A Study of the Relative Efficacy of a Grammatical and a Thought Approach to the Improvement of Sentence Structure in Grades Nine and Eleven," *School Review,* 47 (1939), 663–675.

[38]"Research on Grammar and Usage and Its Implications for Teaching Writing," *Bulletin of the School of Education,* Indiana University, 36 (1960), pp. 13–14.

[39]Meckel. "Research on Teaching Composition and Literature," in *Handbook of Research on Teaching,* ed. N. L. Gage (Chicago: Rand McNally, 1963), pp. 966–1006.

A Critique of Research (Scranton, Penn.: International Textbook, 1969) to the grammar issue, concluding that "instruction in formal grammar is an ineffective way to help students achieve proficiency in writing" (p. 135). Some early experiments in sentence combining, such as those by Donald R. Bateman and Frank J. Zidonnis and by John C. Mellon, showed improvement in measures of syntactic complexity with instruction in transformational grammar keyed to sentence combining practice. But a later study by Frank O'Hare achieved the same gains with no grammar instruction, suggesting to Sandra L. Stotsky and to Richard Van de Veghe that active manipulation of language, not the grammar unit, explained the earlier results.[40] More recent summaries of research—by Elizabeth I. Haynes, Hillary Taylor Holbrook, and Marcia Farr Whiteman—support similar conclusions. Indirect evidence for this position is provided by surveys reported by Betty Bamberg in 1978 and 1981, showing that time spent in grammar instruction in high school is the least important factor, of eight factors examined, in separating regular from remedial writers at the college level.[41]

More generally, Patrick Scott and Bruce Castner, in "Reference Sources for Composition Research: A Practical Survey" (*CE*, 45 [1983], 756–768), note that much current research is not informed by an awareness of the past. Put simply, we are constrained to reinvent the wheel. My concern here has been with a far more serious problem: that too often the wheel we reinvent is square.

It is, after all, a question of power. Janet Emig, developing a consensus from composition research, and Aaron S. Carton and Lawrence V. Castiglione, developing the implications of language theory for education, come to the same conclusion: that the thrust of current research and theory is to take power from the teacher and to give that power to the learner.[42] At no point in the English

[40]Bateman and Zidonis, *The Effect of a Study of Transformational Grammar on the Writing of Ninth and Tenth Graders* (Urbana, Ill.: NCTE, 1966); Mellon, *Transformational Sentence Combining: A Method for Enhancing the Development of Fluency in English Composition* (Urbana, Ill.: NCTE, 1969); O'Hare, *Sentence-Combining: Improving Student Writing without Formal Grammar Instruction* (Urbana, Ill.: NCTE, 1971): Stotsky, "Sentence-Combining as a Curricular Activity: Its Effect on Written Language Development," *RTE*, 9 (1975), 30–72; and Van de Veghe, "Research in Written Composition: Fifteen Years of Investigation," ERIC 157 095.

[41]Haynes, "Using Research in Preparing to Teach Writing," *English Journal*, 69, No. 1 (1978), 82–88; Holbrook, "ERIC/RCS Report: Whither (Wither) Grammar," *Language Arts*, 60 (1983), 259–263; Whiteman, "What We Can Learn from Writing Research," *Theory into Practice*, 19 (1980), 150–156; Bamberg, "Composition in the Secondary English Curriculum: Some Current Trends and Directions for the Eighties," *RTE*, 15 (1981), 257–266; and "Composition Instruction Does Make a Difference: A Comparison of the High School Preparation of College Freshmen in Regular and Remedial English Classes," *RTE*, 12 (1978), 47–59.

[42]Emig, "Inquiry Paradigms and Writing," *CCC*, 33 (1982), 64–75; Carton and Castiglione, "Educational Linguistics: Defining the Domain," in *Psycholinguistic Research: Implications and Applications*, ed. Doris Aaronson and Robert W. Rieber (Hillsdale, N.J.: Lawrence Erlbaum, 1979), pp. 497–520.

curriculum is the question of power more blatantly posed than in the issue of formal grammar instruction. It is time that we, as teachers, formulate theories of language and literacy and let those theories guide our teaching, and it is time that we, as researchers, move on to more interesting areas of inquiry.

Additional Sources

Baron, Dennis. *Grammar and Good Taste: Reforming the American Language.* New Haven: Yale University Press, 1982.

Traces the history of grammar reform in America, arguing that much of the reform appeals to internally contradictory theories of language acquisition.

Kolln, Martha. "Closing the Books on Alchemy." *College Composition & Communication* Vol. 32, 2 (May 1981): 139–51.

Argues that composition studies has too quickly concluded that grammar instruction is futile.

Lazere, Donald. "Orality, Literacy, and Standard English." *Journal of Basic Writing* Vol. 10, 2 (Fall 1991): 87–98.

Discusses the problems which many basic writers have in regard to literacy and orality when coming to college.

Weaver, Constance. *Teaching Grammar in Context.* Portsmouth, NH: Boynton/Cook Publishers, Inc., 1996.

Recommends specific practices for teaching grammar and usage in the context of writing; while intended for secondary teachers, the review of the controversy and recommendations are useful for college teachers.

Chapter 7

Grading and Responding

Probably the least pleasant aspect of directing a composition program is dealing with student complaints, but it is also a very informative aspect. In my experience, most complaints involve the ways in which the instructor has responded to the student's work, and those complaints are often as much about the comments as the grades. Generally, the complaints are the result of miscommunication, or mismatched understandings, of the task of teaching writing, or of the shift between the standards of high school and college. I have found these complaints worth thinking about carefully, for they raise the problem of the teacher's own rhetoric. To put it very simply, we are in an awkward situation if we claim to be teaching students how to express themselves effectively in writing when we cannot express our own reactions to their papers. Yet, we often end up in complicated miscommunications because we and our students have different understandings of the rhetorical situation.

For instance, in regard to grades, many students expect a certain grade simply because they have always gotten that grade. I had one student explain to me that she deserved an 'A' on a paper because she had stayed up *all* night to write it. Just as in all their other courses, students can find it difficult to understand that college writing courses are harder than those in high school, and that they must work harder to get the same grades.

In addition, many students assume that an 'A' is a kind of default grade, and they read the comments on the paper as defending the degree of deviation from that default. Thus they think that fixing every marginal comment will result in an 'A' paper. Or, they see marginal comments as editorial commands, and they believe that substantially revising a paper means changing a word or two in every single place there is a comment in the margin—such changes, they will often argue, should earn them an 'A' since they have done everything they were told to do. (For example, in the midst of a conversation with one student who was explaining that he thought that he deserved an 'A' because he had made a change in every place there was a note in the margin, I pointed out that the teacher had specified in her course handouts that "minimal revision will result in no change in grade." The student believed that "minimal" revision would be responding to very few of the teacher's comments, but he had substantially revised because he had responded to all of them.) Teachers, on the other hand, often see their comments on papers as recommendations for further revisions. They rarely remark on every aspect that needs to be changed (since doing so simply overwhelms the students) and may worry more about "appropriating," or defining the outcome of, the student text than defending the grade. For some teachers and some programs, a 'B' is a kind of default grade, and for others a 'C' is the grade given to an average paper that follows directions.

There are two very different issues in regard to responding to student writing: how to grade the work and how to comment on it. Obviously, the division is somewhat arbitrary, in that grades are a kind of comment, and it is generally expected that the comments will bear some sort of relation to the grade. Still, it is worth trying to retain the distinction, for the distinction can help prevent certain important kinds of confusion.

Peter Elbow, in his very helpful essay "Embracing Contraries," describes the paradoxical roles that a teacher must simultaneously fulfill: While we must be encouraging to students (what Elbow calls the coach), we must also be honest with them by assessing their papers accurately (a role that Elbow calls guardian). Although it is possible to quibble with the specific metaphors that Elbow uses, the general sense that we have obligations in two directions is true.

I have found much of the work done by Edward White and others on program assessment to be very helpful in thinking about that latter role (which I would not call a guardian role). What White and others have argued is that, for assessment to be meaningful, the program must have clearly articulated goals, and there must be an assessment method that can measure progress toward those goals. For instance, if one of the program goals is to teach "critical thinking," a grammar and usage or library skills test will not work—probably some kind of portfolio assessment is the best route. Without any kind of assessment, the program directors cannot make informed decisions about what changes (if any) should be made to the program.

Similarly, for grades to be meaningful, a course (or assignment) needs to have clearly articulated goals, and the grading method must be one that can measure progress toward those goals. If the goal of the course is critical thinking, a grading method that is entirely determined by effort (such as simply how much work a student turned in on time) or a method that evaluates other skills (such as having the grade entirely determined by lack of usage errors) would be useless because teachers could not make informed decisions about what teaching strategies to use, and students could not make good decisions about how to alter their writing processes.

Most programs issue some kind of general guidelines for grades, but it is still extremely useful for an instructor to try to specify his or her more specific goals for each assignment. Trying then to describe in some detail how those goals will be measured will also help teachers reflect thoughtfully on their grading. Many instructors, in fact, include those statements of goals and methods of measurement in their assignment sheets—this strategy helps students not only understand their grades better, but apply their energy appropriately during the writing process. In other words, if the number of sources that a student uses is an important measurement of fulfilling the assignment, then letting the students know that they will need multiple sources is helpful. If, however, the number of sources is irrelevant, but how those sources are handled is important, that distinction should be specified.

Identifying one's goals can help an instructor decide about his or her strategies for commenting on papers. As Elaine Lees notes in the following essay, "Evaluating Student Writing," there are numerous strategies for commenting on papers, and a person is likely to do some combination of the ones she describes. I have found that what she calls "emoting" generates the most complaints—with some reason. The authority relations are already such that students in a class tend to feel imposed upon—emoting to a student (except for enthusiasm) often feels like a personal attack. It is, at best, a kind of venting that should be done toward inanimate objects, and, at worst, a strategy which is likely to lead to a personally antagonistic relationship with students. I have found it interesting that students read other sorts of reactions as emoting. For instance, students will often read questions as snide (so that they read "What do you mean here?" as "What do you mean here?!"). In general, students read ironic comments as sarcastic, and they see comments as highly directive. One of the more common sorts of complaints I have had to handle involves students feeling genuinely attacked or insulted by a comment that I am certain the instructor never imagined would be taken that way.

Thus effectively done peer reviews become a teacher's ally when commenting on papers. Describing what a paper does is most effective when it is coupled with a description of the reader's response. This strategy takes less time than one might think if there are peer reviews to which the instructor can refer: "I notice that all of your reviewers got lost at this point in the paper. It might be because you have raised a new topic, and the connection isn't made clear until the next page."

Evaluating Student Writing
Elaine O. Lees

A sentence may be simple; no writer is. In light of this knowledge, how ought I to envision my responsibility as a commentator on my students' writing? When I sit down at my desk to confront papers which open with sentences like "High school can be a time of total banality for many people," what way of envisioning my role will help me help the writer of the sentence to become a better composer? Familiar terms like "marking," "correcting," and even "evaluating" seem inadequate to describe what I might do with such writing, and yet a term like "counseling," which has the virtue of acknowledging that writing somehow has to do with writers' experience of themselves, clearly reaches beyond my area of expertise. Where, then, can I begin with such papers? On what bases can I decide what their writers need to hear?

Let me examine some of the complexities of responding to student writing by referring to a paper that was written by a graduate student but is not very different in kind from writing I regularly receive in undergraduate General Writing classes. The writer, whom I'll call Edwin Fisher, had been assigned the problem of reviewing Strunk and White's *The Elements of Style* for a journal in his field. His task was to review the book in such a way as to define what a review could be at its best; he was to produce a critical paper that met his own critical standards. Here is part of what he wrote in answer to the assignment:

> William Strunk sounds off from on high throughout his "little book." He throws down such aphorisms as "do not overwrite," "do not explain too much" (which he doesn't), and my favorite, "be clear." Along this road of rigid dogma, Strunk shows himself to be a man who is not only sadly dated, but banality incarnate.
>
> Strunk advises "to achieve style, begin by affecting none—that is, place yourself in the background." It seems to me that advice such as this would produce sterile, lifeless prose. The language of the dead. If a writer isn't supposed to show through his or her writing then who is, Professor Strunk?

The paper continues, in the same vein, for three pages:

As an infinite number of lines can be passed through a given point, so in the marking of papers, the fact that an infinite number of comments can touch upon what appears in a paper may not be sufficient grounds for writing them in the margin. In order to suggest how comments might work in the margin of Edwin Fisher's paper, let me arbitrarily divide the activity of commenting into seven modes—*correcting, emoting, describing, suggesting, questioning, reminding,* and *assigning*—and examine a response to the paper in each of these modes. After examining these responses and the comments I actually wrote on Fisher's paper, I shall return to the problem of the teacher's role as commentator.

Correcting. By "correcting" I mean indicating that what the student has written is erroneous, by inserting a form the teacher believes to be preferable. There is not very much to correct, in the narrowest sense, in the passage from Edwin Fisher's paper. If I were only to make the few corrections possible, I would perhaps convey some factual information to the student, but as others have already pointed out,[1] I would also run a number of risks. By emphasizing the importance of editorial tidiness, I would encourage the student to try to edit fully as he generated sentences. I would then have helped to create an instant writer's block. Worse, I would be suggesting to Edwin Fisher that the best way to improve his writing would be to eliminate a relatively minor set of errors by mastering certain stylistic conventions. Although mastering those conventions is something he ought to do, his doing so would take this composition very little distance from where it began.

Emoting. I might come closer to getting at what bothers me in this paper by giving Fisher a piece of my mind. I might vent my emotions. For our purposes, let me suppose I wrote next to the paragraphs cited above, "I'm offended and bored by all this." Such an approach, applied to any tone, I'll call "emoting." The advantage of emoting over correcting is that it suggests that teachers have feelings as they read student papers and that these feelings are often of the bread-and-butter sort which students and teachers occasionally pretend not to have. But comments that stop at emoting, although they are in one sense about the paper, are more obviously about the teacher. Unless further elaborated on or otherwise given a context, they invite the response, "So what?"—a response that applies as much to the "Nice!" or "I agree" in the margin as to the "I'm bored." And then I am stuck with the job of convincing the student that my boredom or agreement is more than "just an opinion"—that it indicates something he might find worth knowing about the paper as a piece of writing.

Describing. To emphasize what I think is worth knowing about the writing, I might shift my focus to the paper itself. In the case of Edwin Fisher's paragraphs, I might write, "This section is swaggering stuff, exaggerated and imprecise in its attack on Strunk." This comment is certainly likelier than my earlier ones to pique the student, for here I have pointed at what I believe to be the cause of my emoting rather than at the emoting itself. I've asserted that the *paper* behaves in a certain way—namely, swaggering—independent of the possibly crackpot reactions I as a reader may have to it. This comment will sting, then, but it is also likely to do more than that. I am apt to hear the terms "swaggering" and "exaggerated," "precise" and "imprecise" in future classroom discussions of papers, since students pick up the terms their composition teachers use to talk about

---

[1]See, for example, David Bartholomae, "Teaching Ourselves to Teach Basic Writing," *PTCE Bulletin,* (April, 1977), pp. 18–19; Peter Elbow, *Writing without Teachers* (New York: Oxford Univ. Press, 1973), pp. 4–7; Janet Emig, *The Composing Processes of Twelfth Graders* (Urbana, IL: NCTE, 1971), pp. 99–100; and John Warnock, "New Rhetoric and the Grammar of Pedagogy," *Freshman English News,* (Fall, 1976), pp. 15–17.

writing, just as they pick up terms like "dodecaphonic" and "quark" to talk about what matters in their other courses. Acquiring a set of descriptive terms is, after all, a way of beginning to understand. Since my students' understanding of writing is a function of the language they use to describe it, I'd be wise to choose my terms cautiously. But even when I do so, I cannot assume that by understanding how his paper may be described, Fisher will understand how to produce a paper that may be described differently. My description of a paper, even if understood by the student, may be irrelevant to his needs as a writer.

Suggesting. I may attempt to address Fisher's needs more directly by offering editorial suggestions outright. I might write, "Make more of an effort to be fair to Strunk here. After all, he was not 'banality incarnate' to White and many of his other students. You'd better explain what you mean by 'banality' if you expect to make a convincing case against the book." A teacher's suggestions may be valuable at some stages in a student's and a paper's development to increase the strategies available to a writer. But problems enter when teacherly suggestions become merely blueprints for rewriters of particular papers. The more detailed those blueprints are and the more divorced their language is from the principles of structure that they embody, the less they will be transferable, and the likelier they are to produce a better revised paper without producing a better writer.

Questioning. Perhaps I could take a step toward producing a better writer by questioning Edwin Fisher on how the sentences he's written relate to what he now believes. I could try, through questioning, to lead him to see how little he has used his writing to discover something he couldn't have said when he began the paper. By writing, "But the situation isn't as simple as you suggest here, is it? Who decides whether a writer is 'showing through'?" I might begin the process of turning his statements over in his mind. Comments that ask real, and not rhetorical, questions of a student acknowledge that writing can and ought to be worth thinking about. They suggest that students ought to ask themselves, as they write, if they're saying exactly what they think they mean—on one level, in order to answer a teacher's possible inquiries but on another level, to acknowledge and address the complexities of their own thought.

Reminding. I might expand the context of my response to Edwin Fisher's paper by echoing words that students have used in class discussions, words that have become metaphors rather than wisecracks we share in common. If Edwin Fisher has taken part in inventing a phrase like "the Orientation Week Scholar" for voices that substitute bravado for understanding, he may be able to see from a comment like "the Scholar again?" that his paper has fallen into a familiar trap. And something else may be gained in the bargain: when what has been said in class reappears in comments on papers, students come to recognize a coherence among parts of the course. What they say in class then has something to do with what the instructor notices in papers and, in turn, with what appears in the margins.

Assigning. Assigning, the final mode of responding, is seldom regarded as part of commenting on papers at all. Yet creating another assignment based on what a student has written is one way to assure that the student's revisions are just that: ways of reseeing a subject, ways of using what has been said already to discover how to say something new. The importance of this method lies in its forcing students to reconsider what they have written and thus to treat a paper as if it represents a stage in the growth of ideas rather than the only crystallization of them.

Of the seven kinds of responding I've examined, the first three—*correcting, emoting,* and *describing*—put the burden of work on the teacher; the next three— *suggesting, questioning,* and *reminding*—shift some of that burden to the student. The last mode—*assigning*—provides a way to discover how much of that burden the student has taken.

My actual written response to Edwin Fisher's paper, like most responses I write, used a combination of approaches. Next to his sentence, "If a writer isn't supposed to show through his or her writing then who is, Professor Strunk?" I questioned: "But the process isn't as simple as either Strunk or you suggest, is it?"[2] Then I described and questioned again: "For instance, it's possible to turn the statement back on this paper. What sort of writer is speaking in this paper? Do you believe *you* 'show through' in it? What qualities of yours show through? Which ones don't? Which ones are you?" Finally, I assigned: "Write two replies to this paper. Imagine they will also appear in that scholarly journal, as letters to the editor. In the first reply, discuss the paper in the spirit and manner of the 'Edwin Fisher' created in these pages. In the second reply, based on what you've discovered in preparing the first, create another 'Edwin Fisher'—one whose voice would not be inappropriately described as 'powerful' and 'wise.'"

Through these comments and this assignment, I attempted to lead Edwin Fisher to identify the standards he had set for himself as a writer and to compare them with another set of standards I believed he had—standards of "wisdom" and "power" as he would apply those terms to writing. In my note, I hoped to confront him with the problem of reconciling the paper's simplistic notion of "showing through" with the damning of himself which had to occur if he meant what he said. I wrote nothing else on the paper.

Yet the temptation to write a full critique of the paper was difficult to resist. Although for years I heard it said that a teacher need not mark "everything" on a single paper—every lapse in sense, every instance of dead prose, every error in grammar, spelling, or punctuation—I nonetheless clung to the belief that it was somehow safer to do so, as my aunt believes it's safer to rinse the cups when they come from the dishwasher and iron every pair of Levi's she washes. A teacher marks things because they're THERE.

Yet I suspect that much of what can be said about a paper, many of the lines that can be passed through it, make no fresh contact with the student writer and are therefore unnecessary to put into comments. Much emoting, correcting, and describing now seems to me to fall into the same category as Levi's-pressing; not exactly wrong but useless. Worse, since both students and teachers seem to share the presumption that teachers should say what they say for the best of rea-

[2]Had I been pressed for time, I would simply have put an asterisk next to this section of the paper and added my comments at the end.

sons, students may come to assume from certain kinds of comments that learning to write is a matter of learning grammar or learning to describe papers in the way a teacher does or learning what makes a teacher want to write "Nice!" in the margin. Learning these things may, and perhaps on occasion must, accompany learning to write; but since none is at the heart of the enterprise of writing, none is what students ought to be encouraged to put their faith in. By heavily editing a student's paper, a teacher is in a real sense appropriating the student's primary job.[3] Of course we want students to learn how to do such things, as we want them to write grammatically and to produce papers we can describe as "excellent" and "powerful"—but to do so in order to say more eloquently what each alone has to say. Our covering students' papers with suggestions and corrections is not the same thing as leading students to revise for themselves, and—although both activities may be part of a teacher's repertoire—the difference between them is crucial.

In responding to student papers, then, we deal with a paradox: the paper is the only tangible evidence we have of students as writers' and yet, at least in one sense, to base our comments solely on that evidence is to assume that the students have already succeeded in creating personas which suitably represent them—that they have accomplished, in other words, what they have come to us to learn. Yet this paradox is also the source of contrasts on which a teacher may draw in comments. The teacher confronting papers like Edwin Fisher's can foster through comments a tension among predications; a tension between what students have said and who they believe they are; a tension between what they have written and the better, but so far unseen, things they may be capable of writing.

By responding to a paper in this way, teachers accomplish something else. We imply by our example that students need not accept what their work so far suggests about their ability to compose. A serious writer who had made ten tries at a sentence, all of which are clearly not "it," clearly not the sentence the writer had tried to write, faces a body of evidence that looks dishearteningly like grounds for a perfect induction. Ten sentences, all not "it," imply a writer who does not produce "it"; and no additional try before the right one will change the nature of that evidence. But serious writers can't afford to practice that kind of empiricism. Student writers, in learning to be serious, need to learn how to hope—how to ignore the evidence that their ability has so far produced and believe in the possibility of producing something else. Among other things, such belief is a skill: it can be learned, both by students and by teachers, and it ought to be. For in addition to the mastery of syntactic skills and rhetorical strategies, serious writing requires, as its driving force, an ability to believe in the face of evidence to the contrary that one can find language for something that has not yet been said. In precipitating the search among words for one's own meanings, such a belief reaches to the heart of what writing does for writers. We mislead students about the nature of the enterprise if we do not give it room to work.

[3]On the responsibilities of students in such matters, see E. D. Hirsch, Jr., *The Philosophy of Composition* (Chicago: Univ. of Chicago Press, 1977), p. 87; and Warnock, p. 16.

Additional Sources

Anson, Chris M., Ed. *Writing and Response: Theory, Practice, and Research.* Urbana: NCTE, 1989.

Collection of sixteen articles on responding to student writing in various fora (tutoring sessions, electronic media, traditional settings).

Connors, Robert J., and Andrea A. Lunsford. "Teachers' Rhetorical Comments on Student Papers." *College Composition & Communication* Vol. 44, 2 (May 1993): 200–23.

Discusses recurrent patterns in teachers' comments on papers; based on a study involving 3,000 student papers.

Brannon, Lil, and Cy Knoblauch. "On Students' Right to Their Own Texts: A Model of Teacher Response." *CCC* 33 (May 1982): 157–66.

Argues that instructors too often impose their own notion of the "ideal text" on student writing.

Elbow, Peter. "Embracing Contraries in the Teaching Process." *College English* 45 (April 1983): 327–39.

Argues that effective response to student work necessarily involved adopting contrary positions as both guardian of academic standards and student coach.

Sommers, Nancy. "Responding to Student Writing." *CCC* (1982): 148–56.

Argues that a study of teacher comments indicates a problem with lack of specificity.

Part III
Writing Genres and Assignments

Chapter 8
Personal Essays and Exploratory Writing

Many programs and textbooks begin first-year composition courses with personal writing, and there are good reasons for doing so. As Elbow argues, learning private writing and reflection can be a necessary step in learning to write and think about public issues; he notes that some "students often lose interest in an issue that had intrigued them—just because they don't find other people who are interested in talking about it and haven't learned to talk reflectively to *themselves* about it". Students often enjoy talking about themselves, so they often take an interest in the exploratory writing assignment, an interest which may translate into increased interest in the rhetorical dimensions of their writing. And because they are most familiar with the narrative structure that a personal essay often involves, students have an easy time organizing their expressive papers. In addition, some theorists argue that beginning with personal writing enables students to learn about peer review—students know how to read personal writing, and if the intention of the piece is simply to interest an audience of peers, the peer groups can provide useful advice.

There are, however, serious issues in regard to teaching personal writing. In their essay "The Ethics of Requiring Students to Write about Their Personal Lives" (which is included in this chapter), Susan Swartzlander, Diana Pace, and Virginia Stamler discuss the serious ethical and psychological problems of assignments that require students to write about deeply emotional issues. These problems range from instructors who are not trained in psychological counseling behaving like "frustrated therapists" to students who drop out of college due to their discomfort with their writing courses. It is a fundamental precept of counseling that a person must choose to engage it—certain kinds of personal writing assignments can unintentionally violate that precept. There are additional and particularly troubling problems if an instructor is giving these sorts of assignments in a situation in which there will be heavy emphasis on peer review.

As Swartzlander, Pace, and Stamler note, these various potential problems do not preclude personal writing, but they do indicate that writing the assignment requires sensitivity. Perhaps the most important point is simply that personal and emotional are not necessarily the same thing—while emotional topics do sometimes inspire good writing, they sometimes prevent it. Here Elbow's point about inhibiting versus inviting audiences is relevant: Personal writing assignments can be inviting or they can be inhibiting.

Swartzlander, Pace, and Stamler warn against *requiring* that students write about emotional issues; however, they do not suggest that students be prohibited from doing so. Others have argued that personal writing is not appropriate in college writing courses, especially if those courses are supposed to teach academic writing. There is the possibility that too much emphasis on the personal will fail to prepare students for the writing they will have to do in other courses—few of which will permit, let alone encourage, personal writing.

Kate Ronald has described another problem with programs that draw a deep division between personal writing and other sorts of writing. As she has argued, the origins of philosophical and political questions are deeply personal—Gorgias and Socrates argue about what sort of subjects a person should study, Phaedrus and Socrates discuss what sort of lover a person should take, and so on. Ronald has argued that we lose this sense of the connections among issues when we divide personal from public writing, and she has insisted that we retain that connection. Even Elbow, whose argument on ignoring audience is also an apologia for personal writing says that we must "seek ways to heighten both the *public* and private dimensions of writing".

Because of the desire to promote the simultaneous pursuit of the public and private, some teachers have moved toward describing the desired kind of writing as *exploratory* rather than *personal*. As William Zeiger argues in "The Exploratory Essay: Enfranchising the Spirit of Inquiry in College Composition," we can ask that students explore a topic—engage in "speculative and ruminative thinking" rather than "the scientific model of thesis and support". This exploratory writing weaves in some of the best aspects of the personal essay (playfulness with language, a willingness to take risks) with some of the best aspects of public writing (such as that it prepares students for most of their writing situations).

The Ethics of Requiring Students to Write About Their Personal Lives

Susan Swartzlander, Diana Pace, and Virginia Lee Stamler

I like to write journals, but I don't write a lot about myself. The reason is that I have had a terrible life throughout my adolescent years. Therefore, I believe that some things are better left unsaid or unwritten. . . . My English teachers always say that I am too general in my writing. The way I see it, I don't want my teachers to tell other students about me from my writings. I don't even want my teachers to know about me. From my greatest fear to my first date, I just don't feel comfortable writing about some topics.

—from a student's journal

Imagine a university professor asking a student to reveal in class the most intimate details of a childhood trauma like sexual or physical abuse. We would all agree that such behavior would be shockingly unprofessional. And yet, every day in college classrooms and faculty offices across the country, students receive writing assignments requiring inappropriate self-revelation.

We have serious concerns about the impact on students of required writing about their personal lives, whether in journals, freshman compositions, or other writing assignments. Among those who teach composition, the controversy about autobiographical writing focuses on whether personal writing helps students to develop the necessary academic skills—not on any ethical considerations about such assignments.

Advocates contend that having students write on what they care about most and know best is the only way to get them to write well. Opponents argue that such assignments not only fail to help students improve their writing, but also may even deter them from acquiring the skills in critical thinking, research, and writing that are necessary in an academic setting. Students who rely on their own knowledge and perceptions for writing assignments are not asked to engage in the rigorous thinking required to grapple with a world outside their immediate ken, critics say.

Although the ethics of requiring students to write about their personal lives have largely been ignored in the debate over the utility of such writing, we believe that several ethical issues need to be examined.

First, should grading be tied to self-revelation? Theoretically, it may be true that students have options about what they choose to reveal, but the students that we have talked to believe that the papers that receive the highest grades are those detailing highly emotional events or those that display the most drama. At our university, faculty members evaluate essays to place students in composition classes appropriate for their skill levels. The essays that are most moving are often given the highest ratings; the most notable papers usually are about emotionally charged topics such as the death of a parent or the suicide of a teen-aged friend.

At least one of our colleagues refuses to teach a composition course that focuses primarily on autobiographical writing, because she thinks that it is impossible and inappropriate to grade someone's feelings. One might also ask how much we really learn about a student's writing skills when assignments evoke the kind of emotional turmoil that often results from writing about difficult personal topics.

A second ethical issue concerns the extent to which students are able to make judgments about how much to reveal and to whom. For example, students who have been sexually abused often have difficulty understanding appropriate limits in relationships, stemming from the fact that childhood sexual abuse involves a transgression of appropriate boundaries. Such students might respond to a writing assignment by making themselves completely vulnerable or else being extremely distant. Because knowing what to say and how to say it is so difficult for them, dealing with these issues while trying to complete an assignment can be overwhelming. Writing about childhood experiences could cause strong feelings of shame to surface; having others read about their experiences could cause additional trauma.

One student felt so ashamed after submitting an autobiography detailing her abusive background that she never went back to the class. Some student writers find themselves confronting feelings of shame for the first time. Our counseling center has had to aid students who have blocked out unpleasant childhood experience, only to have an intrusive writing assignment elicit a flood of excruciating memories.

Because it is difficult for victims abuse to allow themselves to be emotionally vulnerable with others, course requirements that demand self-disclosure can intensify a student's feelings of abuse and powerlessness. Making themselves vulnerable to an authority figure may be particularly difficult for some students. Some may manage to avoid discussing childhood events by writing superficial essays or by cutting off their feelings during presentation of their essays in class. However, both of these strategies are likely to result in a lower grade.

Gender plays a distinct role in the ethics of autobiographical-writing assignments. Both men and women suffer some of the same discomfort from autobiographical assignments, but required personal writing may particularly perpetuate the "chilly classroom climate" for women, in which a complex of explicit as well as subtle behaviors creates an uncomfortable atmosphere. When the boundaries between professional and personal are blurred by turning personal revelation into course content, paternalism may thrive in the guise of professional guidance when the professor is male and the student female.

One professor with whom we shared our concern about autobiographical assignments told us, with great pride in his sensitivity, that they could be a valuable opportunity for students if it meant that they got the counseling they needed. He did not see that seeking counseling should be *their* choice.

Still another problem lies in the fact that women students are more likely to have horrid tales to tell in their writing, since women more often than men are the victims of rape, incest, and sexual abuse. According to studies, about 85 per cent of incest victims are female, 15 per cent male. For every 10 females who report sexual abuse, one male reports abuse. Some psychologists estimate that 3 out of every 10 female students have been sexually abused as children, and a recent study has reported that 26 per cent of female college students experienced some form of sexual assault at some point in their lives. The fact that the typical abuser is male and the fact that those who encourage them to reveal their stories—that is, their professors—often are men may intensify an unhealthy dynamic.

Finally, the female student required by a male instructor to reveal *anything* about her personal life is surrendering even more control to someone who already has emotional and social power over her. Unscrupulous faculty members could use students' stories as a way of identifying the most vulnerable female students; this is a legitimate concern when we consider that, as some research suggests, about 2 out of 10 women report being harassed by their male professors.

Men, too, may suffer anguish over personal writing assignments. In fact, given the socialization of women to disavow emotions, this type of writing may be very difficult for them. As we discussed this essay with friends outside academe, we heard a number of stories from men who had bad memories of college writing courses because of demands to write about their childhoods. One man recalled that writing about his early years meant reliving the anguishing loss of two siblings.

Consider, too, the possible impact of race, ethnicity, class, or sexual orientation on a student's discomfort with autobiographical writing. Students in their late teens and early 20's are at an age when feeling as if they "belong" is crucial to them. College, particularly if it means leaving home and moving to a campus, is a frightening enough prospect to many students and particularly scary to those who perceive themselves as different from their peers or professors.

Students of color have asked staff members at our counseling center about the appropriateness of their choosing to write about black leaders and activists with whom they personally identify. These students wondered whether the predominantly white world around them would understand and respect *their* world. The novelist Valerie Miner has written eloquently about the constant self-consciousness and feelings of inadequacy that accompany many working-class students into academe (and well into adulthood). She herself admits to feeling that she will be betrayed by "a dropped dialect or fork." Imagine how students who feel out of place to begin with might respond to autobiographical writing assignments.

Many instructors may not recognize students' discomfort in having to reveal personal information. But one wonders how faculty members would feel if they were expected to write personally revealing articles and then share them with colleagues.

Other faculty members may actually use such assignments as a way to gain greater intimacy with students for reasons other than sexual harassment. For example, a faculty member may want a close personal relationship with a student or may be a "frustrated therapist." We know of one faculty member who acted in a therapist role with students who revealed incest in their pasts; she held personal "sessions" after class to discuss the incest. In a different case, one student complained of feeling uncomfortable with an instructor who revealed details of her own childhood with an alcoholic parent and details of her own psychotherapy.

Most often it is a college's counseling staff, rather than faculty members, who end up dealing with students struggling with the issues we've described. In fact, a student often will just disappear from the class that precipitated the discomfort, and the instructor will have no idea why. We wonder what happens to the students who do not find their way to a counseling center.

From our experience at a variety of institutions, public and private, we know that this problem is endemic whenever students are asked to write about themselves. We have seen negative consequences in courses from academic disciplines as varied as arts and humanities, social sciences, and health sciences.

We are not suggesting that all writing about personal experience should be abandoned, but we do have some suggestions for protecting students from overly intrusive activities. Professors should be careful not to foster the perception that students must "deal with" their emotional problems in their writing or that they will succeed in courses if they can write about dramatic personal experiences.

Writing assignments can be oriented more to the future than to the past. Ask students to write about their plans, hopes, and goals, rather than their past experiences. Let students know that you care about their privacy. Tell them that they should never feel pressured in any way to say or write anything that makes them feel uncomfortable.

Also, make it clear that you will not share their writing with colleagues or other students without their permission. Do not return papers at the end of a semester by putting them in a box outside your office where other students might have access to them. Do not ask students to read personal assignments aloud in class unless they volunteer.

We strongly urge that university counseling centers sponsor workshops that will help instructors to understand better the needs of students and the consequences of intrusiveness.

In addition, in elective courses that include personal-writing assignments, such as upper-level psychology courses, faculty members might consider describing the assignments early in the semester so students are aware that an activity is coming up that might be emotionally difficult for them.

Finally, teachers should not require that personal assignments be reviewed by tutors. Tutors rarely are equipped to deal with the emotional revelations and disruption that come with discussing a personal writing assignment. During one recent training workshop for tutors offered by our counseling center, several tutors (undergraduates themselves) asked how to handle students who became emotionally upset while discussing assigned autobiographies. Tutors should never be expected to deal with these difficult issues.

Instructors must become more aware of all the implications of forced revelations. After all, as the writer May Sarton asks in *Journal of a Solitude* (1973), "Is there no one who is not emotionally wounded and in the process of healing?" Our students deserve the respect and dignity we afford other adults. They need to be able to work, on their own psychological issues in their own time and ways. We should be in the business of encouraging emotional development—*not* mandating it.

Susan Swartzlander is assistant professor of English at Grand Valley State University. Diana Pace is a psychologist and director of the counseling center there, and Virginia Lee Stamler is a psychologist and director of training at the counseling center.

The Exploratory Essay: Enfranchising the Spirit of Inquiry in College Composition
William Zeiger

When Michel de Montaigne chose the title "Essaies" for his collection of short prose works, he characterized them as trials or experiments. In his essays, Montaigne made "a trial of himself and his opinions."[1] He sketched out the implications of his thoughts to test their soundness and durability and, ultimately, to know himself. The reader of these essays observes the writer's mind in something like its native workings, driven by its own impulse, led by its own intuitive sense. The essays record a mature, energetic mind exploring avenues to which it is suddenly attracted, as the jungle explorer might turn to follow an exotic bird—

> *I had with me for a long time a man who had lived ten or twelve years in that other world which has been discovered in our time, in the place where Villegaignon landed [Brazil], and which he called Antarctic France. This discovery of so vast a country seems to me worth reflecting on. . . .*
> *—"On Cannibals" (105)*

> *In this chilly season, I was questioning whether the fashion in these lately discovered countries of going entirely naked is forced on them by the heat of the air, as we assume with the Indians and Moors, or whether it is the original custom of mankind. . . .*
> *—"On the Custom of Wearing Clothes" (119–120)*

The sense of the experimental in these essays arises from the curiosity Montaigne displays about his ideas. He teases at an idea, like a cat playing, poking from odd angles, reacting to each novelty. He examines "cannibals," for instance, through the eyes of Plato and then through those of Aristotle; he considers several aspects of the cannibals' society—their intelligence, their health, their building, their recreation, artifacts, religion, warmaking, and personal virtues— and in each aspect compares them, sometimes favorably, sometimes not, with his own European contemporaries. By the end of the essay our notion of cannibals, and of Montaigne's own society, has deepened considerably, and yet Montaigne makes no more assertive conclusion than "All this does not seem too bad. But then, they do not wear breeches." He presents ideas for their own sake, for their power to stimulate the mind and broaden the vision.

During the time that Montaigne was growing up, schools taught a method of theme-writing which approximated the exploratory manner of such essays. Erasmus, the "schoolmaster of Europe," who died when Montaigne was three,

---

[1]Citations from Montaigne's essays are from Cohen's collection.

had revived and popularized the classical modes of varying a topic. Under his influence, young scholars exercised their pens and their wits by developing themes in copious detail. The schoolmaster set the theme topic by assigning an adage (say, "Nothing more lucky can happen to a man than faithful and friendly counsel"), and the young scholars treated the topic in a dozen or more ways, including refutation, confirmation, encomium, vituperation, comparison, characterization, and description. These treatments followed classical models and often made allusion to Greek or Roman history or literature.[2] The students thus demonstrated an understanding of the given adage, a degree of intellectual ingenuity, and an acquaintance with their universe of scholarship. Such school themes were not exploratory in the same way that Montaigne's essays were, for they did not allow the student to set his own topic. But they were exploratory in the sense that they exercised the student's ability to manipulate and examine an idea, to invent arguments, to hit upon effective illustrations, to "find the available means of persuasion."

This practice of experimenting, of trying something out, is expressed in a now uncommon sense of the verb *to prove*—the sense of "testing" rather than of "demonstrating validity." Montaigne "proved" his ideas in that he tried them out in his essays. He spun out their implications, sampled their suggestions. He did not argue or try to persuade. He had no investment in winning over his audience to his opinion; accordingly, he had no fear of being refuted. On the contrary, he expected that some of the ideas he expressed would change, as they did in later essays. Refutation represented not a personal defeat but an advance toward truth as valuable as confirmation. To "prove" an idea, for Montaigne, was to examine it in order to *find out* how true it was.

The Renaissance schoolboys were trained to examine ideas in a similar way. They did not operate on their own ideas, but on borrowed assertions, adages drawn from the common cultural pool; hence, whether an assertion was true was not as important as how ingeniously it could be varied and examined. "Proving" became a sort of academic game, the aim of which was not so much to refute and defend as to scrutinize and tinker.

To "prove" in the fullest of this old-fashioned sense, then, was to express a tentative idea and to perform every imaginable variation of it in order to know it thoroughly and at first hand. When the poet said,

> Come live with me and be my love
> And we will all the pleasures prove,

he meant that he and his beloved should try everything, sample every pleasure, make a personal tour of the ways of loving. He would "put love through its paces."

This sense of *prove* is quite distinct from the rigorous modern sense of demonstrating a truth or establishing the validity of a proposition, and the essays of Montaigne are distinct in kind from those we demand of our composition

---

[2]See Baldwin 122, 243–45, 301; Clark; and Nadeau.

students today. To "prove" an assertion today is to win undisputed acceptance for it—to stop inquiry rather than to start it. There is nothing tentative or playful in this action; we "prove" an idea not to learn about it, but to fix it in certainty. This sense of certainty in proving has arisen in association with science and mathematics (Halloran and Whitburn): geometry "proves" theorems; physics "proves" theories; and the success of science has led us, when we teach students to write essays, to ask them to "prove" their theses in this modern sense. In the words of one critic, Keith Fort,

> In the essay it would seem that . . . [the] key rule is that there must be a thesis which the essay proves. The first question always asked about a prospective paper is whether the idea is "workable" or can be "handled." As I understand these terms, they mean "do you have a thesis that can be proved?" This formal requirement is a *sine qua non* for a paper. (631)

With overwhelming frequency, college composition classes today teach the writing of an essay which conforms to the scientific model of thesis and support. We loosely apply the term "exposition" to this form of writing. In this general category we include the critical essay, which advances a particular reading of a literary work; the argumentative/persuasive essay, which contrives to move its audience to a particular end, and the informative essay, which upholds the truth of a particular proposition. All of these essays employ the basic pattern of thesis and support. They would move the reader to one and only one conclusion. Kitzhaber's *Themes, Theories, and Therapy* (1963) showed that "exposition," thus defined, dominated the composition classes of two decades ago; similarly, a two-year-old survey by Clinton S. Burhans, Jr. finds

> a widespread emphasis on exposition. Across levels, it appears in 59% of basic, 82% of intermediate, and 68% of advanced writing courses. Even though exposition sometimes appears in the company of other rhetorical modes, it more often does not, and it is clearly the most emphasized element in most general writing courses. (646–47)

The domination of the composition class by the expository essay represents a temporary victory of the art of demonstration, the modern way of "proving," over the older way of "proving," the art of inquiry. Inquiry and demonstration, like their classical forebears dialectic and rhetoric, have distinct methods and distinct goals. Demonstration aims to establish the validity of a thesis. To accomplish this goal, it marshals supporting evidence and refutes counterarguments. It creates a logically exclusive, linear progression to a predetermined end. Inquiry, or exploration, on the other hand, aims to discover the fecundity of an idea (like a good post-modernist). It does not pursue a linear sequence, but holds several possibilities in suspension simultaneously, inviting the inquisitive mind to play among them. Rather than refute counter-arguments, it cultivates them. The art of inquiry entails a readiness to entertain alternatives, to examine two sides of an issue, to permit contradictory elements to coexist, the better to appreciate their differences. But when one sets out to prove an assertion in the modern sense, one tolerates no ambiguity: every hint of variance from the preferred line of thought must be solidly rejected. Each of these processes, of course, makes a crucial contribution to the whole of intellectual activity. Demonstration, or "exposition," expresses the sequential activity of the left brain; exploration, or inquiry, expresses the holistic activity of the right brain.[3] In *A Theory of Discourse: The Aims of Discourse* James Kinneavy treats these two processes as equal partners. Exploratory discourse, he says, fundamentally asks a question and suggests a tentative answer, while expository discourse asserts an answer and supplies proof; together; exploration and exposition compose the two complementary stages of scientific method. Inquiry is logically prior to exposition. "Exploration leads to a testable hypothesis which scientific proof then demonstrates as tenable or not" (100). In pure science, the second stage is a process of deducing consequences in order to *test* the validity of the hypothesis; it is "proving" in the old sense. But in classroom practice the aim of exposition is to ratify a thesis, not to test it.

This emphasis on confirming a result contributes to a general trend in American education away from speculative and ruminative thinking. As several prominent educators have recently charged, the spirit of inquiry is ebbing in American colleges and universities; the liberal arts are in disarray. Students do not seek truth for its own sake, but hunger after jobs, scholarships, and other material advancement. Teachers and administrators, anxious about enrollment levels, acquiesce to students' clamor for courses with immediate, obvious relevance to the contemporary environment. The demand for history and philosophy wanes. One commentator associates the hunger for quick results and practical applications with the rapid development of high-speed technological communication, and a corresponding drop in contemplative activity:

> It seems as if the ability to convert knowledge into forms that can be transmitted and utilized by highly technological systems dries up the interpretive capacity to understand other people. When knowledge is bleached into information, it becomes less reliably informing. . . .
>
> High speed methods of transmission must be matched or paralleled by the maintenance and refurbishing of those other patterns of communication that are slower, which are based upon conversation, discussion, and interrogation, and which attempt to cultivate different and deeper forms of understanding. (Carey 48)

Noble local exceptions notwithstanding, the art of thinking, the habit of quizzical reflection, the slow melding of old and new ideas, has yielded its place in the university to the calculation of immediate advantages—just as the old sense of "prove" has given way to the new.

---

[3]"In classical terms, the minor hemisphere seemed to govern invention *(inventio)*, whereas the dominant hemisphere governed rehearsal and reformulation" (Emig 2026).

In recent years, of course, a growing number of teacher-scholars have shown a theoretical interest in the art of inquiry. Within the past few decades, books and articles have appeared which recommend strategies for generating ideas and describe heuristics for examining issues from several angles (Winterowd, *Contemporary Rhetoric;* Tate). The rhetorical department of invention has acquired new meaning as theorists have suggested techniques not only for "finding the available means of persuasion," but for discovering the depths and facets of a seemingly commonplace idea or event. As one's appreciation of these techniques grows, it becomes more and more apparent that the demonstrative composition depends on the process of inquiry not merely for its thesis, but for virtually all of its subordinate concepts and their interrelationships. "Toughing out" an essay in ignorance of the methods of inquiry is tantamount to reinventing the wheel in several drafts. Writers who know that the first step in writing is exploration, and who consciously begin the writing process not in the middle but at the beginning, steal a march on the less well informed.

The invention strategies which have emerged in composition theory, however, have not yet had a great effect in the classroom.[4] Even where inventive strategies are extensively used, they are not usually considered an equal partner to the act of exposition. "Pre-writing," however pleasurable and productive, plays only a preliminary role. It crowds those sheets of longhand which one throws away before submitting the "real" work, the neatly typed exposition.

The ability to construct a logical argument, as in exposition, is of course a critical skill for any educated person. Equally important, however, is the ability to explore—to recognize and weigh alternatives. By concentrating almost exclusively on thesis-support exposition in college composition classes, we are implicitly teaching that the ability to support an assertion is more important than the ability to examine an issue. In doing so, we fall in with the results-oriented popular prejudice and fail in our duties as liberal educators. No doubt we composition teachers extol to our students the need to research a topic carefully and to scrutinize a question from all sides; we even sit in conference over preliminary drafts. But as long as the goal and product of writing is to demonstrate the validity of a thesis, the implicit message is that *proving* is more important than *finding out.*

The overemphasis on the importance of validating and defending a thesis carries a collateral penalty in composition classes: it puts pressure on the student to win an unequal "battle" with the teacher. For when the aim of an essay is to prove or "win" a point, the projected audience become not co-inquirers, or even neutral attendants, but critical opponents. The student conceives the audience as an antagonist. Whatever classroom fiction may be invoked about the essay's readership—whether the essay is addressed to a local newspaper, a friend or relative, or a particular social group—the student knows that the real audience is the teacher. In *The Development of Writing Abilities (11–18),* James

[4]This is Burhan's conclusion.

Britton et al. note how subtly the writing student adjusts to the teacher's expectations. The teacher

> becomes an audience on whom pupils must focus a special kind of scrutiny in order to detect what they must do to satisfy him. The peculiar feature of this relationship is that the pupil will see the teacher's response as a means by which his progress is to be charted. It is part of a larger and more elaborate system of making judgments and not simply a question of the reader's pleasure or understanding or insight. (64)

The teacher's authority as a judge of writing and as a "thinker-at-large" by virtue of age or experience outweighs the student's in almost all cases. To this authority is added the power of the grade, from which there is virtually no appeal. The student either "attacks" an impervious "foe" or "defends" against an irresistible "assailant."

Remedies have been suggested for the imbalance of the teacher's functioning as audience, including the teacher's assuming a variety of other roles and evaluation of essays by students' peers. Although these measures do ease the difficulty of addressing an overpowering audience, the labor of this writing situation continues to sap students' wills. Britton et al. observe,

> The student's writing may be dominated by the sole consideration of meeting *minimum* requirements. In other words it may be shaped solely by the demands of his audience and not by the complementary pressure to formulate ideas in a way which satisfies the writer. (64)

The expectation of severe criticism breeds an excess of caution or an excess of boldness. In the first instance, the student uses information only if it supports the thesis and tacitly suppresses any suggestion contrary to the thesis. This practice tends to close rather than open the mind; it is the antithesis of liberal education. In the second instance, the student dismisses counter arguments with shrill disdain rather than with sober consideration. Here, too, the spirit of liberal edution is lost. In order to learn to express thoughts freely and sincerely, the writer needs to address a tolerant, even friendly audience, an audience disposed to accept and consider ideas rather than to suspect and impeach them.

It would appear, in sum, that concentration on the expository essay has reached a point of severely diminished returns. It continually demands that the writer prove a thesis, even while slighting the exploration that would provide the substance of the proof; it asks the writer to make bricks without straw. It augments this impediment to free creation by confronting the writer with a critical audience, dispelling the congenial atmosphere in which exploration would thrive. I do not challenge the importance of sound exposition to a college career and a liberal education; but as long as the "bottom line" of an essay is a well defended thesis, the art of exploration will continue to languish as the poor stepsister of exposition. If we genuinely wish to promote freedom of thought, to balance demonstration with the inquiry which sustains it, then we must establish the art of exploration as an equally acceptable and worthy pursuit.

I have in mind, of course, teaching the personal or familiar essay in the manner of Montaigne—an essay in an informal, friendly tone, whose aim is to unfold the intellectual potential of an idea—on an equal basis with exposition. The spirit of inquiry which characterized Montaigne's essays waned in the prose of the eighteenth century, but waxed again in that of the nineteenth with the great romantic essayists Charles Lamb, William Hazlitt, and others. In our own time, this spirit informs the work of such essayists as Annie Dillard, Loren Eiseley, Joan Didion, and Garrison Keillor. The genre of the personal or familiar essay embraces a variety of works; but two qualities make it peculiarly appropriate as a medium of exploration—its open form and its friendly tone.

By the "open form" of the familiar essay, I mean the quality of accommodating several viewpoints, even contradictory viewpoints, simultaneously. If the expository essay is essentially an argument, the familiar essay is essentially a conversation. It rambles easily—not really randomly—over a variety of related thoughts. It "proves" an idea in the sense of testing and turning it; and thus it readily embraces contrasting alternatives. Charles Lamb's *Essays of Elia* abound with sly contradictions intended to provoke the reader into thought. In "A Chapter on Ears," for example, Lamb (in the persona of Elia) begins by protesting (with winning modesty) that he has no ear for music.

> I have been practising "God Save the King" all my life; whistling and humming of it over to myself in solitary corners; and am not yet arrived, they tell me, within many quavers of it. (French 55)

> Scientifically, I could never be made to understand (yet have I taken some pains) what a note in music is; or how one note should differ from another. Much less in voices can I distinguish a soprano from a tenor. Only sometimes the thorough bass I guess at, from its being supereminently harsh and disagreeable. (55)

These are only two of the more straightforward assertions in the essay of Elia's insensibility to music. There are others, more subtle and mirthful, such as when Elia gives vent to a secret desire—

> I am not without suspicion, that I have an undeveloped faculty of music within me. For, thrumming, in my wild way, on my friend A's piano, the other morning, while he was engaged in an adjoining parlour,—on his return he was pleased to say, "*he thought it could not be the maid!*" (55)

Elia interprets his friend's remark as a compliment, that at least his musical powers are above those of an unschooled servant. The emphasis on the remark suggests another meaning, however—that "A" could not guess who could be playing the piano so badly.

After so thoroughly establishing Elia's lack of musical talent, and involving the reader in its assertion, later in the essay, with no apparent transition, in the midst of a series of invectives against musical performances, Lamb lets Elia confess, "I deny not, that in the opening of a concert, I have experienced something vastly lulling and agreeable . . ." and likens this sensation to the pleasurable onset of melancholy described by Burton:

> Most pleasant it is to such as are melancholy given, to walk alone in some solitary grove, betwixt wood and water, by some brook side, and to meditate upon some delightsome subject. . . . A most incomparable delight to build castles in the air, to go smiling to themselves. . . . (57)

Soon Elia is at an organ recital in the home of a friend where, at the beginning of the music, "a holy calm pervadeth me. I am for the time —rapt above earth,/And possess joys not promised at my birth."

The great contrast of sensibility to music between the early Elia and the late Elia in the essay constitutes the essay's aesthetic form. Lamb makes no overt knowledgement of this contrast, but has Elia insist throughout that music oppresses him, and closes the essay ambiguously, permitting the opposing character traits to dissolve in beer. This ambiguity permits and invites a number of speculations—about one's yearning to realize a personal talent, as represented by Elia's irrepressible but wayward desire to make music, and about the social conventions which repress personal expression, as represented by Elia's acquired opinion that he is not musical. Thus the essay does not "conclude," but opens at the end.

Lamb is perhaps the foremost practitioner of the familiar essay, and it is typical of his works to toss up a provocative contradiction and to retire from the stage of creation at the moment of greatest wonder. This practice would never do, of course, in the expository essay, which abhors ambiguity and marches to a predictable conclusion. But the scene and scope of the familiar essay is not logic, but intuition; not the rational order of left-brained, linear, sequential procedure, but the free association of right-brained, holistic, simultaneous play of alternatives. It is not the writer's reasoning which governs the familiar essay, but the writer's personality. And while reasoning succeeds only when predictable, the personality charms most with its little irrational leaps. Such a context, moreover, provides a fertile field for creativity, permits the mind to examine without penalty or prejudice the most unlikely and even untenable positions, and makes possible the emergence of new ideas and associations. As Charles Brashers, in "The Aesthetic Form of the Familiar Essay" observes,

> Exposition hopes to fix, to define, to delimit, so that clarity and precision are perfect within a certain scope. Persuasion presses toward assent, conformity, submission, so that force of expression and argument are translated into belief and action. The familiar mode tries to open, to stimulate, to inject multiple overtones, so that insight is expanded and pleasure is aroused. This opening, stimulating, multiplying vision is useful *because* it is opening, stimulating, multiplying, not because it is practical. . . . (155)

Essayists in our time have exploited the familiar mode in their own ways. In "The Judgment of the Birds," Loren Eiseley strings together a series of mystical anecdotes. The naturalist expresses his awe at the glimpses he gets of a world profoundly different from his own, but makes no further attempt to link these episodes: From a high hotel window before dawn he sees pigeons leaving their niches and soaring off above the city, and for a moment he imagines he can fly, and feels the impulse to leap into the void. Walking in a dense fog, he is almost hit by a low-flying crow, and imagines the crow's alarm at seeing so strange a creature apparently walking in the clouds. In a primeval desert at sunset he sees a flock of birds go over and realizes the oneness of their bones and flesh and feathers with the inert chemicals on which he treads. In a remote forest clearing a group of songbirds are silenced at the killing of a nestling, but then take up the song of life again.

The specific lesson of these episodes is not immediately apparent, perhaps not even paraphrasable. There is certainly no obvious induction; the only recurring elements are birds and the alchemy of the naturalist's wonder. Eiseley himself concludes,

> It was better, I decided, for the emissaries returning from the wilderness . . . to record their marvel, not to define its meaning. In that way it would go echoing on through the minds of men, each grasping at that beyond out of which the miracles emerge. . . . (36)

The unity of the essay resides in the writer's personality, and in his implicit assertion and belief that all these apparently disparate episodes do share a common theme and make an important comment on the life we live. Yet no definitive reading of "The Judgment of The Birds" emerges; its interpretation is left to the individual reader, and each may vary from each other and still remain true to the essay.

Umberto Eco's discussion of "open" and "closed" works in *The Role of the Reader* (1979) suggests a theoretical rationale for such an essay. Some art, Eco observes, deliberately refrains from making an uniquivocal statement, but instead presents a number of possibilities for the audience to arrange or distill. For example, in musical works, he says, the "open" technique consists in the composer allowing the performer to choose tempo, duration, or pitch, sometimes even the sequence of passages, so that the performer is involved in constructing the work, which nevertheless remains identifiable. In fiction or drama, this technique consists in creating sufficient complexity and ambiguity to permit a variety of valid interpretations—interpretations which do not exclude, but which complement and inform each other, so that every reader may give a somewhat different "performance" of the text without violating its integrity. Works which permit such free interpretation Eco calls *open* works. Although he does not extend the concept to nonfiction prose, it is easy to see that expository composition—writing whose great virtue is to confine the reader to a single, unambiguous line of thought—is *closed,* in the sense of permitting, ideally, only one valid interpretation. An "exploratory" essay, on the other hand, is an open work of nonfiction prose. It cultivates ambiguity and complexity to allow more than one reading or response to the work.

The creation of such a text differs profoundly from the creation of a "closed" essay. In the latter case, the writer begins knowing precisely to what end the essay must come. In the former case, however, the writer may never know, rationally or objectively, the "conclusion" of the essay, because the essay does "conclude" in the conventional sense. The formal art of the exploratory esselects and expresses viewpoints which cluster around and incline toward a tral idea. The writer's shrewdness and insight guide the deployment of these viewpoints, and the essay as a whole represents the writer's expression of the idea central to it.

The "exploratory" essay refrains from concluding, not so much because its goal is out of reach as because the best resolution of its issue is multiple: any reduction to a definitive conclusion would distort the truer complexity of the vision. Eiseley lets "The Judgment of the Birds" rest in a complexity more satisfying and suggestive than any unity he could express; Lamb ends "A Chapter on Ears" in an ambiguity which prefers both sides of the question. Similarly, Annie Dillard joins the opposite strands of her childhood reminiscence, "God in the Doorway," in one sentence of rich internal conflict:

> Even now I wonder: if I meet God, will he take and hold my bare hand in his, and focus his eye on my palm, and kindle that spot and let me burn? (141)

This exquisite blending of tenderness and pain, love and fear, seeks no further resolution, for it expresses the rich duality of a human condition which persists.

Another quality by which the familiar essay creates a context for exploration is its tone. A text characterized by a severe, analytical tone does not invite thought to flow freely but checks and guides thought into a narrow channel. A text marked by a friendly, conversational tone, on the other hand, persuades the reader that new ideas are safe from censure, that all responses are welcome. As such a text, the familiar essay makes of its reader an intimate audience. The reader of one of Lamb's essays, for example, feels like a confidant, a guest in Elia's home, in an easy chair by the fire after dinner, a glass of port within easy reach. Elia's tone is guileless. Despite his occasional seeming self-deception, Elia would never deceive the reader, except perhaps in fun. Elia talks as to a friend whose assumptions he shares. Thus the familiar essay does not attempt to persuade; the reader and writer are already in essential agreement. The familiar essay aims to extend and enrich the reader's perceptions. It addresses a friend, not an antagonist.

Similarly, Eiseley defines his own audience as others like himself. He records his remarkable stories, he says,

> . . . in the hope that they will come to the eye of those who have retained a true taste for the marvellous, and who are capable of discerning in the flow of ordinary events the point at which the mundane world gives way to quite another dimension. (28)

He does not seem to try to shape the reader's experience, to direct the reader to a particular conclusion or judgment; instead he places before the reader a sample of that which he himself savors, one wonderer to another.

Dillard's voice, too, has the soft, earnest intensity of intimacy, of talk so familiar that names are unnecessary. Her vulnerability demands confidence. To contradict her is simply inappropriate. She suspects, one imagines, that what she says is crazy, yet she must have a hearing; she presents not an argument but a phenomenon, a child with a shell in her hand.

A number of theorists have examined the attitudes which underlie and promote creative thinking. Carl Rogers summarizes these conditions as "psychological safety" and "psychological freedom."[5] Psychological safety means that one feels one's own worth is unconditionally assured, that one fears no judgment or criticism, and that one is understood empathetically. Psychological freedom means that one feels free to express oneself symbolically. These two conditions—safety from censure and freedom to speak—create an atmosphere which encourages speculation. With no penalty for espousing an unpopular thought, with an audience disposed to embrace and good-naturedly entertain unlikely notions, the ideas sleeping in the back of the mind may tentatively emerge. Ideas which one may have withheld, from fear of ridicule or lack of encouragement, one may now bring forth. Ideas of which one may even have been unaware, ideas yet unformed, ideas new-born now arise and grow and take on color, nurtured and animated by an answering receptivity. We are not describing here only the love of the parent which inspirits the shy child. This loving receptivity is the same which Socrates commends, in the *Phaedrus,* as the most appropriate and fruitful context for philosophy—an intimacy conducive to "stargazing." When such an audience awaits, a writer writes most frankly and truly and easily. When an essay creates a sense of such security and friendliness, the reader participates most willingly in the essay's ambiguity.

A friendly tone, together with a flexibly open form, creates a context in which the mind may play freely within broad bounds. Thus, the familiar essay, characterized by a friendly tone and an open form, provides a literary vehicle for the act of exploration. A propensity to explore is exactly what composition classes, with their habitual emphasis on proving a point, now lack.

We cannot expect our composition students to write on a par with Dillard or Eiseley or Lamb, but we can teach them the familiar essay as a means of exploration. We can lead them to express and explore their own internal contradictions in an open form; we can encourage a trusting, inquisitive tone in their writing. In a two-semester writing program, the first semester could focus on the exploratory essay, the second on exposition. First-semester students would grow in the confidence of their own opinions, would come to appreciate the ephemeral nature of opinion, would tolerate more readily the opinions of others. Approaching the second-semester expository writing with this preparation, students would realize the folly of bludgeoning an audience, or of kowtowing to it, or of deceiving it; would accept that "proofs" are never better,

[5]Winterowd makes this observation in "Brain, Rhetoric, and Style" (161). His source is Rogers, 71.

but need not be worse, than the premises from which they derive. Teaching the exploratory essay would contribute to the larger effort of revitalizing the humanities by restoring the spirit of inquiry to a place of currency and honor, and by educating people to communicate freely with one another.

Works Cited

Baldwin, T. W. *William Shakespeare's Small Latine and Lesse Greek*. Urbana: U of Illinois P, 1944.

Brashers, Charles. "The Aesthetic Form of the Familiar Essay." *College Composition and Communication* 22 (1971): 147–55.

Britton, James, Tony Burgess, Nancy Martin, Alex McLeod, and Harold Rosen. *The Development of Writing Abilities* (11–18). London: Macmillan Education, 1975.

Burhans, Clinton S., Jr. "The Teaching of Writing and the Knowledge Gap." *College English* 45 (1983): 639–56.

Carey, James W. "High-Speed Communication in an Unstable World: What happened to conversation and discussion that attempt to cultivate deeper forms of understanding?" *Chronicle of Higher Education* 27 July 1983: 48.

Clark, Donald Lemen. "The Rise and Fall of Progymnasmata in Sixteenth and Seventeenth Century Grammar Schools," *Speech Monographs* 19 (1952): 259–63.

Cohen, J. M., ed. *Michel de Montaigne: Essays*. Baltimore: Penguin, 1958.

Dillard, Annie. "God in the Doorway." *Teaching a Stone to Talk*. New York: Harper, 1982.

Eco, Umberto. *The Role of the Reader*. Bloomington: Indiana UP, 1979.

Eiseley, Loren. "The Judgment of the Birds." *The Star Thrower*. San Diego: Harcourt, 1978.

Emig, Janet, "Writing, Composition, and Rhetoric." *Encyclopedia of Educational Research*. 5th ed. New York: Free, 1982.

Fort, Keith. "Form, Authority, and the Critical Essay." *College English* 32 (1971): 629–639.

French, J. Milton, ed. *Charles Lamb: Essays and Letters*. New York: Doubleday, 1937.

Halloran, S. Michael, and Merrill D. Whitburn. "Ciceronian Rhetoric and the Rise of Science: The Plain Style Reconsidered." *The Rhetorical Tradition and Modern Writing*. Ed. James J. Murphy. New York: MLA, 1982. 58–72.

Kinneavy, James. *A Theory of Discourse: The Aims of Discourse*. Englewood Cliffs, NJ: Prentice, 1971.

Kitzhaber, Albert R. *Themes, Theories, and Therapy: The Teaching of Writing in College*. New York: McGraw, 1963.

Nadeau, Ray. "The Progymnasmata of Apthonius in Translation." *Speech Monographs* 19 (1952): 264–85.

Rogers, Carl R. "Toward a Theory of Creativity." *Creativity and its Cultivation.* Ed. Harold H. Anderson. New York: Harper, 1959. 69–82.

Tate, Gary, ed. *10 Bibliographical Essays.* Fort Worth: Texas Christian UP, 1976.

Winterowd, W. Ross. *Contemporary Rhetoric.* New York: Harcourt, 1975.

———. "Brain, Rhetoric, and Style." *Linguistics, Stylistics, and the Teaching of Composition.* Ed. Donald McQuade. Akron: Dept. of English, U of Akron, 1979. 151–181.

Additional Sources

Belenky, Mary Field, et al. *Women's Ways of Knowing: The Development of Self, Voice, and Mind.* New York: Basic Books, 1986.

Studies the cognition processes of women, ending with a discussion of the implications for teaching.

Bridwell-Bowles, Lillian. Freedom, Form, Function: Varieties of Academic Discourse. *College Composition & Communication* Vol. 46, 1 (February 1995): 46–61.

Referring to the author's own "literacy history," criticizes the narrative of college composition as transforming.

Halloran, S. Michael. "Rhetoric in the American College Curriculum: The Decline of Public Discourse." PRE/TEXT 3 (Fall 1982): 245–69.

Criticizes current neglect of public argument in composition instruction and argues for a more rhetorical grounding to discourse.

Peterson, Linda H. "Gender and the Autobiographical Essay: Research Perspectives, Pedagogical Practices." *College Composition and Communication* 42 (May 1991): 170–83.

Studies the connection between gender and "good" autobiographical writing.

Ronald, Kate. A Reexamination of Personal and Public Discourse in Classical Rhetoric. *Rhetoric Review* Vol. 9, 1 (Fall 1990): 36–48.

Argues that classical rhetoric provides a useful model for connecting the personal and public.

Stotsky, Sandra. "The Uses and Limitations of Personal or Personalized Writing in Writing Theory, Research, and Instruction." *Reading Research Quarterly.* Vol. 30, 4 (October–December 1995): 758–76.

Using recent research on writing, argues that personal writing should be balanced with other kinds of writing.

Chapter 9
Argument

Probably one of the best resources for teaching argumentation is the Monty Python skit "The Argument Clinic." In that skit, a person becomes deeply frustrated because he pays for argument, but gets nothing more than contradiction. The distinction made in this skit is one that can help students understand the difference between argumentation and disagreements; it also serves as a basis for presenting other distinctions that can help students distinguish productive disagreements from shouting matches (such as arguments versus fights, arguments versus debates, arguments versus assertions). These distinctions are also helpful for teachers of writing to understand, for argument remains a difficult subject for many people to teach as long as they insist upon perceiving it as something different from what they spend much of their day doing.

There are two very different traditions in the teaching of argument. One is to insist upon it as a formal art, with special rules. This is essentially the debate, or forensic tradition, and it is extremely useful for students who intend to go into law. (Its utility for other students remains somewhat obscure to me.) The other tradition is the dialogic tradition, which presents argument as something that people tend to engage in whether or not they are formally trained in it. In this tradition, argument is simply what happens when people have a point of view that they are trying to get someone else to share—it is discourse in a community with some agreement and some disagreement.

The detractors of this dialogic view of argument complain that it makes argument too universal, which is an important criticism. The proponents, however, argue that the narrower form of argumentation (which is typically modeled on debate) is, as Catherine Lamb notes in "Beyond Argument in Feminist Composition," deeply frustrating for people engaged in postmodern pedagogies. If we perceive argument as getting what we want, and we "acknowledge the other side's position but only to refute it", we almost certainly behave that way in our classroom discourse. Dialogic argument is, as Lamb notes, a form of engaging in disagreement that does not involve one side dominating another; it is an approach to disagreement that permits (even requires) difference.

Many graduate students in English are hesitant when it comes to teaching argument because they rarely have training in logic, but the relation of formal logic and dialogic argument is fairly complicated. Interestingly, though, Lamb's use of negotiation models for argument sidesteps the issue of formal logic altogether. And in "Teaching Argument: A Theory of Types," Fahnestock and Secor describe an approach to reasoning which someone with virtually no training in logic can apply.

Central to the different approaches to argument is the difference in the role that the audience plays in the writing process. In the debate model, one invents an argument and then considers audience objections. These objections are mentioned and refuted at some point in the discourse, and the intended audience is some more or less hypothetical "neutral" audience. In the dialogic approach, the writer is required to consider the audience's expectations and assumptions when inventing the argument. The audience to be considered includes the opposition, and finding effective enthymemes means finding shared ground with the opposition.

There are numerous forms of dialogic argument, but they all share certain qualities. First, dialogic argument emphasizes the importance of understanding the people with whom one is arguing. For this reason, some topics do not work very well for some students—particularly difficult topics include those about which students refuse to acknowledge any good reasons for disagreement. (Hence, I never let students write about abortion or the death penalty, and I often recommend to students that they consider changing the topic if they genuinely believe that anyone who disagrees with them is inherently evil.) In addition, dialogic argument tends to rely on informal reasoning, making the enthymeme more important than the syllogism. Because it relies on probability, dialogic argument is most exciting in regard to topics about which there is disagreement among experts, or about which the students themselves can easily become expert.

Although argumentation does not require "political" topics, some instructors find it useful to restrict students to topics where a course of action is recommended or criticized. This latter sort of topic might range from whether or not readers should blame Willy Loman for his predicament to whether or not employers should intervene in an employee's personal life if substance abuse is suspected. Thus these topics may be literary, personal, philosophical, or political. A good argument is a good discussion, and it requires nothing more than intelligent people who disagree.

Currently, the dominant forms of dialogic argument are: mediation-based (like Lamb's); classical (such as is promoted by Gage); Toulmin-based (Fahnestock and Secor); Rogerian (discussed by Lunsford). Each of these approaches has its disadvantages. Mediation-based argument requires conflict within the class, and some teachers are uncomfortable with that conflict. Some instructors have trouble understanding the terminology of either classical or Toulmin-based argument. And, as Lamb mentions, some feminists dislike Rogerian argument since it seems feminine rather than feminist. Despite these problems, dialogic argument seems to many people to be a more productive approach than monologic arguments, and the main reason is that it works.

Monologic argument works to persuade some audiences in some situations, but it rarely works to persuade the opposition. It is most effective with people who already agree, second most effective with the uninformed and neutral, and third most effective with the informed and neutral. The committed opposition will rarely listen because monologic argument quickly conveys that the rhetor has not listened to the opposition, and listening is usually treated as a reciprocal obligation. Thus monologic argument works well in situations like political rallies (which people will usually not attend unless they are already in agreement) or formal situations like courtrooms (in which the audience is required to be neutral).

The most important rhetorical situations in which our students will find themselves, however, involve being face to face with a committed opposition. Trying to persuade a police officer not to give a ticket, trying to persuade a teacher to change a grade, trying to persuade a roommate to change behavior, and so on are all instances in which the student will fail if she or he tries to appeal to a hypothetical audience. Teaching students to write effective arguments, then, means teaching them to work *with*—not *on*—people who disagree.

Teaching Argument: A Theory of Types
Jeanne Fahnestock and Marie Secor

The climax of many composition courses is the argumentative essay, the last, longest, and most difficult assignment. An effective written argument requires all the expository skills the students have learned, and, even more, asks for a voice of authority and certainty that is often quite new to them. Aware of the difficulty and importance of argument, many composition programs are devoting more time to it, even an entire second course. At Penn State, for example, the second of our required composition courses is devoted entirely to written argument, out of our conviction that written argument brings together all other writing skills and prepares students for the kinds of writing tasks demanded in college courses and careers.

We know what we want our students to do by the end of our second course: write clear, orderly, convincing arguments which show respect for evidence, build in refutation, and accommodate their audience. The question is, how do we get them to do it? What is the wisest sequence of assignments? What and how much ancillary material should be brought in? The composition teacher setting up a course in argument has three basic approaches to choose from: the logical/analytic, the content/problem-solving, and the rhetorical/generative. All of these approaches teach the student something about argument, but each has problems. Our purpose here is to defend the rhetorical/generative approach as the one which reaches its goal most directly and most reliably.

The teacher who uses the logical/analytic approach in effect takes the logic book and its terminology into the classroom and introduces students to the square of opposition, the syllogisms categorical and hypothetical, the enthymeme, the fallacies, induction and deduction. It has not been demonstrated, however, that formal logic carries over into written argument. Formal logic, as Chaim Perelman and Stephen Toulmin have pointed out, is simply not the same as the logic of discourse;[1] students who become adept at manipulating fact statements in and out of syllogisms and Venn diagrams still may not have any idea how to construct a written argument on their own.

Another supposed borrowing from logic is the distinction between induction and deduction as forms of reasoning and therefore as distinct forms of written argument. Induction and deduction are sometimes seen to be as different as up and down, induction reaching a generalization from particulars and deduction affirming a particular from a generalization. Actually the exact distinction

---

[1]Chaim Perelman and L. Olbrechts-Tyteca, *The New Rhetoric: A Treatise on Argument* (Notre Dame, IN: University of Notre Dame Press, 1969), pp. 1–4; Stephen Toulmin, *The Uses of Argument* (Cambridge, England: Cambridge University Press, 1958), p. 146.

between the two is a matter of some controversy. In his *Introduction to Logic* Irving M. Copi defines the two not as complementary forms of reasoning, but as reasoning toward a certain conclusion (deduction) and reasoning toward a probable conclusion (induction).[2] And Karl Popper in *Conjectures and Refutations* obliterates the distinction by showing that induction, as traditionally defined, is not valid.

> But in fact the belief that we can start with pure observations alone, without anything in the nature of a theory, is absurd; as may be illustrated by the story of the man who dedicated his life to natural science, wrote down everything he could observe, and bequeathed his priceless collection of observations to the Royal Society to be used as inductive evidence. This story should show us that though beetles may profitably be collected, observations may not.
>
> Twenty-five years ago I tried to bring home the same point to a group of physics students in Vienna by beginning a lecture with the following instructions: 'Take pencil and paper; carefully observe, and write down what you have observed!' They asked, of course, *what* I wanted them to observe. Clearly the instruction, 'Observe!' is absurd. . . . Observation is always selective. It needs a chosen object, a definite task, an interest, a point of view, a problem. And its description presupposes a descriptive language, with property words; it presupposes similarity of classification, which in its turn presupposes interests, points of view and problems.[3]

Thus according to Popper, the observations that supposedly lead to a conclusion are, in fact, controlled by a prior conclusion. There is no pure form of reasoning which goes "example + example = conclusion," as it is represented in many rhetorics. We cannot reason "x chow is vicious + y chow is vicious = z chow is vicious = most chows are vicious" unless we assume "Chows x, y and z are typical chows." The conclusion of a so-called inductive argument depends not on the number of examples but on their typicality. The reasoning in such an argument does not leap from particular to general but proceeds from an assumption of typicality and particular evidence (in this case three examples of vicious chows) to a conclusion. This process is not essentially different from deduction. Students are misled if they think their minds work in two gears, inductive forward and deductive reverse, or if they believe it is possible to argue purely from evidence without assumptions. But students who recognize the necessity for typical evidence can fruitfully consider whether their audience will accept their evidence as representative or whether they must explicitly argue that it is.

[2]Irving M. Copi, *Introduction to Logic,* 5th ed. (New York: Macmillan, 1978), pp. 23–26.

[3]Karl Popper, *Conjectures and Refutations: The Growth of Scientific Knowledge* (New York: Harper & Row, 1963), pp. 46–47.

Another continually attractive if indirect way of teaching argument in the composition classroom is the content/problem-solving approach, which assumes that students will absorb the principles and methods of written argument simply by doing it. In such content-based courses, which may use a case book (now rare) or a group of related readings or even the lectures and readings of another course, the instructor may not even define the writing as argument. Instead, students write papers with "theses" which grow naturally out of their readings or are suggested by the instructor. Another variety of this approach is the problem-solving method, as in *Cases for Composition* (by John P. Field and Robert H. Weiss, Boston: Little, Brown & Co., 1979), which frames assignments not only by specifying topics but also by defining rhetorical situations. Students write their way out of problems, arguing in letters, memos, reports, and brief articles.

The content/problem-solving approach effectively approximates real-life writing situations which supply both purpose and content. Moreover, a course that teaches writing this way is attractive because the instructor can present for discussion a coherent body of material from philosophy, sociology, psychology or even literature; if such a course works well, invention is not a problem because students are directly stimulated by the content, and they do practice writing arguments. And at best students may learn a method of problem-solving which they can apply to other writing situations when their instructor is no longer suggesting topics nor the controlled reading stimulating invention. However, the content in such courses tends to crowd out the writing instruction or, increasingly, it is given away to the real experts in other departments and the composition teacher reduced to an overseer of the revision process, a police officer with a red pencil.

The composition course which does not organize itself around a body of content can take what we will call the "rhetorical/generative" approach and explicitly teach invention. Now the composition course devoted entirely to argument can turn to the classical sources which are still the only scheme of invention purely for argument. These sources (definition, comparison, cause and effect, and authority) do help students find premises for the proposals and evaluations they usually come up with when left on their own to generate theses for arguments. But the sources are less help when we ask students to take one step further back and support the very premises which the sources have generated. If, for example, the student wants to argue that "the federal government should not subsidize the airlines," thinking about definition might yield a premise like "because airline subsidies are a form of socialism," and thinking about cause and effect might yield a premise like "because once an industry is subsidized, the quality of its service deteriorates." But how is either of these premises to be supported? How does one actually argue for a categorization such as the first or a cause and effect relationship such as the second? To tell the student to continually reapply the four sources is rather discouraging advice. Thus while the classical sources are powerful aids to invention in the large-scale arguments that evaluations and proposals require, they do not help students construct smaller-scale supporting arguments.

It is possible to give students more specific aid in inventing arguments if we begin by distinguishing the basic types of arguments and the structures characteristic of each. We derived this approach when confronted by the variety of propositions our students volunteered as subjects for argument. After collecting scores of these, we found they could be sorted into four main groups answering the questions 1. "What is this thing?" 2. "What caused it or what effects does it have?" 3. "Is it good or bad?" and 4. "What should be done about it?" Propositions which answer these questions are, respectively, categorical propositions, causal statements, evaluations, and proposals. The thesis of any argument falls into one of these categories. The first two, which correspond to the classical sources of definition and cause and effect, demand their own forms of argument with distinctive structures. Arguments for the third and fourth, evaluations and proposals, combine the other two. If we take students through these four types of argument, from the simpler categorical proposition to the complex proposal, we have a coherent rationale for organizing a course in argument.

Any statement about the nature of things fixed in some moment of time can be cast as what logicians call a categorical proposition (CP), a sentence which places its subject in the category of its predicate. The pure form of a CP is

Subject	Linking Verb	Predicate
All art	is	an illusion
Caligula	was	a spoiled brat
Ballet dancers	are	really athletes

Statements about the nature of things do not always come in such neat packages, but even a proposition without a linking verb, like "Some dinosaurs cared for their young," is still a CP which could be recast into pure form, "Some dinosaurs were caring parents."

Whenever a CP is the thesis of an argument, it makes certain structural demands. Since supporting a CP is always a matter of showing that the subject belongs in the category of or has the attributes of the predicate, that predicate must be defined whenever its meaning cannot be assumed, and evidence or examples must be given to link the subject up with that predicate. The arguer for a CP, then, works under two constraints: the definition of the predicate must be acceptable to the audience and the evidence or examples about the subject must be convincing and verifiable. We can see these two constraints operating on the arguer constructing support for a CP like "America is a class society." For most audiences, the definition of "class society" cannot be assumed. If our arguer defined a "class society" as one in which people live in different sized towns, he or she could produce plenty of evidence that Americans do indeed live in towns small, medium, and large, but "class society" has been defined in what speakers of English would intuitively recognize as a completely unacceptable way. It may be a vague term, but there are some meanings it cannot have. On the other extreme, the writer could define "class society" more acceptably as "a society structured into clearly defined ranks, from peasantry to nobility," but where could he or she find the non-metaphoric American duke or serf? Obviously, the arguer must construct a definition which is acceptable to its audience while it fits real evidence.

But suppose a student writes a brief argument supporting a CP like "My roommate is generous." He or she will bypass definition and go straight to examples of the roommate's generosity: the lending of money, clothes, shampoo, and time. The student can go right to such evidence because he or she has a clear definition of "generous" in mind and cannot imagine any audience having a different one. Still a definition of "generous," whether or not articulated in the argument, controls the choice of examples. It was not the roommate's behavior which led to the label "generous," but a definition of "generous" which led to the categorization of the behavior. Because we tend to forget the controlling power of definition, we delude ourselves into thinking that the examples come first and lead inductively to the thesis when in fact the process goes the other way.

Once the student understands that definition and specific evidence are the structural requirements of a CP argument, several organizational options become available. The controlling definition can sit at the beginning of the argument, can emerge at the end, or can have its elements dispersed.[4] In this last option, the definition of the predicate is broken down into components, each supported with appropriate evidence. Take a CP like "Wilkie Collins's *Armadale* is a sensation novel." An arguer for this proposition might specify a multi-part definition of "sensation novel" which would supply the whole structure of the paper: "a sensation novel is characterized by its ominous setting, grotesque characters, suspenseful plot, and concern with the occult." Each of the elements from this definition becomes the predicate of its own CP (again requiring definition where necessary) and the topic sentence of its own paragraph," e.g. "*Armadale* has grotesque characters," "Collins dabbles in the occult in *Armadale*."

Once students have learned the fundamentals of the CP argument, they have the tools to support a comparison or a contrast as well. An arguer for a single comparison, "Kissinger is like Metternich," for instance, finds one or more traits that the two subjects have in common. "Both Kissinger and Metternich had no chauvinistic pride." This is simply a CP with a compound subject which can be divided into two simple CPs ("Kissinger had no chauvinistic pride," "Metternich had no chauvinistic pride"), each supported, as much as the audience requires, by definition and evidence.

A second type of proposition needs quite a different kind of argument. An assertion of cause and effect adds the dimension of time and is therefore not supported with definition but with another kind of ruling assumption, that of *agency,* a basic belief about what can cause what. Just as users of the same language

[4]Here perhaps is the only legitimate use of the terms "inductive" and "deductive" in written argument. They can be used to describe the organization of arguments, the deductive setting out the thesis at the beginning and the inductive disclosing it at the end.

share a set of definitions, so do people in the same culture share many causal assumptions. We have a common-sense understanding, for instance, of such natural agencies as light, heat and gravity, as well as many accepted human agencies whose operation we believe in as readily as we believe in the operation of physical law. Philosophers, psychologists, anthropologists and social scientists debate about what to call these agencies—motives, instincts, or learned patterns of behavior. But we recognize a believable appeal to the way human nature works, just as we recognize an appeal to the way physical nature works; we no more accept happiness as a motive for murder than we would accept the power of rocks to fly.

Definition and agency, then, are the warrants (to use Toulmin's term) behind the two basic kinds of arguments.[5] If we make a claim about the nature of things (a CP), we rely on an assumption about the nature of things, a definition. If we make a claim about causal relations, we rely on an assumption about what can cause what, an agency. And whether or not we articulate agency in a causal argument depends largely on audience. For example, if we argue that a significant cause of teenage vandalism is violence on TV, the agency between these two is imitation. Since most audiences will readily accept imitation as a human motive, we would not have to stop and argue for it. But if we claimed that wearing a mouth plate can improve athletic performance (*Sports Illustrated*, 2 June 1980), we will certainly have to explain agency. (The article did.)

Students have two problems with causal argument. First, they need help thinking up the possible causes of an event. Students tend to overlook the complex interaction of factors, conditions, and influences that yield an effect; they will seize on one cause without understanding how that cause works in connection with others. We have to teach them to think backwards along the paths of known causal agencies, and we can help them do this by introducing the existing terminology of causality. Causes can be identified as necessary and sufficient, as remote and proximate, or as conditions and influences acted on by a precipitating cause. Or sometimes any linear model of causality is a falsification and we have to look at causes and effects as reciprocal, as acting on each other; inflation urges pay raises and higher wages fuel inflation. And, oddly enough, students have to consider what was missing when they think about causes, for an event can take place because a blocking cause was absent. Finally, whenever people are involved in a consideration of causes, the question of responsibility arises. We look for whoever acted or failed to act, or at the person in charge, as causes (usually with the ribbon of praise or the stigma of blame in our hands). In the

---

[5]Stephen Toulmin, finding the syllogism ambiguous, created a new pattern for analyzing arguments. In his terminology, a "claim" is supported by "data" linked to the claim by a "warrant." Warrants are "inference licences," "the general hypothetical statements which can act as bridges between the data and the claim" (Toulmin, p. 98). Warrants often require backing themselves. They are not always interchangeable with the minor premise of a syllogism, which may be either a warrant or its backing.

aftermath of the Three Mile Island reactor breakdown, for instance, the operators in the control room, the engineers who designed the reactor, and even the Nuclear Regulatory Commission officials whose safety regulations controlled its operation were all considered in varying degrees as causes of the accident. Students who are familiar with these possible frames or sets of causes, from necessary cause to responsible cause, can put together models of how causes interacted to bring about the effect they are interested in.

Convincing an audience that a particular cause did in fact operate is the second problem students need help with. The writer of a causal argument can choose from several tactics for presenting evidence that two events are connected as cause and effect. A remote cause, for instance, can be linked to an effect by a chain of causes. NASA provides us with a good example of this technique in their argument claiming that sunspots caused Skylab's fall. Sunspots are storms on the sun which hurl streams of electromagnetic particles into space; these streams, the solar wind, heat up the earth's outer atmosphere. The heated atmosphere expands into Skylab's orbit, increasing the drag on the craft; the craft therefore slows down and falls. Identifying such a chain of causes in effect replaces an implausible leap from cause to effect, a leap an audience is not prepared to take, with a series of small steps they are willing to follow.

Although proximity in time is by itself insufficient evidence of a causal relationship (indeed this is the *post hoc* fallacy), nevertheless, in the presence of plausible agency, time sequence is another tactic for supporting a causal assertion. So is causal analogy, a parallel case of cause and effect; we believe for instance that saccharin or red dye no. 2 causes cancer in humans because it causes cancer in animals. And in the case of a causal generalization such as "Jogging increases self-confidence," a series of individual cases, so long as agency is plausible (and in this instance a definition of self-confidence established), will lend support.

John Stuart Mill's four methods for discovering causes are also powerful aids to invention in causal argument. If the student can find at least two significantly parallel cases, one in which an effect occurred and one in which it didn't, the *single difference* between them can be convincingly nominated as a cause. Or if the same effect occurs several times, any *common factor* in the antecedent events is possibly a cause; this was the method of the health officials searching for the cause of Legionnaire's disease. Another method, that of *concomitant variation,* is the favorite of the social scientist who looks for influences and contributing factors; when two trends vary proportionately, when the hours of TV watching increase over a decade as SAT scores decline, a causal relationship is suggested, especially when a plausible agency can be constructed between the two. Mill's fourth method, *elimination,* is the ruling-out of all but one possible sufficient cause. It is the favorite of Sherlock Holmes and other detectives faced with a limited number of possible causes.

The student who uses one of Mill's methods can construct a convincing causal argument by repeating the process in writing. Take our sample proposition, "Violence on TV encourages teenage vandalism." Support may come from concomitant variation if we can document an increase in TV violence and a corresponding increase in vandalism perpetrated by teenagers. (The propositions that teenage vandalism exists and has increased along with TV violence can be supported with CP arguments, which the student knows by now require careful definition. What, for instance, precisely constitutes "violence" on TV?) And since this causal claim is a generalization, it could also be supported by citing specific acts of violence clearly inspired by similar acts on TV.

Arguments for CPs and causal statements are the two basic types. Once students have learned to construct these simpler arguments they can combine them into the more complex arguments required for evaluations and proposals. An evaluation is a proposition which makes a value judgment: e.g. "The San Diego Padres are a bad team," "*Jane Eyre* is a great novel," "The open classroom is a poor learning environment." We have to encourage our students to see such propositions as genuinely arguable, as claims which an audience can be convinced of and not merely as occasions for the expression of personal taste. The key is, once again, finding and, when necessary, articulating and defending the sharable assumptions or criteria on which the evaluation is made. Just as the CP argument rests on definition and the causal on agency, so do all evaluations rest ultimately on criteria or assumptions of value.

Students can be taught to construct evaluations by first learning to distinguish the various subjects of evaluations. We evaluate objects both natural and man-made, including the practical and the aesthetic. We also judge people, both in roles and as whole human beings, and we evaluate actions, events, policies, decisions and even abstractions such as lifestyles and institutions which are made up of people, things and actions. Constructing a good evaluation argument is a matter of finding acceptable criteria appropriate to the subject. Our students are already familiar with the typical standards behind the "consumer" evaluations of practical objects. They are far less familiar with the formal criteria used or implied in aesthetic judgments. Most challenging of all are the evaluations of people, actions, and events which require the application of ethical criteria. Students must be encouraged to see that arguing about ethics is not the exclusive province of religion or law, but that we all have beliefs about what is right, proper, or of value which an arguer can appeal to in an evaluation.

In form, an evaluation proposition looks exactly like a CP and, overall, the argument is carried on like a CP argument. Our example above places *Jane Eyre* in the class "great novel." An arguer for this proposition must construct a plausible "definition" or set of criteria for "great novel" which fits the evidence from the book. But the criteria or standard of an evaluation can easily include good or bad consequences as well as qualities, and thus evaluations often require causal arguments showing that the subject does indeed produce this or that effect. If we want to argue, for example, that it was right to bring the Shah to the U.S. for medical treatment, we could do so by classifying that decision as an humanitarian one in a CP argument; or we could argue that the decision was wrong by exploring its consequences in a causal argument. (Of course, whether a consequence can be labeled good or bad gets us right back to ethical assumptions which must be either appealed to or defended, depending on one's audience. Evaluations can lead us into an infinite regress unless we stop eventually on an appeal to shared values.)

The fourth and final type of proposition is the proposal, the call to action. The specific proposal which recommends an exact course of action requires a special combination of smaller CP and causal arguments. We can imagine this argument's structure as something like an hour glass, preliminary arguments funneling in from the top, proposal statement at the neck, and supporting arguments expanding to the base.

We can see how that structure works if we imagine ourselves carrying through an argument for a proposal such as, "Wolves should be reestablished in the forests of northern Pennsylvania and a stiff fine levied for killing them." No one will feel a desire to take action on this proposal unless first convinced that some problem exists which needs this solution; that is the work of the preliminary arguments. An opening CP argument establishes the existence of a situation, in this case the absence or extreme rarity of wolves in certain areas. But an audience may agree that a situation exists yet not perceive it as a problem; it may take a further causal argument to trace the bad consequences (i.e. deer herds are out of control) or show the ethical wrongness of the situation (i.e. a species has been removed from its rightful habitat). These opening parts amount to a negative evaluation. Another preliminary step might be a causal argument singling out the dominant reason for the problem, for ideally the proposal should remove or block this cause or causes, rather than simply patch up the effect alone. If wolves have become nearly extinct in northern Pennsylvania because of unrestricted hunting, then a ban on hunting wolves ought to take care of that.

After the specific proposal is disclosed, it can be supported with another series of CP and causal arguments. The proposal will lead to good consequences (the causal: deer population will be controlled), and it will be ethically right (CP: the balance of nature will be as it ought to be). And most important, the proposal is feasible; the time, money, and people are available (CP), and the steps to its achievement are all planned out (causal).

Just how much of this full proposal outline is actually needed for the writer to make a convincing recommendation depends entirely on audience and situation. A problem may be so pressing that preliminary arguments can be dispensed with entirely; after the last flood, the people of Johnstown did not have to be convinced they had a problem. And not every call to action requires a full proposal argument. One which ends with an unspecified plea, "We really ought to do something about this," is actually a negative evaluation. Such a vague call to awareness is really a coda resting on the widely-held assumption that if something is wrong it ought to be corrected.

In addition to dealing with the four types of arguments we have described, any course in argument must treat the two elements common to all arguments: accommodation and refutation. Consideration of audience (accommodation) and consideration of potential or actual opposition (refutation) inform all argument, affecting invention, arrangement, and style. Where do they sensibly come in a course? The only answer is first, last, and all the way through, worked into every discussion of every type of argument.

Once students have learned the necessary structures of CP and causal arguments and learned how these types combine in support of evaluations and proposals, they have not only the help they need for constructing arguments but tools for the critical analysis of argumentative discourse as well. They can recognize what type of proposition an argument is trying to support, identify the necessary structural elements both explicit and implied and, considering the argument's audience, determine whether all was skillfully done. We might illustrate how this process works by taking a brief look at James Madison's *Federalist* No. 10, reprinted in Corbett's *Classical Rhetoric for the Modern Student* and followed by a careful analysis of its logical elements and the arguments from the sources (2nd edition, New York: Oxford University Press, 1971, pp. 239–256). Madison's argument is an all but perfectly symmetrical full proposal with preliminary arguments (pars. 1–13), explicit proposal (par. 14), and supporting arguments (pars. 15–23). Given his audience and purpose, Madison needs no lengthy demonstration of the existence of a problem; he has only to appeal to "the evidence of known facts." He turns quickly, therefore, to a causal analysis of the problem and finds it in "faction," rooted in the corrupt nature of man. The ethical problem facing his audience is that of preserving two self-evident goods, the control of faction and some form of popular government. The solution which will bridle the effects (for the causes, as he cogently argues, are untouchable) is the federal union, which Madison then goes on to support by tracing the good consequences that will flow from it. Its feasibility has of course been argued elsewhere. Such an analysis is possible to the student who recognizes types of arguments and can thus identify the necessary structural elements in a given argument and even come to a satisfying understanding of why they are where they are.

The approach to argument we have outlined, then, makes it possible to teach argument coherently while avoiding some of the pitfalls of existing approaches. We can avoid extensive and unnecessary diversions into formal logic while keeping to the principles of sound reasoning. And the overall method of building from simple, basic types of argument to types requiring a combination of steps gives the student transferable structures which are suitable for any subject but are not so automatic as to preclude the student from doing his or her own thinking.

Beyond Argument in Feminist Composition
Catherine E. Lamb

Current discussion of feminist approaches to teaching composition emphasizes the writer's ability to find her own voice through open-ended, exploratory, often autobiographical, writing in which she assumes a sympathetic audience. These approaches are needed and appropriate: they continue to show us the richness and diversity of women's voices. My intent in this essay is to suggest a means by which one can enlarge the sphere of feminist composition by including in it an approach to argument, ways to proceed if one is in conflict with one's audience—in other words, the beginning of a feminist theory of composition. The place to start is not with particular forms—those close off options too easily—but by understanding the range of power relationships available to a writer and her readers. One then determines which are consistent with the emphasis on cooperation, collaboration, shared leadership, and integration of the cognitive and affective which is characteristic of feminist pedagogy (Schniedewind 170–179). This line of exploration has taken me to the study of negotiation and mediation, and how these well-established forms of oral discourse can be adapted for a feminist composition class. Argument still has a place, although now as a means, not an end. The end—a resolution of conflict that is fair to both sides—is possible even in the apparent one-sidedness of written communication.

Broadening the Scope of Feminist Modes of Discourse

Much has now been written about women writing and feminist modes of discourse. To illustrate representative approaches, I have selected two essays that have appeared recently in composition journals—one by Elizabeth Flynn describing patterns in women's narratives; the other by Clara Juncker playing out some of the implications if one applies French feminists' theories in the classroom, especially those of Hélène Cixous. Neither pretends to be an exhaustive treatment of the subject. However, because both deal in the content and form that we have come to associate with the broad topic of women and writing, one could quite easily get the idea that these are the only areas in which feminist composition has a contribution to make.

In "Composing as a Woman," Elizabeth Flynn uses what we know about gender differences in social and psychological development to interpret the content of narratives her students wrote. The four essays she uses, two by women and two by men, are not meant to be definitive proof that women write one way and men another, but rather to show that the connections between psychological theory and narrative content are there and may illuminate each other. Her findings are not surprising: women write "stories of interaction, of connection, or of frustrated connection"; men write "stories of achievement, of separation, or of frustrated achievement" (428). This essay and one which followed it fourteen months later, "Composing 'Composing as a Woman': A Perspective on Research," emphasize the open-ended, provisional nature of Flynn's thinking—another quality that has come to be associated with (and prized in) feminist composition.

What I have learned from Flynn's essay and others like it helps me when I am working with women students and reading some literature by women. I need something else, though, if I am to develop a comprehensive approach to feminist composition, guidelines that could be used throughout a course, including the emphasis I used to give argument as a mode in which one's goal is to persuade another to one's point of view. I would also like to be as free as possible from the charge of essentialism, to which an essay like Flynn's is vulnerable. A feminist composition class could easily be a place where matriarchal forms are as oppressive as the patriarchal ones once were; even if in different ways.

Clara Juncker's essay "Writing (with) Cixous" is quite a different piece, written in the exuberant manner of the theorists whose work she is describing. Like them, she is much less interested in women as gendered beings possessing certain characteristics (a possible extension of Flynn's argument) than she is in "woman" as a feminine linguistic position from which to critique phallogocentrism, "the fantasy of a central, idealized subject and the phallus as signifier of power and authority" (425). If this order is dislocated, students may be able to find their own voices on the margins. Playing with language, as well as stressing pre-writing and revision, can sensitize students to the open-endedness of writing. And if they read material sufficiently outrageous, they are more likely to empathize with otherness, whether "racially, politically, sexually, herstorically" (433).

With Flynn's essay, in spite of its value, I see its potential for reductiveness. My concerns with Juncker's essay are theoretical and practical in a different way. I admire the energy in her essay and, having heard her read a shortened version of it at CCCC in 1988, I don't doubt she is able to convey the same to her students. But after the disruptions, then what? I can imagine an essay written this way that is every bit as combative as the masculinist discourse we are seeking to supplant. Further, how can students take these forms and use them in other classes or in the world of work? If we are serious about the feminist project of transforming the curriculum and even affecting the way students think, write, and act once they leave us, we need an approach to teaching composition that is more broadly based and accessible to our students.

Without such a framework, we are also left battling the dichotomies that Cynthia Caywood and Gillian Overing identify in the introduction to their anthology *Teaching Writing: Pedagogy, Gender, and Equity*. Noting that "the model of writing as product is inherently authoritarian," they continue, "certain forms of discourse and language are privileged: the expository essay is valued over the exploratory; the argumentative essay set above the autobiographical; the clear evocation of a thesis preferred to a more organic exploration of a topic; the impersonal, rational voice ranked more highly than the intimate, subjective one" (xii). I don't know anyone who would deny that these dichotomies exist and are evaluated in the manner described. Neither do I deny the value of continuing to emphasize and explore the potentials of the categories in the second half of each of these dichotomies, as do Flynn and Juncker, along with the contributors to this anthology. We need as well, however, to consider a feminist response to conflict, at the very least to recast the terms of the dichotomy so that "argumentation" is opposed not to "autobiography" but, perhaps, to "mediation."

One half of the problem I am addressing is the narrow range of feminist composition as defined so far. The other is its incompatibility with the values of what I am calling here "monologic argument," the way most (all?) of us were taught to conceptualize arguments: what we want comes first, and we use the available means of persuasion to get it, in, one hopes, ethical ways. We may acknowledge the other side's position but only to refute it. We also practice what we were taught. Keith Fort, in a 1975 essay that uses language we have come to expect in feminist critiques, sees stating a thesis as a competitive act, a way to claim mastery over the subject matter. Similar competition may be generated between the reader and the text (179).[1] More recently, Olivia Frey demonstrates that the antagonism in our writing is much more overt than Fort implies. Using a sample that included all the essays published in *PMLA* from 1975 to 1988 as well as articles in a variety of other professional journals, she found some version of the "adversarial method" in all but two of the essays she examined (512). We have uncritically assumed there is no other way to write—at least that attitude was present in much of the discussion about ways to respond to conflict at the 1990 Wyoming Conference on English. Even a text like Gregory Clark's *Dialogue, Dialectic, and Conversation,* which does a superb job of laying out the theory for a cooperative, collaborative approach to writing and reading that is consistent with much of what I shall present later in this essay, sees the act of writing as by definition authoritarian in an even broader sense than do Caywood and Overing. Thus, it is the reader, not the writer, who has the primary responsibility for how a text functions in a community (see especially 49–59). Ideally, wouldn't we want the reader *and* the writer to share that responsibility?[2]

[1]Fort's essay is cited by William Covino in *The Art of Wondering.* Fort's solution for the critical essay is to recommend "process criticism," where one might explore the correctness of a particular thesis rather than begin with it and show only how the work being analyzed fits. Fort notes that, to some extent, such essays are about the *process* of criticism; in the same way, the form I have students use when they are using negotiation as an alternative to argument is about the process of negotiation.

[2]S. Michael Halloran works under assumptions similar to Clark's in "Rhetoric in the American College Curriculum: The Decline of Public Discourse." He is arguing for returning the practice of teaching public discourse to our teaching of rhetoric (a goal I support, as does Clark, for the ways it would reinforce the social function of writing). Although the form of the discourse is not his major concern, the examples he gives all assume a debate model of interaction.

If we as teachers pass on without reflection what we have been taught and ourselves practice concerning argument, whether the rest of our pedagogy intends it or not, we are contributing to education as "banking," Paulo Freire's metaphor for education that is an act of "depositing" information into students who are only to receive and have no say in what or how something is taught (58–59). We are doing so because we are teaching students to form "banking" relationships with their readers, resisting dialogue, which, for Freire, means they are precluded from any possibility of naming the world, the essential element of being human (76). One of my first-year students this past year knew at some basic level what Freire was talking about when he described himself as a writer at the beginning of the semester: "For myself writing as a whole is not very important . . . I would much rather interact with someone by voice rather than writing. Writing is one-sided where no argument or opinion from others can be intervened."

In my discussion thus far of monologic argument, I have intentionally avoided associating it with classical rhetoric, especially Aristotle's. While the connections can surely be made and have been for more than two thousand years, recent scholarship is much more likely to explore ways in which both Plato and Aristotle comment on the social, dialogical context in which knowledge is acquired and exchanged. (See, for example, chapter 2 in Clark, "Rhetoric in Dialectic: The Functional Context of Writing.") Here, I wish only to remind readers of some of those connections without discussing them in detail. The feminist alternatives I am advocating do not follow necessarily, but they are clearly consistent with them. With respect to Plato, what is most important is the example of his dialogues themselves illustrating the dialectic he is advocating, even though the goal, immutable truth, may not be one we share. In the *Phaedrus,* Socrates criticizes writing (in writing), seeing it as something static which inhibits dialectic (95–103). However one interprets his condemnation,[3] the dissonance resulting from an attack on writing itself, also made directly by Plato in *Letter VII* (136), contributes to the dialectic. Aristotle is much more explicitly connected to monologic argument, especially if one stops at his definition of rhetoric as no more than dealing with "the available means of persuasion," a set of techniques to be used. Andrea Lunsford and Lisa Ede have refuted the contradictory claims that Aristotelian rhetoric over-emphasizes the logical and is manipulative ("On Distinctions"), making use of William Grimaldi's work on Aristotle. Grimaldi maintains that in Aristotle's *Rhetoric* one person is speaking to another *as a person;* the rhetor's task is to put before the audience the means by which the

---

[3]For examples of the range of interpretations possible, see Ronna Burger, *Plato's Phaedrus,* in which she argues for Plato's developing a "philosophic art of writing"; Jasper Neel, on the other hand, in *Plato, Derrida, and Writing,* argues that Plato is not using writing but trying to "use it up," appropriating both Socrates's voice and then his means of expression (1–29). Walter Ong, in *Orality and Literacy,* is more relaxed. He notes that Plato's criticisms of writing are the same that were made with the advent of printing and now of computers (979).

audience can make up his or her mind, but it is then up to the audience to decide. The enthymeme is most often cited by these writers and others as illustrating Aristotle's recognition of the proper use of both reason and emotion. The speaker, in constructing an enthymeme, must take the audience into account since it is the audience who supplies the unstated premise. As Lloyd Bitzer says, the audience in effect persuades itself (408).

A Feminist Theory of Power

While it is helpful to view Plato and Aristotle in the ways I have just summarized, neither provides ways to get to concrete alternatives to monologic argument. Considering writer/reader relationships in the context of a feminist theory of power allows us to see more clearly the disjuncture between monologic argument and the modes of discourse advocated by Flynn and Juncker. It also provides a framework for evaluating any alternatives to resolving conflict. Because the emphasis is on values available to men as well as women, essentialist aspects of this approach are minimized.

In an earlier essay, I note that we understand power in a common-sense way as "the ability to affect what happens to someone else" (100). Monologic argument fits in here easily. There are, however, a number of feminist theorists who view power not as a quality to exercise on others, but as something which can energize, enabling competence and thus reducing hierarchy.[4] More than thirty years ago, Hannah Arendt, in her discussion of "action" in *The Human Condition,* showed us what this use of power might look like. She wrote about the *polis* in classical Greece, in which rhetoric as a spoken art, and therefore argument, would have functioned to maintain the *polis* as she describes it. Its essential character is not its physical boundaries, but "the organization of the people as it arises out of acting and speaking together, and its true space lies between people living together for this purpose" (198). Power maintains this space in which people act and speak: no single person can possess it (as an individual can possess strength). It "springs up" when people act together and disappears when they separate. This sort of power is limitless; it can, therefore, "be divided without decreasing it, and the interplay of powers with their checks and balances is even liable to generate more power" (200–201). I am reminded here of Bakhtin's familiar image of the carnival as the place where hierarchy is suspended and with it the distance between people (e.g., *Problems of Dostoyevsky's Poetics* 122–126). The image is much less dignified than Arendt's idealized description of the *polis,* but the impulse that drives and sustains them is, I believe, the same.

[4]In addition to the theorists discussed in this essay, I also refer to Jean Baker Miller, *Toward a New Psychology of Women,* and Elizabeth Janeway, *Powers of the Weak.* Another important source is Nancy Hartsock, *Money, Sex, and Power.*

In discussing Dostoyevsky's world view, Bakhtin says its governing principle is "To affirm someone else's 'I' not as an object but as another subject" (10). Some feminist theorists contribute to articulating how such a relationship might develop through insights gained from studying women's experience. They are arguing from what has come to be called a "feminist standpoint," defined by Sara Ruddick as "a superior vision produced by the political conditions and distinctive work of women" (129). The superiority of the standpoint derives from the manner in which it is acquired. An oppressed group, in this case, women, gains knowledge only through its struggle with the oppressor, men, who have no need to learn about the group they are oppressing. With this experience, women's knowledge has at least the potential to be more complete than men's (Harding, "Conclusion" 184–185). There are, admittedly, dangers in using standpoint theory: It can imply the moral superiority of women, easily become essentialist,[5] and ignore the reality that many of the qualities we ascribe to women can just as accurately be called non-Western—possibilities that my anthropologist friends have pointed out to me and that Harding notes in a later essay ("Instability" 29–30). I continue to use this approach, however, because of the teaching power of concrete experience reflected on, to which the success of a book like Belenky et al.'s *Women's Ways of Knowing* is eloquent testimony.

The most complete feminist discussion of the thought and action which makes possible the use of power described above, in individual relationships as well as those between nations, is Sara Ruddick's *Maternal Thinking*. Ruddick deliberately uses "maternal" because women still have most of the responsibility for raising children; mothering work, she says, can be done as well by men as by women (xi). One need not be a biological parent either. I want to summarize the main features of maternal thinking and then apply them to writer/reader relationships. (They are also readily applicable to teacher/student relationships—but that is another essay. One of the pleasures of teaching this approach to conflict resolution is that it invites attention to the congruence between what and how one teaches.) Central to the idea and experience of maternal thinking is "attentive love, or loving attention" (120). Loving attention is much like empathy, the ability to think or feel as the other. In connecting with the other, it is critical that one already has and retains a sense of one's self. The process requires, ultimately, more recognition and honoring of difference than it does searching for common ground. The vulnerability of the child, combined with the necessity for it and the mother to grow and change, place apparently contradictory demands on the relationship. On the one hand, maternal work requires an attitude of "holding," in which the mother does what is necessary to protect the child without

---

[5]I invite readers to consider whether Ruddick's approach as I go on to summarize it is essentialist. Perhaps in the final analysis it is, although in her book she goes to considerable lengths to discuss varieties of mothering experiences. The potential oppression of any essentialist features is also reduced because the process she describes is available to men as well as women and has as its hallmark a deep respect for the other as person.

unduly controlling it. On the other hand, she must continually welcome change if she is to foster growth (78–79, 89–93, 121–123).

In the second half of her book, Ruddick shows how maternal thinking can be applied to conflict resolution more generally. One begins by recognizing that equality often does not exist in relationships; even with this reality, individuals or groups in unequal relationships do not have to resort to violence to resolve conflicts. Making peace in this context requires both "giving and receiving while remaining in connection" (180–181). In *Composing a Life,* a discussion of the shaping of five women's lives, Mary Catherine Bateson reflects on these asymmetrical, interdependent relationships and how ill-prepared we are to function in them. Typically, we value symmetrical relationships—buddies and colleagues—which happen also to promote competition. Instead of honoring difference, which makes interdependence possible (both are qualities which "loving attention" cultivates), we want to reduce difference to inequality (102–106).

Monologic argument, even at its best, inevitably separates itself very quickly from the qualities I have just described because of its subject/object, I/it orientation. As I shall demonstrate later, where we still need this kind of argument is at the early stages of resolving a conflict, where both parties need to be as clear as possible about what they think and feel. Our students need to learn it for their survival in other contexts, and, more fundamentally, as part of the process of becoming adults. It promotes differentiation, the sense of self that Ruddick says must precede maternal thinking or integration more generally. This essay is itself a kind of monologic argument because I am asking readers to consider a different (and better, I believe) approach to resolving conflicts in writing. For any change to occur, however, readers first need to know what it is I am proposing.

At this point, readers might be thinking of Rogerian argument as an alternative to monologic argument. In it, the writer goes to great lengths to show the audience that he understands their point of view and the values behind it. The hope is that the audience, feeling less threatened, will do the same. My experience using Rogerian argument and teaching it to my students is that it is feminine rather than feminist. It has always been women's work to understand others (at Albion, it is women, not men, who sign up for The Psychology of Men); often that has been at the expense of understanding self. Rogerian argument has always felt too much like giving in. (In "Feminist Responses to Rogerian Argument," Phyllis Lassner makes these points and others about the difficulties of using Rogerian argument, and the hostilities it may arouse in users, especially if they do not yet have a clear sense of self.)

Mediation and Negotiation as Alternatives

What we need as an alternative to the self-assertiveness of monologic argument is not self-denial but an approach which cultivates the sense of spaciousness Arendt describes in the working of the *polis.* My very brief comments on Plato and Aristotle were intended as another way of saying they are concerned with knowledge as something that people do together rather than something anyone possesses (Gage 156). In a reversal of Bacon's dictum, we could say that Arendt's notion of power makes possible knowledge realized this way. We are ready now to apply this relationship of knowledge and power more specifically to a conflict situation. In it, both parties can retain the interdependence that permits connectedness while also going through the giving and receiving necessary if they are to resolve their conflict. The result is a paradoxical situation where the distance between writer and audience is lessened (as they explore the dimensions of the conflict together) while the "space" in which they are operating has enlarged because they see more possibilities (Lamb 102–103). Jim Corder, in "Argument as Emergence, Rhetoric as Love," also asks us to visualize the writer/audience relationship in terms of physical space. Argument, he says, is too often a matter of "presentation" and "display." Instead, it should just "be." Rather than objectifying the other, we need to "emerge" toward it. In a corollary to the idea of creating more space in which writer and audience can operate, he says we should expect to have to "pile time" into our arguments: we can do so by relying less on closed, packaged forms and more on narratives that show who we are and what our values are (26–31).

When I read Fisher and Ury's *Getting to Yes,* a layperson's version of how the process of negotiation works, I saw that here were some new (to me, as a composition teacher) ways of thinking about argument and conflict resolution. I later attended a seminar on mediation and have mediated cases of sexual harassment at Albion, as one of the people designated by the College to hear these complaints. What quickly became apparent, in both negotiation and mediation, is that the goal has changed: it is no longer to win but to arrive at a solution in a just way that is acceptable to both sides. Necessarily, the conception of power has changed as well: from something that can be possessed and used on somebody to something that is available to both and has at least the potential of being used for the benefit of both. When negotiation and mediation are adapted for a writing class, talk is still central for either process. Writing marks critical stages but cannot occur without conversation that matters, before and after. With all of the currently fashionable and often obscure discourse about writing as dialogue, here is a simple, concrete way of actually doing it.

Central to understanding this broadened and re-focused "practice" of power—how it creates more space and the possibility for loving attention—is articulating the place of conflict in it. As a culture, we learn much more about how to repress or ignore conflict than how to live with and transform it. When we practice and teach monologic argument as an end, we are teaching students that conflict can be removed by an effort that is fundamentally one-sided. Morton Deutsch, in *The Resolution of Conflict,* reminds us that conflicts arise in order that tensions between antagonists might be resolved. They can be healthy ways of finding a new stability and of clarifying values and priorities (9), especially if both parties participate in the resolution in ways that are mutually satisfactory. Negotiation and mediation are *cooperative* approaches to resolving conflicts that increase the chances of these goals occurring. They focus on the future, not the past (as does the law), and seek to restore trust between the two parties. A win-lose orientation encourages narrowness and a wish to use resources only for the goal one has already identified. Deutsch notes that the outcomes of a cooperative approach are those which encourage creative problem-solving: "openness, lack of defensiveness, and full utilization of available resources" (363). Negotiation and mediation are also *collaborative,* with both parties using the process to identify interests and outcomes they share. (See Clark, xvi, for distinctions between cooperation and dialogue on the one hand and collaboration and dialectic on the other.) Finally, both cooperation and collaboration are facilitated by negotiation and mediation as *structured* forms of conflict resolution. The point is important, for the guidelines which provide the structure are the mechanism whereby space between the two parties can be increased, making it possible for the distance between them to lessen as they move toward each other.

Negotiation as it is described in *Getting to Yes* begins with a recognition that focusing on the particularities of the *positions* of both parties will get them nowhere. Instead, identifying underlying *interests or issues* is a way to get at root causes of the problem as well as seeing where there might be common ground. The parties brainstorm a number of possible solutions, evaluating them using criteria both sides can accept. For Fisher and Ury, the ideal outcome is to reach a solution to which both sides can unequivocally answer "yes." Mediation extends and elaborates the process of negotiation with the introduction of an impartial third party. The nature of the outcome is still the responsibility of the disputants, as is carrying out the settlement. The parties in a dispute often appeal to a mediator when they believe they cannot resolve the conflict themselves. The presence of a mediator is also extremely valuable if there is a power imbalance between the two parties, as with, in my experience, cases of sexual harassment involving a student and professor. One of the mediator's main functions, especially at the beginning, is collecting information: What are the problems for each side? What are the interests these problems reflect? Where are the areas of agreement? What are the outcomes each side wants? The mediator's goal is a written agreement, which all parties sign, consisting of concrete statements describing actions both parties will take to resolve the conflict.[6]

I am not yet prepared to recommend one process of conflict resolution over the other in a composition classroom. Mediation may be somewhat more accessible because the roles of negotiator and disputant are separate. I have also taught both only in upper-level writing courses, negotiation in Advanced Expository Writing and mediation in Technical Writing. (I originally used mediation in Technical Writing because a good mediation agreement is also a model of good

---

[6]I have taken this very abbreviated description of the mediation process from Christopher Moore, *The Mediation Process,* and from the *Mediator Training Manual for Face-to-Face Mediation* (Boston: Department of Attorney General, 1988), used at the Mediation Institute taught each spring at the University of Massachusetts at Amherst by staff of the Mediation Project.

technical writing: its function is instrumental, and it must be straightforward, concrete, and unambiguous.) In both courses, the pedagogy is feminist, but only in the expository writing class do I use the theoretical orientation I describe in this paper as a guiding principle for the entire course. Here, I shall describe my use of mediation first to show how the roles operate separately. It also illustrates how a traditional-looking, writing-as-product piece of discourse actually functions quite differently because of the context out of which it comes.

Students work in groups of three, deciding what problem they will work with and who will take what role. Projects come from their reading or current college issues. Last semester, they were as disparate as mediating a property settlement between Donald and Ivana Trump and a dispute between the Inter-Fraternity Council and the administration at Albion College over the social function fraternities serve on campus. Much of the training for being a mediator (or a disputant) goes on in role plays. Of the many skills a mediator needs, I concentrate on just a few: getting as complete a picture as possible from both sides, separating the facts of the situation from the issues, and getting the parties they are working with to come up with as many options as possible in the process of arriving at a solution.

The first piece of writing is one they do individually after they have met several times as a group. If they are one of the disputants, they write a memo to the mediator in which they explain the problem as they see it, including an attempt to separate the immediate ways in which the problem has exhibited itself from the underlying issues or interests. They gain more from the experience if they are willing to take on a role opposite from their own actual position: a fraternity member representing the administration; or a woman playing a man whose spouse has just been offered a high-paying position hundreds of miles away— accepting it would mean serious disruptions in the family and in his career. If a student is the mediator, he or she writes a memo to a supervisor, summarizing the issues for both parties as they appear at that point. Here, all three are using the analytical skills we associate with monologic argument, although not with the goal of persuasion. The memos are part of what will give the mediator a sense of the dimensions of the conflict. For the disputants, they act to "pile time." All of these actions encourage maternal thinking, which is especially desirable between the mediator and both disputants; one hopes it also occurs between the disputants by the end of the process. The second piece of writing is the mediation agreement itself, which all three prepare together. Here are two of ten clauses in an agreement the Inter-Fraternity/administration group reached to resolve their differences:

1. Fraternities agree to restrict the number of house parties to two per semester for the spring 1990 and fall 1990 terms.
2. The administration agrees to begin free shuttle services to cities (Ann Arbor and Lansing) to widen the available social possibilities.

All these pieces of writing in the mediation process are products and not, as will be seen in the discussion of negotiation, a record of a process. Because of the interaction that must occur, particularly when the agreement is being developed, and because everyone involved is both writer and audience, I am not willing to accept Caywood and Overing's judgment that "writing as product is inherently authoritarian." The group's inventing has quite literally been a collaborative, social act, as Karen LeFevre has urged us to see invention more generally (see especially 35–40). Developing and carrying out a mediation agreement is clearly an illustration of what Arendt is getting at when she describes how power works, a point LeFevre also makes. The mediator and disputants, acting together in good faith, can move beyond the conflict that divides them. They are likely to have the experience described by one of the professionals Andrea Lunsford and Lisa Ede interviewed for their book on collaborative writing, *Singular Texts/Plural Authors:* "Working with someone else gives you another point of view. There is an extra voice inside your head; that can make a lot of difference" (29). If, however, one disputant pulls out, or the mediator gives up her neutrality, the energizing power is gone.

When I teach negotiation, it, like mediation, comes in the second half of the course when students trust me and one another and are accustomed to working in groups on various projects. Many of the features of teaching mediation (sources for topics, how to do the training, using writing in different ways at various stages of the process) apply as well to negotiation. Students work in pairs, selecting an issue of some substance in which they are both interested and which will require outside research. Individually, they each write a paper in which they take a contrasting position on the issue. I expect a monologic argument in the best sense of that term. Students see they cannot hope to negotiate a solution with integrity unless they are first clear about the characteristics and values of the viewpoint they are presenting, especially critical if it is one with which they do not agree. When the students have finished the first paper, I meet with the pairs to discuss their arguments. Sometimes, students on their own will take the initiative to begin negotiating a resolution during the conference, ignoring me. We can all then see the process occurring; their next essay, which they write together, is a record of it. They have little trouble differentiating the effect of reading it, its greater sense of spaciousness, from the much more linear effect of reading a monologic argument. The most common form of resolution is some kind of compromise, for example, merit pay for teachers, with the conditions limiting its application making it acceptable to its opponents. (The dynamics of power between the students working together are something I have not yet tried to identify in any systematic way. My impression, from anecdotal evidence, is that most pairs function in a fairly egalitarian way. Of course, they also know that's what I want to hear them say.)

Taking together my discussion of mediation and negotiation, these several features of a feminist alternative to monologic argument are apparent: (1) Knowledge is seen as cooperatively and collaboratively constructed (what the groups have created has come out of the relationships among their members). (2) The "attentive love" of maternal thinking is present at least to some degree (or they would not have been able to come up with a solution acceptable to both of them). (3) The writing which results is likely to emphasize process. (4) Finally, overall, power is experienced as mutually enabling.

These forms, along with the contexts in which they are produced, may also be ways to respond to Lunsford and Ede's call for written discourse which reflects dialogic collaboration in the texts themselves (*Singular* 136). They will not necessarily be of interest to all feminists. Sandra Gilbert and Susan Gubar, among the best known feminist collaborators, have said in a public discussion that they do not see any particular value to writing in a way that would reflect their collaboration and, by extension, more overtly invite the reader into the text. For those of us who *are* interested, these forms show how the writing of a text need not be "an inherently unethical act" (Clark 61), saved only by its readers and their responses. The forms are expressions of writer/reader relationships which reflect an understanding of power consistent with feminist values. As we use them, the forms themselves will change to mirror our evolving understanding of what we are constructing. We *can* move beyond argument. It may not even be foolish to hope for a time when wanting to do so is beyond argument.

Works Cited

Arendt, Hannah. *The Human Condition.* Chicago: U of Chicago P, 1958.

Bakhtin, Mikhail. *Problems of Dostoyevsky's Poetics.* Trans. and ed. Caryl Emerson. Theory and History of Literature 8. Minneapolis: U of Minnesota P, 1984.

Bateson, Mary Catherine. *Composing a Life.* New York: Atlantic Monthly, 1989.

Belenky, Mary Field, et al. *Women's Ways of Knowing.* New York: Basic Books, 1986.

Bitzer, Lloyd F. "Aristotle's Enthymeme Revisited." *Quarterly Journal of Speech* 45 (1959): 399–408.

Burger, Ronna. *Plato's Phaedrus.* University, AL: U of Alabama P, 1980.

Caywood, Cynthia L., and Gillian R. Overing. Introduction. *Teaching Writing: Pedagogy, Gender, and Equity.* Albany: State U of New York P, 1987, xi–xvi.

Clark, Gregory. *Dialogue, Dialectic, and Conversation.* Carbondale: Southern Illinois UP, 1990.

Corder, Jim W. "Argument as Emergence, Rhetoric as Love." *Rhetoric Review* 4 (1985): 16–32.

Covino, William. *The Art of Wondering.* Portsmouth: Heinemann, 1988.

Department of Attorney General. *Mediator Training Manual for Face-to-Face Mediation.* Boston: Department of Attorney General, 1988.

Deutsch, Morton. *The Resolution of Conflict.* New Haven: Yale UP, 1973.

Fisher, Roger, and William Ury. *Getting To Yes: Negotiating Agreement Without Giving In.* New York: Penguin, 1983.

Flynn, Elizabeth A. "Composing as a Woman." *College Composition and Communication* 39 (1988): 423–435.

——. "Composing 'Composing as a Woman': A Perspective on Research." *College Composition and Communication* 41 (1990): 83–91.

Fort, Keith. "Form, Authority, and the Critical Essay." *Contemporary Rhetoric.* Ed. W. Ross Winterowd. New York: Harcourt, 1975. 171–183.

Freire, Paulo. *Pedagogy of the Oppressed.* Trans. Myra Bergman Ramos. New York: Seabury, 1970.

Frey, Olivia. "Beyond Literary Darwinism: Women's Voices and Critical Discourse." *College English* 52 (1990): 507–526.

Gage, John. "An Adequate Epistemology for Composition: Classical and Modern Perspectives." *Essays on Classical Rhetoric and Modern Discourse.* Ed. Robert J. Connors, Lisa S. Ede, and Andrea A. Lunsford. Carbondale: Southern Illinois UP, 1984. 152–169, 281–284.

Grimaldi, William M. A. *Aristotle, Rhetoric I: A Commentary.* New York: Fordham UP, 1980.

Halloran, S. Michael. "Rhetoric in the American College Curriculum: The Decline of Public Discourse." PRE/TEXT 3 (1982): 245–269.

Harding, Sandra. "Conclusion: Epistemological Questions." *Feminism and Methodology.* Ed. Sandra Harding. Bloomington: Indiana UP, 1987. 181–190.

——. "The Instability of the Analytical Categories of Feminist Theory." *Signs* 11 (1986). Rpt. in *Feminist Theory in Practice and Process.* Ed. Micheline R. Malson et al. Chicago: U of Chicago P, 1989. 15–34.

Hartsock, Nancy. *Money, Sex, and Power.* Boston: Northeastern UP, 1983.

Janeway, Elizabeth. *Powers of the Weak.* New York: Knopf, 1980.

Juncker, Clara. "Writing (with) Cixous." *College English* 50 (1988): 424–436.

Lamb, Catherine E. "Less Distance, More Space: A Feminist Theory of Power and Writer/Audience Relationships." *Rhetoric and Ideology: Compositions and Criticisms of Power.* Ed. Charles W. Kneupper. Arlington: Rhetoric Society of America, 1989, 99–104.

Lassner, Phyllis. "Feminist Responses to Rogerian Argument." *Rhetoric Review* 8 (Spring 1990): 220–232.

LeFevre, Karen Burke. *Invention as a Social Act.* Carbondale: Southern Illinois UP, 1987.

Lunsford, Andrea, and Lisa Ede. "On Distinctions Between Classical and Modern Discourse." *Essays on Classical Rhetoric and Modern Discourse.* Ed. Robert J. Connors, Lisa S. Ede and Andrea A. Lunsford. Carbondale: Southern Illinois UP, 1984. 37–49, 265–267.

——. *Singular Texts/Plural Authors: Perspectives on Collaborative Writing.* Carbondale: Southern Illinois UP, 1990.

Miller, Jean Baker. *Toward a New Psychology of Women.* Boston: Beacon, 1975.

Moore, Christopher. *The Mediation Process.* San Francisco: Jossey-Bass, 1987.

Neel, Jasper. *Plato, Derrida, and Writing.* Carbondale: Southern Illinois UP, 1988.

Ong, Walter. *Orality and Literacy.* New York: Methuen, 1982.

Plato. *Phaedrus and Letters VII and VIII*. Trans. Walter Hamilton. London: Penguin, 1973.

Ruddick, Sara. *Maternal Thinking*. Boston: Beacon, 1989.

Schniedewind, Nancy. "Feminist Values: Guidelines for Teaching Methodology in Women's Studies." *Freire for the Classroom*. Ed. Ira Shor. Portsmouth: Heinemann, 1987. 170–179.

Additional Sources

Gage, John. "An Adequate Epistemology for Composition: Classical and Modern Perspectives." *Classical Rhetoric and Modern Discourse*. Eds. Robert J. Connors, Lisa S. Ede, and Andrea A. Lunsford. Carbondale: So. Illinois UP, 1984. xiii, 152–169.

Argues that classical conception of rhetoric contains two views, formalist and dynamic, with the latter most productively modelled in Aristotle's theory of the enthymeme.

Kneupper, Charles. "Teaching Argument: An Introduction to the Toulmin Model." *College Composition & Communication* 29.3 (October 1978): 237–41.

Important article for relating Stephen Toulmin's theory of argument to specific pedagogical practices.

Lassner, Phyllis. "Feminist Responses to Rogerian Argument." *Rhetoric Review* 8 (Spring 1990): 220–232.

Discusses the problems faced by female students in regard to Rogerian approaches to argument, especially the sense of denial which appears to be implied.

Lunsford, Andrea A. "Aristotelian vs. Rogerian Argument: A Reassessment." *College Composition & Communication* 30.2 (May 1979): 146–51.

Discusses similarities between Rogerian and Aristotelian approaches to argument, with emphasis on the notion of common ground.

Chapter 10

Research

The most common complaint that teachers have about research papers is that they are boring collections of only vaguely related data, about which neither the writer nor reader cares. As Richard Larson argues in "The 'Research Paper' in the Writing Course: A Non-Form of Writing," talking as though there is an abstract entity "The Research Paper" is both inaccurate and unproductive. Research, he argues, is not a product, but an activity. That is, research is not a collection of data, but a process by which people try to answer a question that matters. Instructors who describe success with research papers generally propose methods by which research (whether or not it is library research) is part of a recursive writing process.

But, damning the Research Paper can seem to be a condemnation of teaching students how to use the library. And, obviously, that would be doing students a disservice. All papers require support for their assertions, and the library can be an excellent resource for finding that support, whether or not the paper is a Research Paper. Thus, as Larson and others have argued, one error with having a separate entity called the Research Paper is that students will mistakenly conclude that no other paper requires research.

Simply presenting information to students about doing research, or simply leaving it to students to figure it out for themselves, will not work as well as sequencing the coursework so that research is thoughtfully integrated into the writing processes. However, there are certain problems inherent in teaching the Research Paper, especially if the topics are "open." We do a disservice to our students if we think of research in narrow terms, leaving them (and us) with boring papers on topics about which they cannot make meaning. Others have noted the problems presented by term-paper mills, or paper files (a problem worsened by the availability of pre-written papers on the Internet). As with the teaching of grammar or reasoning, a poorly designed assignment sequence can land us in a situation about which we know little—trying to evaluate a paper on a topic about which we are utterly ignorant, or trying to assist a student when our own library skills might be deficient in that area.

Thinking imaginatively and practically about what we want to happen when teaching research can enable us to incorporate some of the most interesting and productive recent developments from rhetoric and composition into our courses. Loosely, there are four facets of research which programs might emphasize: critical thinking and reading, library skills, documentation and presentation of source material, and skills regarding synthesizing and organizing source material.

Before planning a class or assignment, the instructor needs to know if there is a programmatic decision regarding how much time and instruction must be spent on each facet. If there is not a programmatic dictate, an instructor should decide for him or herself which of those facets seem most important, as it is difficult to provide thorough instruction in all of them.

For instance, if library skills seem most important, the instructor may choose to have students work on creating bibliographies. And the major thrust of at least one large section of the assignment sequence would be ensuring that students must use a variety of research tools available at the library. The best resource for designing such a sequence is a reference desk librarian, who can give assistance regarding exactly what materials are available, in what form (i.e., hard copy, computer, telnet), and at what times. A librarian can also warn against certain kinds of pitfalls, such as sending students to databases that will be inappropriate, having too many students relying on too few resources (so that a large number of students will not be able to get access to it), sending students looking for materials the library does not have.

One pitfall of teaching bibliographic methods is confusing the process with a procedure. In the days before photocopy machines and highlighters, it made sense for instructors to teach about using notecards. The purpose of the notecards was to ensure that researchers quickly abstracted information, so that they could move easily into the process of synthesizing. That process is what matters—now that many students are capable of doing the same process with laptop computers, photocopiers and highlighters, or methods of downloading, instructors can afford to be less rigid about notecards. That is not to say that we can afford to be less rigid about the process, in that we still need to help students understand the importance of stepping away from the research material to get a good perspective.

Teaching critical thinking and reading is most easily done if students are working on topics on which the instructor knows the source material. It is both arrogant and unnecessary to assume that people trained in English or Rhetoric can teach source evaluation in all fields without preparation. We do not, for instance, necessarily know which are the most prestigious journals in the field of physics and which are considered likely to publish less reliable research.

But the ability to evaluate sources is extremely important in research. Classes (even in the social sciences) do not always provide instruction regarding what makes one study more reliable than another, yet that is a skill which many courses simply assume. Thus taking considerable time to talk about scientific method, ranking of journals, and reasoning will help students understand why some sources carry more credibility than others. Some journals, like *Scientific American,* are popular enough that undergraduates can read them, yet present the results of studies that are susceptible to methodological analysis. In groups, as a class, or as individuals, students can present conflicting studies on the same topic in order to discuss methods, evidence, and reasoning within the experimental and human sciences.

Many students have never used a library that has scholarly journals, and they have only used material from popular journals. So, a discussion of what makes one journal scholarly, or more and less appropriate for citation in an academic setting, can be one way to pursue what it means to know something in various disciplines. Similarly, there are numerous kinds of journals that are not written for scholars within the field but are not accurately called "popular" either (such as *Scientific American* or *New York Review of Books*). Having the class look at how such journals handle a recent discovery or philosophical theory in contrast to something like *Time, Newsweek,* or *Vogue* can also lead to productive discussions of audience.

Teaching documentation and presentation of source material is another place where process can become procedure. Documentation methods not only vary among fields but continually change within them. While it is important for instructors to emphasize that readers have specific expectations regarding documentation, it often seems unproductive to spend too much time on exactly what those expectations are. If we get a class of students to memorize the specifics of a particular set of documentation standards, we have spent a lot of time teaching them something they will have to re-learn the next time those standards change. If, on the other hand, we teach them how to use a handbook, and why that use is important, they will be prepared for the next time the standard changes.

The more subtle skill involved in presenting documentation involves the sophisticated skill of knowing when to quote, how much to quote, how much to paraphrase, and how to combine quotes from various sources. The best method for this issue, I have found, is to spend time with the class brainstorming revision strategies for sample paragraphs (taken from class members' papers).

The inability to handle specific quotes well can be a sign of confusion at the more abstract level. If the student has not intellectually synthesized the information that has been gathered into a specific argument or interpretation, then it is very difficult for him or her to know how to synthesize specific words. Requiring that students free-write after every time they research can provide them with ideas to discuss with their peers.

A good paper, like good bread, needs time to sit. The students need to have time to think about the research which they have gathered. This means that instructors need to organize the assignment sequence both so that there is time between when the research is done and when students need to turn a paper in, but also that there is some way for the instructor to know if students are getting themselves into trouble with procrastinating. And, as teachers well know, one often learns something best when one tries to explain it to someone else. Many instructors find class presentations very helpful to students—they can see what aspects of a topic are interesting to other class members, what aspects are easy to explain and what aspect of an explanation is fragmented. These presentations can take the form of describing the prospective paper or reporting on research.

The "Research Paper" in the Writing Course: A Non-Form of Writing
Richard L. Larson

Let me begin by assuring you that I do not oppose the assumption that student writers in academic and professional settings, whether they be freshmen or sophomores or students in secondary school or intend to be journalists or lawyers or scholars or whatever, should engage in research. I think they should engage in research, and that appropriately informed people should help them learn to engage in research in whatever field these writers happen to be studying. Nor do I deny the axiom that writing should incorporate the citation of the writer's sources of information when those sources are not common knowledge. I think that writers must incorporate into their writing the citation of their sources—and they must also incorporate the thoughtful, perceptive evaluation of those sources and of the contribution that those sources might have made to the writer's thinking. Nor do I oppose the assumption that a writer should make the use of appropriate sources a regular activity in the process of composing. I share the assumption that writers should identify, explore, evaluate, and draw upon appropriate sources as an integral step in what today we think of as the composing process.

In fact, let me begin with some positive values. On my campus, the Department of English has just decided to request a change in the description of its second-semester freshman course. The old description read as follows:

> This course emphasizes the writing of formal analytic essays and the basic methods of research common to various academic disciplines. Students will write frequently in and out of class. By the close of the semester, students will demonstrate mastery of the formal expository essay and the research paper. Individual conferences.

The department is asking our curriculum committee to have the description read:

> This course emphasizes the writing of analytical essays and the methods of inquiry common to various academic disciplines. Students will write frequently in and out of class. By the close of the semester, students will demonstrate their ability to write essays incorporating references to suitable sources of information and to use appropriate methods of documentation. Individual conferences.

I applauded the department for requesting that change, and I wrote to the college curriculum committee to say so.

While thinking about this paper—to take another positive example—I received from the University of Michigan Press a copy of the proofs of a forthcoming book titled *Researching American Culture: A Guide for Student Anthropologists,* sent to me because members of the English Composition Board of the University of Michigan had decided that the book might be of use as a supplementary text at Michigan in writing courses that emphasize writing in the academic disciplines. Along with essays by professional anthropologists presenting or discussing research in anthropology, the book includes several essays by students. In these essays the students, who had been instructed and guided by faculty in anthropology, report the results of research they have performed on aspects of American culture, from peer groups in high school to connections between consumption of alcohol and tipping in a restaurant, to mortuary customs, to sports in America. If anyone was in doubt about the point, the collection demonstrates that undergraduate students can conduct and report sensible, orderly, clear, and informative research in the discipline of anthropology. I am here to endorse, indeed to applaud, such work, not to question the wisdom of such collections as that from Michigan or to voice reservations about the capacity of undergraduates for research.

Why, then, an essay whose title makes clear a deep skepticism about "research papers"? First, because I believe that the generic "research paper" as a concept, and as a form of writing taught in a department of English, is not defensible. Second, because I believe that by saying that we teach the "research paper"—that is, by acting as if there is a generic concept defensibly entitled the "research paper"—we mislead students about the activities of both research and writing. I take up these propositions in order.

We would all agree to begin with, I think, that "research" is an activity in which one engages. Probably almost everyone reading this paper has engaged, at one time or another, in research. Most graduate seminars require research; most dissertations rely upon research, though of course many dissertations in English may also include analytical interpretation of texts written by one or more authors. Research can take many forms: systematically observing events, finding out what happens when one performs certain procedures in the laboratory, conducting interviews, tape-recording speakers' comments, asking human beings to utter aloud their thoughts while composing in writing or in another medium and noting what emerges, photographing phenomena (such as the light received in a telescope from planets and stars), watching the activities of people in groups, reading a person's letters and notes: all these are research. So, of course, is looking up information in a library or in newspaper files, or reading documents to which one has gained access under the Freedom of Information Act—though reading filed and catalogued documents is in many fields not the most important (it may be the least important) activity in which a "researcher" engages. We could probably define "research" generally as the seeking out of information new to the seeker, for a purpose, and we would probably agree that the researcher usually has to interpret, evaluate, and organize that information before it acquires value. And we would probably agree that the researcher has to present the fruits of his or her research, appropriately ordered and interpreted, in symbols that are intelligible to others, before that research can be evaluated and can have an effect. Most often, outside of mathematics and the sciences (and outside of those branches of philosophy that work with nonverbal symbolic notation), maybe also outside of music, that research is presented to others, orally or in writing, in a verbal language.

But research still is an activity; it furnishes the substance of much discourse and can furnish substance to almost any discourse except, possibly, one's personal reflections on one's own experience. But it is itself the subject—the substance—of no distinctively identifiable kind of writing. Research can inform virtually any writing or speaking if the author wishes it to do so; there is nothing of substance or content that differentiates one paper that draws on data from outside the author's own self from another such paper—nothing that can enable one to say that this paper is a "research paper" and that paper is not. (Indeed even an ordered, interpretive reporting of altogether personal experiences and responses can, if presented purposively, be a reporting of research.) I would assert therefore that the so-called "research paper," as a generic, cross-disciplinary term, has no conceptual or substantive identity. If almost any paper is potentially a paper incorporating the fruits of research, the term "research paper" has virtually no value as an identification of a kind of substance in a paper. Conceptually, the generic term "research paper" is for practical purposes meaningless. We can not usefully distinguish between "research papers" and non-research papers; we can distinguish only between papers that should have incorporated the fruits of research but did not, and those that did incorporate such results, or between those that reflect poor or inadequate research and those that reflect good or sufficient research. I would argue that most undergraduate papers reflect poor or inadequate research, and that our responsibility as instructors should be to assure that each student reflect in each paper the appropriate research, wisely conducted, for his or her subject.

I have already suggested that "research" can take a wide variety of forms, down to and including the ordered presentation of one's personal reflections and the interpretations of one's most direct experiences unmediated by interaction with others or by reference to identifiably external sources. (The form of research on composing known as "protocol analysis," or even the keeping of what some teachers of writing designate as a "process journal," if conducted by the giver of the protocol or by the writer while writing, might be such research.) If research can refer to almost any process by which data outside the immediate and purely personal experiences of the writer are gathered, then I suggest that just as the so-called "research paper" has no conceptual or substantive identity, neither does it have a procedural identity; the term does not necessarily designate any particular kind of data nor any preferred procedure for gathering data. I would argue that the so-called "research paper," as ordinarily taught by the kinds of texts I have reviewed, implicitly equates "research" with looking up books in the library and taking down information from those books. Even if there is going on in some departments of English instruction that gets beyond those narrow boundaries, the customary practices that I have observed for guiding the "research paper" assume a procedural identity for that paper that is, I think, nonexistent.

As the activity of research can take a wide variety of forms, so the presentation and use of research within discourse can take a wide variety of forms. Indeed I cannot imagine any identifiable design that any scholar in rhetoric has identified as a recurrent plan for arranging discourse which cannot incorporate the fruits of research, broadly construed. I am not aware of any kind or form of discourse, or any aim, identified by any student of rhetoric or any theorist of language or any investigator of discourse theory, that is distinguished primarily—or to any extent—by the presence of the fruits of "research" in its typical examples. One currently popular theoretical classification of discourse, that by James Kinneavy (*A Theory of Discourse* [Englewood Cliffs, N.J.: Prentice-Hall, 1971]), identifies some "aims" of discourse that might seem to furnish a home for papers based on research: "referential" and "exploratory" discourse. But, as I understand these aims, a piece of discourse does not require the presence of results of ordered "research" in order to fit into either of these classes, even though discourse incorporating the results of ordered research might fit there—as indeed it might under almost any other of Kinneavy's categories, including the category of "expressive" discourse. (All discourse is to a degree "expressive" anyway.) The other currently dominant categorization of examples of discourse—dominant even over Kinneavy's extensively discussed theory—is really a categorization based upon plans that organize discourse: narration (of completed events, of ongoing processes, of possible scenarios), causal analysis, comparison, analogy, and so on. None of these plans is differentiated from other plans by the presence within it of fruits from research; research can be presented, so far as I can see, according to any of these plans. And if one consults Frank J. D'Angelo's *A Conceptual Theory of Rhetoric* (Cambridge, Mass.: Winthrop, 1975) one will not find, if my memory serves me reliably, any category of rhetorical plan or any fundamental human cognitive process—D'Angelo connects all rhetorical plans with human cognitive processes—that is defined by the presence of the fruits of research. If there is a particular rhetorical form that is defined by the presence of results from research, then, I have not seen an effort to define that form and to argue that the results of research are what identify it as a form. I conclude that the "research paper," as now taught, has no formal identity, as it has no substantive identity and no procedural identity.

For me, then, very little is gained by speaking about and teaching, as a generic concept, the so-called "research paper." If anything at all is gained, it is only the reminder that responsible writing normally depends on well-planned investigation of data. But much is lost by teaching the research paper in writing courses as a separately designated activity. For by teaching the generic "research paper" as a separate activity, instructors in writing signal to their students that there is a kind of writing that incorporates the results of research, and there are (by implication) many kinds of writing that do not and need not do so. "Research," students are allowed to infer, is a specialized activity that one engages in during a special course, or late in a regular semester or year, but that one does not ordinarily need to be concerned about and can indeed, for the most part, forget about. Designating the "research paper" as a separate project therefore seems to me to work against the purposes for which we allegedly teach the research paper: to help students familiarize themselves with ways of gathering, interpreting, drawing upon, and acknowledging data from outside themselves in their writing. By talking of the "research paper," that is, we undermine some of the very goals of our teaching.

We also meet two other, related difficulties. First, when we tend to present the "research paper" as in effect a paper based upon the use of the library, we misrepresent "research." Granted that a good deal of research in the field of literature is conducted in the library among books, much research that is still entitled to be called humanistic takes place outside the library. It can take place, as I mentioned earlier, wherever "protocol" research or writers' analyses of their composing processes take place; it can take place in the living room or study of an author who is being interviewed about his or her habits of working. It can take place in the home of an old farmer or rancher or weaver or potter who is telling a student about the legends or songs of his or her people, or about the historical process by which the speaker came from roots at home or abroad. Much research relies upon books, but books do not constitute the corpus of research data except possibly in one or two fields of study. If we teach the so-called "research paper" in such a way as to imply that all or almost all research is done in books and in libraries, we show our provincialism and degrade the research of many disciplines.

Second, though we pretend to prepare students to engage in the research appropriate to their chosen disciplines, we do not and cannot do so. Faculty in other fields may wish that we would relieve them of the responsibility of teaching their students to write about the research students do in those other fields, but I don't think that as teachers of English we can relieve them of that responsibility. Looking at the work of the students who contributed to the University of Michigan Press volume on *Researching American Culture,* I can't conceive myself giving useful direction to those students. I can't conceive myself showing them how to do the research they did, how to avoid pitfalls, assure representativeness of data, draw permissible inferences, and reach defensible conclusions. And, frankly, I can't conceive many teachers of English showing these students what they needed to know either. I can't conceive myself, or very many colleagues (other than trained teachers of technical writing) guiding a student toward a report of a scientific laboratory experiment that a teacher of science would find exemplary. I can't conceive myself or many colleagues guiding a student toward a well-designed experiment in psychology, with appropriate safeguards and controls and wise interpretation of quantitative and nonquantitative information. In each of these fields (indeed probably in each academic field) the term "research paper" may have some meaning—quite probably a meaning different from its meaning in other fields. Students in different fields do write papers reporting research. We in English have no business claiming to teach "research" when research in different academic disciplines works from distinctive assumptions and follows distinctive patterns of inquiry. Such distinctions in fact are what differentiate the disciplines. Most of us are trained in one discipline only and should be modest enough to admit it.

But let me repeat what I said when I started: that I don't come before you to urge that students of writing need not engage in "research." I think that they should engage in research. I think they should understand that in order to function as educated, informed men and women they have to engage in research, from the beginning of and throughout their work as writers. I think that they should know what research can embrace, and I think they should be encouraged to view research as broadly, and conduct it as imaginatively, as they can. I think they should be held accountable for their opinions and should be required to say, from evidence, why they believe what they assert. I think that they should be led to recognize that data from "research" will affect their entire lives, and that they should know how to evaluate such data as well as to gather them. And I think they should know their responsibilities for telling their listeners and readers where their data came from.

What I argue is that the profession of the teaching of English should abandon the concept of the generic "research paper"—that form of what a colleague of mine has called "messenger service" in which a student is told that for this one assignment, this one project, he or she has to go somewhere (usually the library), get out some materials, make some notes, and present them to the customer neatly wrapped in footnotes and bibliography tied together according to someone's notion of a style sheet. I argue that the generic "research paper," so far as I am familiar with it, is a concept without an identity, and that to teach it is not only to misrepresent research but also quite often to pander to the wishes of faculty in other disciplines that we spare them a responsibility that they must accept. Teaching the generic "research paper" often represents a misguided notion of "service" to other departments. The best service we can render to those departments and to the students themselves, I would argue, is to insist that students recognize their continuing responsibility for looking attentively at their experiences; for seeking out, wherever it can be found, the information they need for the development of their ideas; and for putting such data at the service of every piece they write. That is one kind of service we can do to advance students' humanistic and liberal education.

Research, Expressivism, and Silence
Matthew Wilson

The research paper is a perennial problem in the composition course, and there are those who maintain, as Richard Larson has argued, that it is not even a separate form of writing. Larson and others also insist that English departments have no business teaching the research paper, because the techniques and methodologies of research are so site-specific that they should be taught only within particular disciplines. On the other hand, we cannot ignore an institutional setting where almost 85 percent of all composition courses include a research paper component (Ford and Perry 827). The gap, however, between research paper writing and composition has never been successfully bridged, and that gap has only been widened by many of our prevailing orthodoxies about teaching the two forms. The incompatible paradigms and discursive practices of our teaching strategies illustrate the incoherence of Composition Studies as a field. For instance, working within the paradigm of composition as a genre, Lad Tobin can say that the preferred kind of essay is "the autobiographical narrative of a self-actualizing event" (337). In contrast, Schwegler and Shamoon have argued that most students view the research paper as a test and the teacher as "the audience . . . who already knows about the subject and is testing the student's knowledge and information-gathering ability" (819). In addition, students "view the research paper as a close-ended, informative, skills-oriented exercise" rather than an "act of discovery" (820, 819). Even if we grant that most students are incorrect in their assessment of our assumptions about the research paper, there would seem to be a certain incompatibility between writing that is overtly autobiographical and writing that demands that students suppress the autobiographical, between expressive writing and writing that is assumed to be the antithesis of expressive. No wonder students become confused. We spend half or two-thirds of a composition course encouraging students to reflect on and shape autobiographical experience, then we introduce them to the research paper and assume that, because both activities involve writing, skills will transfer from one discursive practice to another. When the skills fail to transfer, we either blame the students or give up teaching the research paper. Rarely have we thought it necessary to examine the incoherence of our own disciplinary assumptions.

Responding to this incoherence, Richard Larson has argued that, because of its institutional setting, "the generic 'research paper' as a concept, and as a form of writing taught in a department of English, is not defensible" (812). The skills of research should be taught in individual departments because "research in different academic disciplines works from distinctive assumptions and follows distinctive patterns of inquiry" (815–16). Larson's point about the particularity of academic inquiry is one that we should not forget, but his washing-his-hands-of-the-whole-mess solution is certainly an inadequate one where the great majority of composition programs *do* teach research paper writing, and where the great majority of academic departments are unprepared to teach it. His solution, as radical as it sounds, is a response to a sense of profound unease about the kinds of texts students produce when writing research papers. As a former colleague remarked about the research paper course at Rutgers University: "There's a poltergeist haunting this course!" Less hyperbolically, Schwegler and Shamoon register the results of this sense of unease when they begin their essay by stating that "many members of our department—and yours too, we suspect—have stopped teaching the research paper in composition courses" (817). Whether research paper courses have been dropped because of their perceived "failure" or because they are seen to perpetuate a set of false distinctions, this gesture of abnegation is, I believe, a potentially self-defeating one for Composition Studies. If we can teach students nothing about how to write a multiple source paper, what makes us think that we have anything to say to colleagues in other disciplines that they should listen to? If we can teach students nothing about how to write a paper using research in an art history course, or an evaluation of the causes for the outbreak of World War I, then why should our colleagues think of us as more than the language police, as those who fix up "the dinglers and the danglers"? I think we can deal with the research paper neither by orphaning it nor by benign neglect, but by looking more closely and critically at our own pedagogical practices in teaching the research paper and in composition courses.

Writing Technologies of the Research Paper

When I began teaching twenty years ago, practically the first class I taught was a required course in research writing. The texts were interesting and "relevant," the students earnest, the class discussions lively, and the papers uniformly dull. After teaching the course for three consecutive years, I had no interest in ever teaching a research writing course again. My experience, I am sure, was a typical one: teachers and students dread that part of the first-year course given over to the research paper. After teaching research paper writing again for the past few years, I have begun to suspect that our theoretical neglect of this form is connected to the quality of the texts that the students produce for us. What we have done is to treat a form, which has its own history, as if it were a given, an immutable and "natural" fact. As David Russell has observed, "this genre has come to be ubiquitous, relatively uniform, and almost synonymous with extended school writing" (78). Once we realize, in the words of Steven Mailloux, that the research paper is "a methodology . . . used for the classroom practices derived from the German scientific model," then we are in the position to rehistoricize not only the research paper but the function it plays in contemporary composition courses (23). Russell has shown in his *Writing in the Academic Disciplines* that when the research paper was introduced into the American university system, the institutional gap between teachers and students was narrow enough that the students' research paper writing bore some resemblance to that of their teachers', and the roles of teacher and student were conceived as practitioner and apprentice. But as the research paper became institutionalized and routinized, and as scientific knowledge simultaneously exploded and segmented, the pedagogical uses of the research paper

> narrowed, moving from apprenticeship to production. If a discipline was primarily a storehouse of accumulated knowledge (not an active, socially constituted discourse community), then what counted in a research paper was the information it contained, not the methodological processes that led students (or the discipline) to find and value the information, (89)

Very soon in its history, the research paper became an "imitation of the writing that the institution valued most," but an imitation devoid of the *raision d'être* of the original (72). For if in the model of the German scientific paper, the scientist is to communicate the results of his objective research, the student, using the same model can only communicate a second order truth, can only re-discover what has already been discovered. Russell argues that the

> research idea derived its tacit understanding of the nature of written communication from John Locke. . . . [L]anguage is merely a conduit for transmitting preexisting, preformed truth. . . . Expository prose, like the science it communicated, was not the site of a rhetorical struggle among shifting interests for impermanent victories, it was objective and fixed. Those who shaped writing in the curriculum held an abiding faith in the power of written knowledge to defeat ignorance and error and bring permanent progress. Truth would triumph without rhetoric—or in spite of it. (73)

If knowledge is objective and fixed, all the student has to do is simply reproduce it, or in the terms that my students seem to favor—to regurgitate it.

If we look at what textbooks say about research paper writing, their pervasive and fundamental assumption is positivist—that the work a student does in writing a research paper is like the work of a scientist. The writers of these textbooks, in using the model of what they conceive of as scientific research, adopt a "scientific" vocabulary ("observations," "facts," "experimentation," "evidence") which denies uncertainty and ambiguity and which completely excludes the act of writing from their discussion. For these writers, facts are unambiguous, either true or false, and this belief has its basis in their assumption about the unambiguous nature of scientific research. If we accept Thomas Kuhn's definition of the scientist as one "concerned to understand the world and to extend the precision and scope with which it has been ordered," then the project of the student writer bears no relation to that of the scientist (42). Most scientists, Kuhn argues, are engaged in the "mopping-up operations" which constitute "normal science" (24). The scientist's ability to "do" normal science is predicated on his or her acceptance of a "paradigm," and those scientists "whose research is based on shared paradigms are committed to the same rules and standards for scientific practice. That commitment and the apparent consensus it produces are prerequisites for normal science, i.e., for the genesis and continuation of a particular research tradition" (11). Within that research tradition, Kuhn's "mopping-up operations" consist almost wholly of "three classes of problems— determination of significant fact, matching facts with theory, and articulation of theory" (34).

When they work within this paradigm, scientists accept a set of assumptions which make that work possible, assumptions which define the nature of the questions they can ask. In Foucault's terms, this means that "the founding of a science can always be reintroduced within the machinery of those transforma- tions that derive from it" ("Author" 115). Kuhn would probably argue that the "founding act" of a paradigm is always "present," but Foucault makes a crucial distinction between "science" and "discursive practice" which is "heterogeneous to its subsequent transformations" ("Author" 115). Science, since it incorporates the founding act, does not demand, what Foucault calls, a "'return to the origin.' This return, which is part of the discursive field itself, never stops modifying it. The return is not a historical supplement which would be added to discursivity . . . on the contrary, it constitutes an effective and necessary task of transform- ing the discursive practice itself" ("Author" 116). A reexamination of Galileo's writing, Foucault says, may change our sense of "the history of mechanics, but it will never be able to change mechanics itself" ("Author" 116), while a reexam- ination of Freud or Marx would, of necessity, modify Freudianism or Marxism.

Kuhn and Foucault allow us to see how the writers of research textbooks who use the scientific model are at once relying on a simplistic notion of science, and how they ignore differences in discursive practices. The return which Fou- cault speaks of, for instance, has its necessity buried in the word "research" itself. As the *OED* states the prefix *re* has "the general sense of 'back' or 'again,'" while the origin of the word "search" is in the late Latin "circare" which means "to go round." The return of research, within the scientific model, renders no modifica- tion; one can only report on Galileo or mechanics or Egyptian education, and that is why this model relegates the act of writing to the periphery. After all, the scientist writes her report, the model implies, *after* the conclusion of her experi- ments, *after* all the important work has been done. The scientist may indeed write only after the work is done (although writing, I suspect, is continuous throughout the process), but for the scientist the paradigm governs practice. The student researcher, on the other hand, is not consciously working within a research tradition; she has no access to informing theory, and the "rules and standards" of research are particularly opaque. In fact, the practice of the student writer is quite similar to that of the scientist *before* a paradigm has been estab- lished; without a "paradigm . . . all . . . facts . . . are likely to be seen equally relevant" (Kuhn 15). The student, then, is *nothing* like a scientist working within the tradition of normal science. The student, without the comfort of a theoretical envelope, a paradigm, faces the bewildering equality of "facts," and it is only *in* the writing, and not *before* it, that the student can find a way to distinguish among and weigh those facts and thus shape her research.

The scientific assumptions undergirding research paper pedagogy are so strong that even common sense can be claimed as a form of science. In Gaston and Smith's *The Research Paper: A Common Sense Approach,* the authors claim that

> research does not even use any special forms of thought. It only system-
> atizes and extends the common sense of everyday life. At bottom, all
> research consists of four simple operations: (1) making relevant obser-
> vations, (2) making intelligent guesses about the relations among
> observed facts, (3) testing these guesses, and (4) revising them in the
> light of test results. (11–12)

The writers then spend two paragraphs attempting to demonstrate that the four
processes constituting research are as "natural to humans as breathing" (12).
After this somewhat startling assertion, they develop an analogy that research, in
a university, is just like trying to figure out why a car fails to start on a cold
morning. Trying to start the car, the student is enjoined to do

> [i]n effect . . . what a scientist does. You interpret your findings in light
> of the probabilities and trust conclusions based on your experimenta-
> tion until contrary evidence turns up. . . . [A]*ll* specialized techniques of
> research, humanistic as well as scientific, are simply methods for
> increasing the range and accuracy of observation and for tracing more
> precisely the relationships among them. (12)

In their rush to make research seem "user-friendly," Gaston and Smith simplify
some very complicated issues, and they (paradoxically) exclude the students
from a discourse they call "natural . . . as breathing."

The first oversimplification in this passage is the writers' supposition that
research is simply "common sense" (the subtitle of their textbook). As Clifford
Geertz has argued, common sense is, in its content, neither transcultural, nor can
it be used, unproblematically, as a kind of foundational principle. "[I]t is an
inherent characteristic of common sense thought . . . to affirm that its tenets are
immediate deliverances of experience, not deliberated reflections upon it"
Geertz writes (75). Common sense, he goes on to say,

> is as much an interpretation of the immediacies of experience, a gloss
> on them, as are myth, painting, epistemology, or whatever, [and] it is
> like them, historically constructed and, like them, subjected to histori-
> cally defined standards of judgment. It can be questioned, disputed,
> affirmed, developed, formalized, contemplated, even taught, and it can
> vary dramatically from one people to the next. It is, in short, a cultural
> system. (76)

What may appear to be common sense to writers of textbooks may not appear
to be so to student writers who, although they feel at home in cars, may feel
alienated in the methodologies and discourses of the university. The local knowledge they bring to our classes makes them see research as arcane and
formalized, which is, in part, why they write essays which strive to be "objective"
but which are actually mechanical and empty. To assume, as Gaston and Smith
do, that researching and writing are natural and commonsensical, and then go
on to link that common sense to "what a scientist does," is to disable the student

by assuring her that wildly incompatible discourses share, at heart, the same homey impulses.

If the analogies that the textbooks employ (research is common sense, research is like science) are less than useful, the pedagogical assumptions of these books are often quite archaic. As an example, take the matter of outlines: composition textbooks from earlier in this century placed heavy emphasis on outlines. These outlines are always to be crafted *before* any writing of sentences begin, and outlining is often troped as the activity of an architect as in this sentence from a 1926 textbook, Claxton and McGinniss' *Effective English:* "Did the paper read as if a good outline had been made at the outset, and as if the writer had referred to it in preparing this paper, as the builder refers to the architect's plans? It not, it lacks *coherence*" (10). For Claxton and McGinniss, writing itself is not so much an act of thought as it is a transcription of thought or a remembering of thought. The conceptual work in producing an essay, as Porter Perrin claims in his 1950 *Writer's Guide and Index to English,* precedes the writing: "The real process of composing is gathering ideas together [and] grouping them" (13). A more recent text, like Lunsford and Connor's *The St. Martin's Handbook* (1989), discusses the formal outline *only* in the context of the research paper, and stresses that it is "a double-edged sword" because, on one hand, it allows a writer to see how "ideas relate [and] what the overall structure of your argument will be," while, on the other hand, "most people find a full formal outline devilishly hard to write" (575). Not only can the outline, in its rigid structure, be an impediment in writing, but Lunsford and Connors also acknowledge that insight often occurs in the act of writing: "Whatever form your organizational plan takes . . . you may want or need to change it as you begin drafting. Writing has a way of stimulating thought, and you may find yourself getting ideas in the process of drafting" (29). Those shifts from Claxton and McGinniss to Lunsford and Conners are telling; the latter pair do not discuss the outline at all in reference to "composition," and what they do say is more balanced and informed by revisionary work in Composition Studies from the last twenty years.

When one contrasts, however, the advice of older composition textbooks with more recent textbooks devoted solely to research paper writing, it becomes obvious that very little has changed. For instance, Manley and Rickert, in their 1923 book, *The Writing of English,* stress two stages in the outlining process for research papers: first, "when you have in mind the general bearing and content of your subject, do not fail to jot it down in the form of a rough, preliminary outline" (170). Second, "when you have read and taken notes to the limit of available material or of time, you are ready to make the final outline of your paper. If the work of reading and of arranging notes has been carefully done, the outlining is almost automatic," and, it would be fair to say, once the outline is crafted, the writing itself is also "almost automatic" (172). If one looks at Lester's 1990 *Writing Research Papers,* one sees a similar stress on outlining, but in addition one also sees a set of working pedagogical assumptions that appear at first very close to those of Lunsford and Connors. Although he writes that "before progressing very far into note-taking you should prepare a preliminary outline"

(65)—advice consonant with that of Manley and Rickert—when it comes to the formal outlines, Lester writes: "Understand that not all papers require the formal outline. . . . After all, the outline and first draft are preliminary steps to discovering what needs expression" (114). Such advice would seem to signal a shift in pedagogical assumptions, and it would, except for Lester's apparatus: almost six pages on how to outline. Even though Lester makes gestures toward a pedagogy based on process and on discovery, the overall thrust of his advice is even more retrograde than that of Manley and Rickert from 1923. They, at least, have a paragraph on revision in which they admit that significant work can be done at this stage; new paragraphs should be written, and the student's "main attention" should be "focused on general revision of structure" (177). In his single page on revision, Lester nowhere recognizes that revision might mean more than tinkering with and adjusting the paper. It is astonishing how little has changed in this pedagogy in almost seventy years.

Because so little has changed over these seventy years, the form of the research paper has fossilized. Too often, though, we fail to look at our own practice in teaching research papers, and instead scapegoat and blame the students. I have heard it said, derisively, at the Conference on College Composition and Communication, that most college research writing involves "carting dead bones from one graveyard to another." After our rueful laugh of recognition, we should also recognize that we have provided and, in many cases, continue to provide, the cart and the destination, a place of interment, a destination that brings the students full circle. This cart, the model of a scientific and objective paper, can be so disabling that many students find a course in writing research essays one of their most difficult and frustrating experiences in the university. This disabling is probably, at the last remove, a product of a general cultural resistance to conceding, as Edward Said has written, that all knowledge "has been historically constituted and constructed," and that research is not a matter of collecting "facts," but a matter of "constituting and constructing" knowledge (211). This resistance means that students are unaware of how knowledge is "made"; instead, they are inculcated with a "scientific" model of knowledge and research writing. This model of the research "paper" has remained largely resistant to the kind of intellectual move in which knowledge is constituted and constructed by the overlappings of institutional boundaries, a move that Clifford Geertz has written of in an essay entitled "Blurred Genres: The Refiguration of Social Thought": "[T]here has been an enormous amount of genre mixing in intellectual life in recent years, and it is, such blurring of kinds, continuing apace. . . . Something is happening to the way we think about the way we think" (20, 21). But something is *not* happening to the way we expect students to think in the research paper. Research paper pedagogy has been resistant to "genre mixing" and the critical self-awareness Geertz discusses.

A symptom of this resistance is the use of the term "research paper" by most writing textbooks and by our students. When they use and hear the term "research paper," they conceive of it as something like a scientific report, objective and neutral. I sometimes wonder what would happen if we called the form a "research essay." The semantic shift would not be a frivolous one; it would emphasize that the "essay" does not, as Adorno has observed "obey the rules of the game of organized science and theory; . . . [it] does not strive for closed, deductive or inductive, construction" (158). It should strive, I would argue, for a kind of openness, a delight in the unexpected and incongruous. As Hayden White has argued of historical writing, the intention of the essay is to render the "unfamiliar, or the 'uncanny' in Freud's sense of the term, familiar; of removing it from the domain of things felt to be 'exotic' and unclassified into one or another domain of experience encoded adequately enough to be felt humanly useful, nonthreatening, or simply known by association" (5). White also argues that this is "only one side of . . . [a] two-fold operation," and the "other side 'to render the familiar strange'" is also a move essential to the essay (256).

The research paper is seen by the students then as a closed and monologic form, one that prevents them from rendering either the familiar strange or the strange familiar. The reason they view the research paper in this light is social: it is not only a product of their previous schooling, but also a result of the insistence of American culture on binaries, on point-counterpoint. There can be only two views on any possible subject, and when the students adopt a "scientific" model, it conflates with their cultural presuppositions to think in binaries. So rather than the research paper being a hermeneutical process in which one begins with certain tentative questions, ones which are subsequently modified by the process of investigation and of writing, the research paper is conceived in a positivistic sense, as a method that produces binary results, which either confirm or deny. These "scientific" presuppositions are encoded in Packer and Timpane's advice that "a tentative thesis can help you organize your thoughts and direct your research. A tentative thesis is like a working hypothesis in a scientific experiment. It is the 'idea' the research will examine, so it serves as the basis for further investigation" (341). This advice not only simplifies the necessary messiness of research by implying that "a tentative thesis," like "a working hypothesis," can serve as a way of controlling the process of research, but also, in ignoring the differences between the scientist and the student writer, it falsifies the situation of the student. The scientist's "hypothesis" comes out of praxis, the set of assumptions linking theory and practice, but our students, in thinking of science, focus exclusively on practice, and thus understand the scientific method as less than tentative, as something that bears little resemblance to Kuhn's idea of normal science. In their view, the hypothesis is either confirmed or denied, and the scientist goes on from there. What they fail to see is how the process of trying to answer a question raises a whole set of unforeseen questions. So in their hurry to provide students with writing technologies, the authors of textbooks advise students to set aside tentativeness and purge it from the process of their research because it can only serve as an impediment.

The "closed" model proposed by the textbooks implies to the student that the outcome of writing a research essay can be controlled and is relatively predictable, and that it provides the comforting illusion that a process is under control (remember, a "tentative thesis can help . . . organize . . . and direct").

When we begin to write, though, we relinquish control; real writing is a complicated and unpredictable interaction between the writer and the texts of her research, a dynamic suppressed by most writers of textbooks. This interaction, however, can only be initiated once the student begins to write. Essentially, an essay must be able to be eventful, must be able to turn back on itself and interrogate its own assumptions, a quality that Adorno helps us to understand when he writes that the essay does not achieve "something scientifically, or . . . artistically":

> [It] reflects a childlike freedom that catches fire, without scruple, on what others have already done. . . . Luck and play are essential to the essay. It does not begin with Adam and Eve but with what it wants to discuss; it says what is at issue and stops where it feels itself complete— not where there is nothing left to say. (152)

This freedom and openness is what I find missing in many of the research essays I read because luck and play happen only in the act of writing, not in an arid formulating of hypotheses and recording of results.

The Juncture Between Research and Composition

If writing technologies govern the practice of research writing, then the autobiographical essay seems to govern composition pedagogy. Maxine Hairston has claimed (somewhat infamously) that having students "write about other people's ideas doesn't work well" (B1). If this is a composition teacher's working assumption, then the only possible subject for writing would be the students' own ideas as reflected in their own experience. As Lad Tobin has written: "There is . . . a certain type of essay (I will call it the autobiographical narrative of a self-actualizing event) that most of us in this interpretative community prefer" (337). Contrast Tobin's claim with Larson's statement that research "furnishes the substance of much discourse and can furnish substance to almost any discourse except, possibly, one's personal reflections on one's own experience" (813). This juxtaposition illustrates perfectly a basic incoherence in composition pedagogy. Students, taught to write expressivist essays, cannot extend that interest in the autobiographical when they are asked to write about something outside the self. In fact, the anecdote that Tobin uses to open his essay illustrates this bind perfectly. A student who was doing well, apparently, in Tobin's composition course was struggling with the writing in her humanities course. In a final essay in Tobin's course on her image of herself as a writer, this student

> argues that a writer can only think clearly when she is allowed to use a voice and style that she has mastered. In my course, she felt that she had been able to think through important issues in original ways; however in her humanities class she had trouble developing and organizing her ideas about Homer, Cicero, and the Hebrew prophets. . . . [I]n this

translation from her own form of expression to the academic language required in that course, her actual ideas were lost or distorted. (333)

Only later do we discover that Tobin prefers essays that are "autobiographical narrative[s] of a self-actualizing event," a preference that has more than a little to do with the confusion that this student is experiencing. Because she has been taught to valorize what David Bartholomae has characterized in his 1989 CCCC debate with Peter Elbow as the sovereign, a historical Emersonian "I" (or as he has said in another context, "the writer as free agent, as independent, self-authorizing, a-historical, [and] a-cultural"), this student has absolutely no experience of struggling with the ideas of others, or of placing herself in a tradition of writing (123). Her "own form of expression" has been valued to such a degree that when she is faced with the ideas of other and with the demands of academic prose, she is effectively silenced.

Both Tobin and the student argue, however, that her difficulty in the humanities course was a result of two incompatible conceptions of the function of writing. In Tobin's words, she was empowered "by the encouragement I gave her to explore ideas that mattered to her in personal and informal language. Her humanities professor, she complained, had denied her this access by insisting on numerous references to the text and 'impeccable English prose' (333). It may be that the humanities professor was simply being over-prescriptive and that he was acting as an agent of the language police rather than as a reader within a discipline, but even if the case is this extreme there is still a problem with Tobin's expressivist pedagogy. Are students who are taught to write autobiographical narratives of self actualizing events unable to switch gears? Are they unable to adapt to the demands of different audiences? By Tobin's account, his pedagogy may have succeeded at "helping another student establish her identity," but it has not given her much flexibility as a writer (335).

Furthermore, if we assume that the humanities professor was *not* overly prescriptive, then there is an even more disturbing implication to Tobin's narrative. He seems to assume, along with his student, that the transition from expressivist writing ("her own form of expression") to academic discourse means that the student's "actual ideas were lost or distorted." This example leads to my first conclusion about the relation between composition and the research paper: expressivist pedagogy of Tobin's variety is a kind of shell game that in promising to empower students actually disempowers them, and we see this disempowerment in their struggles with research paper writing. Susan Miller has argued much the same point in a wider context in her *Textual Carnivals: The Politics of Composition;* she claims that composition marginalizes students, and she asserts that "the purposes and practices for the composition course . . . indicated that it was set up to be a national course in silence" (55). It is here, at this juncture between an expressivist composition pedagogy and the research paper, that the silence falls. David Bartholomae has spoken to this problem when he observed that, "I think it wrong to teach late-adolescents that writing is an expression of individual thoughts and feelings. It makes them . . . powerless . . . blind to tradition, power and authority as they are present in language and culture" (128–129). Taught to value her own form of expression, taught to develop her own ideas at the exclusion of all else, the student fails utterly to write a productive essay dealing with the ideas of others.

Since we live in a culture that views itself as largely ahistorical and that has been founded on a repudiation of the past (the kind of ideology found in Emerson's early essays), I am tempted, at this point, by the "junking" solution because I find the ahistorical, visionary impulse a dangerously narrow one (as indeed did Emerson himself later in his career). But I have also been warned by my former colleague, Kurt Spellmeyer, that the opposite is just as dangerous: that students have to be more than just slaves to history and discourse communities. What we see, though, in the presently impossible transition from composition to the research paper is a double silencing; the student, in composition, is left in a world of solipsism. Her narrative of self-actualization may well give her greater insight into her personal life, but she has no ability to connect those narratives to history, culture, or community. On the other hand, if the student were to write a research paper on "Homer, Cicero, . . . [or] the Hebrew prophets," she would remain unable to converse with them, because her experience (narrowly construed) would be totally irrelevant. One way out of this bind of double silence, which would preserve some of the visionary quality of the best of the expressivist pedagogy, would be to have students continue to reflect on their experience, but to do so within a context of cultural studies, using what I have come to call an ethnographic perspective. In the absence of any such context, all that a student can be taught, as David Bartholomae said in his debate with Peter Elbow, is to write reasonably competent sentimental narratives, with nothing to provide resistance to or complication of these narratives.

The Model of Postmodern Ethnography

In contrast to both expressivist and "scientific" research paper writing, I would like to offer another disciplinary model for research, that of the contemporary ethnographer who, in renouncing the role of the "objective" scientist, has found a way to position herself not outside of, but in the midst of, her research. In an essay entitled "On Ethnographic Authority," James Clifford has written that in the early part of this century the authority of the "fieldworker-theorist" replaced that of the "earlier 'men on the spot'–the missionary, the administrator, the trader, and the traveller–whose knowledge of indigenous peoples, they argued, was not informed by the best scientific hypotheses or a sufficient neutrality" (27). This fieldworker-theorist as "objective" scientist saw no need to call into question her status as observer or the cultural dominance of her Eurocentric point-of-view, and in constructing the others of her field work as a text, this traditional ethnographer, Clifford argues "transforms the research situation's ambiguities and diversities of meaning into an integrated portrait. The research process is separated from the texts it generates, and . . . [t]he dialogical, situational aspects of ethnographic interpretation tend to be banished from the final representative text" (40). Our students are like this traditional ethnographer in valuing integration over ambiguity and diversity, in separating the "research process" from the text, and in their inability to see the relevance of the "dialogical [and] situational aspects of . . . interpretation."

The traditional ethnographer and the student in a research essay course are further allied in the way in which they assume the authority of "objective" knowledge. The traditional ethnographer assumes—takes on—the authority of representation, while the student assumes—takes for granted—the authority of all such representations. Neither, it seems to me, aspires to what Hayden White has defined as "genuine discourse," that is discourse which is "as *self* critical as it is critical of others" (4). Both, through an exclusionary tactic, try to govern the texts they write through "monologic authority" (Clifford 52), which simplifies by defining certain questions, certain textual practices, as irrelevant. This tactic of exclusion, of course, differs in intentionality: the student, imitating "monologic authority," unreflectingly excludes, while the traditional ethnographer consciously excludes. For instance, in writing about Malinowski and the difference between his 1922 *Argonauts of the Western Pacific* and his posthumously published *Diary* (1967), Clifford remarks on the "anger" and "ambivalence" which was excluded from the ethnographic text. In the *Diary,* Malinowski was

> frequently depressed, prey to constant fantasies about European and Trobriand women, trapped in an endless struggle to maintain his morale, to pull himself together. He was mercurial, trying out different voices, personae. The anguish, confusion, elation, and anger of the *Diary* seem to leave little room for the stable, comprehending posture of relativist ethnography. (97)

The fiction of a "stable, comprehending posture" banishes all this ferment from the representative text. Students, imitating this posture, separate the "research process . . . from the text it generates" out of obeisance to the authority of science and "objectivity" as a model for the research paper. They believe that their encounter with the texts of their research must reproduce, magisterially and neutrally, the stance and tone of those texts. In doing so, they exclude as irrelevant, what is probably most important—what Clifford has called a representation of the "discursive complexity" of "research as an on-going negotiation" (44). Clearly, the researcher experiences this ongoing negotiation as she searches out texts, rejecting some as not useful, reading others, ruminating, and often flailing around for a focus for the research. A pedagogy that would shift the emphasis from a "scientific" to an "ethnographic" model would have to find ways to uncover and foreground this negotiation. What I am suggesting here is that the ethnographic model would provide students with the tools to work in the territory between the scientific model of the research paper and the expressivist, autobiographical essay.

An ethnographic model would give students—allow students to take—the authority to claim the borderland, the liminal space between discourses, something that the scientific model actually prevents. As an example of how the monologic, scientific model can be disabling, a female student of mine once wrote a well-researched essay, exploring various theories of the incest taboo, and another student, after reading her essay, commented: "I distinctly missed the author's own feelings on the subject." The writer's rather puzzled response to this comment is revealing:

> Perhaps my next essay can involve a more personal position. Unfortu-
> nately, since I don't have a personal position towards the incest origin, I
> didn't feel it was necessary to make something up. Does a research
> paper necessarily have to have a personal position? Maybe more
> emphasis should be placed in what I was really trying to accomplish in
> this paper, which was to integrate several sources & show the different
> concepts & theories out there.

This student's assumption that a "personal position" has to be "made up" (That it is, in other words, somehow extrinsic to the research) expresses her idea of her task with her sources, which is to "integrate" and to "show" something which is "out there," unconnected intellectually to herself. As she said when we discussed her essay, she thought of her role as that of "moderator," the person who sets and keeps debating voices in motion. Discussing this draft with her, I pointed out the problem with the vocabulary of "position" that she had adopted. She assumed that she had to decide which of these theories was "right" (confirm or deny), and given her status as novice, she felt (and rightfully so) that she did not have enough knowledge or authority to make that judgement. As we discussed her essay, though, it became clear that she had excluded the process of the ongoing negotiation of her research from the text of her essay. She had found individual theories to be more or less plausible, and she even had observations about particular bits of data. But in conceiving of herself as "moderator," she thought it would be a violation of the conventions for these negotiations to become a foreground of her essay.

One way to try to encourage students to include the ongoing negotiation of research in their writing and to foster an ethnographic view of research might be to focus a research paper course on another culture. Such a course could begin by using an autobiography from a radically different culture, such as Wole Soyinka's *Aké: The Years of Childhood,* as a way of immediately providing a cultural contrast to the students' first autobiographical narratives. As the course continued, the students' sense of their place in the world could be complicated by reading ethnographies, like Michael Moffat's *Coming of Age in New Jersey* or Douglas Foley's *Learning Capitalist Culture: Deep in the Heart of Tejas.* The advantages of a course like this would be obvious. Most importantly, the students' experience would not be jettisoned as irrelevant, rather it would be problematized and historicized by having been seen through various academic lenses. Furthermore, when it came to writing a research paper, a context would already exist for the student to work in. As a researcher into her own experience, history, and culture, the student would be motivated in a way that she often is not in writing a research paper. The project would seem, inevitably, less of an exercise. The student could begin to see some of the reasons for, and the relevance of, academic inquiry, and there would be an organic connection between composition and the research paper. As Nancy Barnes has written, "the most impressive, breathtaking developments in students' thinking often happen as they move back and forth between individual experience (their own, and also that of unfamiliar people and remote places) and structural analyses or theories" (149).

What I am advocating here is not so much a particular course content (ethnography or cultural studies) as I am advocating a conceptual shift. When students write expressivist essays, they conceive of themselves as the Emersonian, sovereign, ahistorical individual; when they write research papers, they think of themselves as objective conduits for information. In both forms, they are absolutists. An ethnographical model would encourage them to move back and forth among experience, conviction, and theory. But to move intellectually in this way, there has to be more at stake than what I called earlier a "second order discovery"; liminality can not be fostered when students are assigned ersatz writing. As Brown, Collins, and Dugid have written in "Situated Cognition and the Culture of Learning," teaching often fails to "provide the important insights into either the culture or the authentic activities of that culture that learners need" (33). This ersatz quality is as equally pronounced in composition as it is in the research paper. In composition based on the expressivist model, students write autobiographical narratives, which we can feel safely superior to, in part because our writing is of a very different sort. Even Peter Elbow has acknowledged that there is a kind of professonalized self-protection involved in our expectation of student writing. Usually, Elbow has written, a teacher "isn't in a position where he can be genuinely affected by your words. He doesn't expect your words actually to make a dent on him. He doesn't treat your words like real reading. He has to read them as an exercise" (Elbow 127).

If we are able to respond to our students' autobiographical writing with readerly empathy (although as writers within the academic discourse community we only very rarely write this way ourselves), the divorce from the work of practitioners is especially marked in that portion of a composition course given over to the research paper. For instance, James Lester in *Writing Research Papers* tries to illustrate how to use one's imagination to develop a topic:

> *Ask Questions.* Stretch your imagination with questions. Some may have ready answers and others may need investigation:
>
> How is dissent defined?
>
> Who benefits?
>
> Is dissent legal? Is it moral? Is it patriotic?
>
> Should dissent be encouraged by government? Stifled?
>
> Is dissent a liberal activity? Conservative?
>
> What is "civil disobedience"? (5)

There's nothing intrinsically wrong with these questions, except that they're the kinds of questions that one would ask when one is writing what Larson has called the "generic" research paper as opposed to a discipline-specific research paper. A student in a political science course would not need to ask herself "What is 'civil disobedience'"? Even if she had never read Thoreau or Ghandi, she would have a sense of the discourse and know that questions are generated from the discourse; she would also know, rather than asking contextless questions, to go and to read the basic texts. Only in a content-less course like first year composition could such questions be asked. Looking at Lester's questions from another angle, that of the practitioner, one *never* starts with the large questions. Only when a practitioner has dealt with a number of specific cases over a long period of time (civil disobedience in liberations struggles, civil disobedience in anti-war movements) can she begin to take on the big questions. From my experience in teaching literature, I suspect that our colleagues in other disciplines do not start their students with the big questions either. My point here is that we have to move away from the generic research paper assignment toward an integrated composition course, one that has a content focus, both for the short papers and the long, multiple-source paper. Whatever the context the students would be encouraged to explore the connections between their life worlds and their experience and academic understandings of the world.

An Alternative Intellectual Lineage

At the heart of the problem I am trying to articulate is a set of different attitudes toward reading and consequently toward knowledge. Current-traditionalists and conservatives of Maxine Hairston's ilk do not believe in the efficacy of reading in a college composition course. As Hairston wrote in the May 1992 issue of *College Composition and Communication:* students "do not need to be assigned essays to read so that they will have something to write about—they bring their subjects with them. The writing of others, except for that of their fellow students, should be supplementary, used to illustrate or reinforce" (186). Students should only read, according to Hairston, in order to provide themselves with models; she does not want other people's writing to distract them from their own ideas. But because her pedagogy makes no place for other people's ideas, the students are hamstrung when asked to write research papers. Their previous writing experience acts as an impediment; their personal experience is irrelevant. Consequently, they fall back on summary—they act as "text processors"—and we excoriate them for "carting dead bones." As Donald Lazare has pointed out in the essay that followed Hairston's, this attitude in Composition Studies toward reading and knowledge emphasizes "basic writing and the generation and exposition of one's own ideas to the neglect of more advanced levels of writing that involve critical thinking in evaluating others' ideas" (194). And, of course, the primary sustained site in the academy for students to evaluate others' ideas and to think critically is the research paper.

As a way of trying to bridge the gap between attitudes like Hairston's and the pedagogies of the traditional research paper, Ken Macrorie has argued in *The I-Search Paper* for an approach to writing research papers that would recontextualize knowledge. Instead of "the ideas, methods, principles, and knowledge of authorities . . . [being] abstracted and detached from the experience that generates them," (Preface), Macrorie advocates something he calls the I-Search paper which "tells stories of quests" (Preface). In this type of paper, the student is not doing an exercise, but rather is recovering something of the origins of the form in the nineteenth century German university. The students do "original searches," and thus they become "authors reading authorities," a process that allows them to become authorities themselves, "however limited and naive" (14). This quest as a narrative, Macrorie argues, restores the cultural and affective context within which all researchers work, a context that we, as purveyors of academic discourse have been trained to eliminate from our own writing.

As appealing as this model might be in its effort to overcome binaries—the split between subjective and objective, expressivism and the research paper—the I-Search paper strikes me as an expressivist and romantic version of research-paper writing, and I seriously doubt how effectively its lessons transfer to other writing contexts. This model establishes the same dynamic I described at work with Tobin and his student who is powerfully enabled within the course, and is equally powerfully disabled outside it. For instance, I suspect that when the student is asked to write a more traditionally academic research paper she would founder, and furthermore I suspect that few if any of my colleagues in my interdisciplinary Humanities Division would accept a quest-narrative as a research paper. In other words, Macrorie's model does not take the demands of academic discourse fully enough into consideration; indeed, one could argue that the I-Search paper, like expressivism itself, is a liberatory response to the oppressiveness of academic discourse. But the liberation it promises is illusory, in part because of Macrorie's romantic (one might even say mystical) notions of how one begins to define a research paper topic. "Allow something to choose you that you want intensely to know or possess," Macrorie intones, and his examples of what to research are telling: a stereo or tape player, a motorcycle, a technical school, a vacation spot (62). Here, Lazare's criticism of Hairston is particularly apposite; this model neglects "more advanced levels of writing that involve critical thinking in evaluating other's ideas" (194). Furthermore, the process of being "chosen" simplifies what Flower and Hayes point to when they say that even though "a teacher gives 20 students the same assignment, *the writers themselves create the problem they solve*" (93). Macrorie's model gives the students no experience in defining a problem that interests them within a field of inquiry, nor does it give them any training in how to chart a course among competing voices and points of view.

What we see in the incompatibility of pedagogies like expressivism, the traditional research paper, and the I-Search paper is a larger struggle over what constitutes knowledge, a struggle that conceals an underlying congruity. One might want to argue, for instance, that I have described a struggle between subjective and objective ways of knowing and conceptions of the truth, a struggle that began with the humanistic disciplines trying to become scientific in the late nineteenth and early twentieth centuries, but I would like to argue that both pedagogies, expressivism and the research paper, are both absolutist and assume that Truth is knowable (albeit in different fashions), and because of their absolutism neither form can speak to the other. I would like tentatively to suggest that these seeming binaries can trace their absolutist heritage back to Plato, who formulates for the Western Tradition a theory of the oneness of Truth (as opposed to the plurality of truths). The expressivists, for instance, share an assumption, in the words of Foucault, that "truth, lodged in our secret nature, 'demands' only to surface; that if it fails to do so, this is because a constraint holds it in place, the violence of power weighs it down, and it can finally be articulated only at the price of a kind of liberation" (*History of Sexuality* 60). Tobin's student was brought to establish "her identity" through the liberation of expressivism; her truth is incontestable, just as is the truth of positivism is incontestable. What I am proposing here is a third way, a way of knowing allied with the Sophists for whom, Richard Enos argues, "meaning . . . [was] an act of abstraction through social consensus" (99).

I realize that this sounds like social construction under another name, but I see the example of the Sophists as being crucially different from twentieth century social constructionists. For social constructionists, discourse communities are monolithic and disciplining. Students, as Pat Bizzell has argued in several essays, must subject themselves to the authority of the discipline; only once they've become initiates have they acquired the authority to speak. For the Sophists, on the other hand, knowledge is a product of social negotiation open to all, even to students and their teachers. Susan Jarratt has observed (quoting Havelock's *The Liberal Temper in Greek Politics*) that the "sophist 'did not seek to place the pupil at an intellectual disadvantage as compared with the teacher,' waiting instead to hear a response which the teacher would take into serious consideration toward the outcome of the discussion" (106). The openness to the negotiation of knowledge is a product of the early alliance of rhetoric and democracy (see Enos), and also of the Sophists' ethnographic observations as they traveled throughout the Greek-speaking world (Jarratt 11). As Jarratt and others have recognized, the Sophists can provide us with an alternative intellectual lineage, a perspective from which we can begin to critique absolutist claims in both expressivism and the research paper.

If I have argued here for a move toward a borderland, an ethnographic center between composition and research pedagogies, I am also forced to recognize that research paper pedagogy has been much more conservative than composition pedagogy. Part of the reason for this fossilized pedagogy is that the juncture between composition and the research paper illustrates our failure to think through the issue of process and product. Clearly, research paper pedagogy has not been able to integrate process theory because a tyranny of the product reigns in research paper pedagogy. Conversely, as Susan Miller has argued, process theory, as presently constructed, has not taken "responsibility for showing students the variability of writing processes, nor has it shown how their variety connects to contingencies in larger cultural systems that privilege some writers over others" (119). And it is here, in the juncture between the paradigms of composition and the research paper, that we must examine how process theory and how expressivist writing connect to "larger cultural systems" as discovered in the research paper, and it is also here, in this backwater of research paper pedagogy, that we must begin to integrate process and product—so that students can see the research paper as an *act* rather than a transcription or a test. Not until we find a way to bring these paradigms closer together will we be able to present ourselves as members of a field which has important insights for teachers in all disciplines.

Pennsylvania State University
Harrisburg, Pennsylvania

Acknowledgement

This essay grew out of my experience as coordinator of the Research Paper course at Rutgers University. I would like to take this opportunity to thank Kurt Spellmeyer not only for the wonderful sustained office conversation in those years, but also for his subsequent support, in particular his many helpful readings of this essay.

Works Cited

Adorno, T.W. "The Essay as Form." *New German Critique* 32 (1984): 151–171.

Barnes, Nancy. "The Fabric of a Student's Life and Thought: Practicing Cultural Anthropology in the Classroom." *Anthropology & Education Quarterly* 23 (1992): 145–159.

Bartholomae, David. "A Reply to Stephen North." *PRE/TEXT* 11 (1990): 122–130.

Brown, John Sella, Alan Collins and Paul Dugid. "Situated Cognition and the Culture of Learning." *Educational Researcher* 18 (1989): 32–42.

Claxton, Philander P., and James McGinniss. *Effective English.* Boston: Allyn, 1926.

Clifford, James. *The Predicament of Culture: Twentieth Century Ethnography, Literature, and Art.* Cambridge: Harvard UP, 1988.

Compact Edition of the Oxford English Dictionary. New York: Oxford UP, 1980.

Elbow, Peter. *Writing Without Teachers.* New York: Oxford UP, 1973.

Enos, Richard Leo. *Greek Rhetoric Before Aristotle.* Prospect Heights, IL: Waveland P, 1993.

Flower, Linda, and John R. Hays. "The Cognition of Discovery: Defining a Rhetorical Problem." *The Writing Teacher's Sourcebook.* Ed. Gary Tate and Edward P.J. Corbett. 2nd ed. New York: Oxford UP, 1988. 92–102.

Ford, James E. and Dennis R. Perry. "Research Paper Instruction in the Under-graduate Writing Program." *College English* 44 (1982): 825–831.

Foucault, Michel. "What Is an Author?" *The Foucault Reader.* Ed. Paul Rainbow. New York: Pantheon, 1984. 101–120.

——. *The History of Sexuality.* Vol. 1. Trans. Robert Hurley. New York: Vintage, 1978.

Gaston, Thomas E., and Bret H. Smith. *The Research Paper: A Common-Sense Approach.* Englewood Cliffs, NJ: Prentice, 1988.

Geertz, Clifford. *Local Knowledge: Further Essays in Interpretive Anthropology.* New York: Basic, 1983.

Hairston, Maxine, C. "Required Writing Courses Should Not Focus on Politically Charged Social Issues." *The Chronicle of Higher Education* January 23, 1991 B1+.

Jarratt, Susan. *Rereading the Sophists: Classical Rhetoric Refigured.* Carbondale: Southern Illinois UP, 1991.

Kuhn, Thomas. *The Structure of Scientific Revolutions.* 2nd ed. Chicago: U of Chicago P, 1962.

Larson, Richard L. "The 'Research Paper' in the Writing Course: A Non-Form of Writing." *College English* 44 (1982): 811–816.

Lester, James. *Writing Research Papers: A Complete Guide.* 6th ed. Glenview, IL: Scott/Little, 1990.

Lunsford, Andrea, and Robert Connors. *The St. Martin's Handbook.* New York: St. Martin's, 1989.

Macrorie, Ken. *The I-Search Paper.* Portsmouth, NH: Boyton/Cook, 1988.

Mailloux, Steven. *Rhetorical Power.* Ithaca: Cornell UP, 1989.

Manley, John Matthews, and Edith Rickert. *The Writing of English.* Rev. ed. New York: Holt, 1923.

Miller, Susan. *Textual Carnivals: The Politics of Composition.* Carbondale: Southern Illinois UP, 1991.

Packer, Nancy Huddleston, and John Timpane. *Writing Worth Reading: A Practical Guide with Handbook.* 2nd ed. New York: St. Martin's, 1989.

Perrin, Peter G. *Writer's Guide and Index to English,* Chicago: Scott, 1950.

Russell, David *Writing in the Academic Disciplines. 1870–1990: A Curricular History.* Carbondale: Southern Illinois UP, 1991.

Said, Edward. "Representing the Colonized: Anthropology's Interlocutors." *Critical Inquiry 15* (1989): 205–225.

Schwegler, Robert A, and Linda Shamoon. "The Aims and Processes of the Research Paper." *College English* 44 (1982): 817–24.

Tobin, Lad. "Reading Students, Reading Ourselves: Revising the Teacher's Role in the Writing Class." *College English* 53 (1991): 333–48.

White, Hayden. *Tropics of Discourse: Essays in Cultural Criticism.* Baltimore: Johns Hopkins UP, 1978.

JAC On-Line, a hypertextual version of the print journal, is located at http://nos-feratu.cas.usf.edu/jac/index.html.

This WWW site is best accessed by browsers such as mosaic.

Additional Sources

Capossela, Toni-Lee. "Students as Sociolinguists: Getting Real Research from Freshman Writers." *College Composition & Communication* Vol. 42, 1 (February 1991): 75–79.

Argues that teachers should make topics like sociolinguists the basis of semester-long research papers.

Macrorie, Ken. *The I-Search Paper.* Portsmouth, NH: Boynton/Cook Publishers, Inc. 1988.

Revised edition of a ground-breaking textbook on research writing, putting emphasis on connecting thinking and research.

McGlinn, Marguerite M. "Moving and Grooving on the Information Highway: One Teacher's Experience with the Internet. *English Journal* Vol. 84, 6 (October 1995): 45–47.

Describes one teacher's experience with having students use the Internet for research, with emphasis on the advantages and disadvantages.

Acknowledgments

Marilyn M. Cooper, "The Ecology of Writing" from *College English*, Vol. 48, April 1986, pp. 364–375. Copyright © 1986 by the National Council of Teachers of English. Reprinted with permission.

Lisa Ede and Andrea Lunsford, "Audience Addressed/Audience Invoked: The Role of Audience in Composition Theory and Pedagogy" from *CCC*, Vol. 35, May 1984, pp. 155–171. Copyright © 1984 by the National Council of Teachers of English. Reprinted with permission.

Peter Elbow, "Closing my Eyes as I Speak: An Argument for Ignoring Audience" from *College English*, Vol. 49, Jan. 1987, pp. 50–69. Copyright © 1987 by the National Council of Teachers of English. Reprinted with permission.

Jeanne Fahnstock & Marie Secor, "Teaching Argument: A Theory of Types" from *CCC*, Vol. 34, Feb. 1983, pp. 20–30. Copyright © 1983 by the National Council of Teachers of English. Reprinted with permission.

Linda Flower and John R. Hayes, "The Cognition of Discovery: Defining a Rhetorical Problem" from *College Composition and Communication*, Vol. 31, Feb. 1980, pp. 21–32. Copyright © 1980 by the National Council of Teachers of English. Reprinted with permission.

Geoffrey H. Hartmann, "Blessing the Torrent: On Wordsworth's Later Style." Reprinted by permission of the author.

Patricia Hartwell, "Grammar, Grammars, and the Teaching of Grammar" from *College English*, Vol. 47, No. 2, Feb. 1985, pp. 105–127. Copyright © 1985 by the National Council of Teachers of English. Reprinted with permission.

Catherine E. Lamb, "Beyond Argument in Feminist Composition" from *CCC*, Vol. 42, Feb. 1991, pp. 11–24. Copyright © 1991 by the National Council of Teachers of English. Reprinted with permission.

Richard L. Larson, "The Research Paper in the Writing Course: A Non-Form of Writing" from *College English*, Vol. 44, Dec. 1982, pp. 811–816. Copyright © 1982 by the National Council of Teachers of English. Reprinted with permission.

Elaine O. Lees, "Evaluating Student Writing" from *CCC*, Vol. 30, Dec. 1979, pp. 370–374. Copyright © 1979 by the National Council of Teachers of English. Reprinted with permission.

Erika Lindemann, "Three Views of English 101" from *College English*, Vol. 57 No. 3, pp. 287–302, March 1995. Copyright © 1995 by the National Council of Teachers of English. Reprinted with permission.

Mike Rose, "Rigid Rules, Inflexible Plans, and the Stifling of Language: A Cognitivist Analysis of Writer's Block" from *CCC*, Dec. 1980 pp. 389–400. Copyright © 1980 by the National Council of Teachers of English. Reprinted with permission.

Peter Smagorinsky & Pamela K. Fly, "A New Perspective on Why Small Groups Do and Don't Work" from *English Journal*, Vol. 83, No. 3, pp. 54–58, March 1994. Copyright © 1994 by the National Council of Teachers of English. Reprinted with permission.